The
Reference Shelf®

Representative Speeches
2013–2014

The Reference Shelf
Volume 86 • Number 6
H. W. Wilson
A Division of EBSCO Information Services
Ipswich, Massachusetts
2014

GREY HOUSE PUBLISHING

The Reference Shelf

The books in this series contain reprints of articles, excerpts from books, addresses on current issues, and studies of social trends in the United States and other countries. There are six separately bound numbers in each volume, all of which are usually published in the same calendar year. Numbers one through five are each devoted to a single subject, providing background information and discussion from various points of view and concluding with an index and comprehensive bibliography that lists books, pamphlets, and articles on the subject. The final number of each volume is a collection of recent speeches. Books in the series may be purchased individually or on subscription.

Library of Congress Cataloging-in-Publication Data

Representative speeches, 2013-2014 / [compiled by H. W. Wilson]. --
[First edition].
    pages : illustrations ; cm. -- (The reference shelf ; volume 86, number 6)
    Includes bibliographical references and index.
    ISBN: 978-1-61925-437-4 (v. 86, no. 6)
    ISBN: 978-1-61925-261-5 (volume set)
    1. Speeches, addresses, etc.--21st century. 2. Social problems--History--21st century--Sources. 3. Marine resources conservation--History--21st century--Sources. 4. Educational change--History--21st century--Sources. 5. Income distribution--United States--History--21st century--Sources. 6. World politics--21st century--Sources. 7. United States--Politics and government--2009---Sources. I. H.W. Wilson Company. II. Series: Reference shelf ; v. 86, no. 6.
PN6122 .R46 2014
815/.6

Cover: Leonardo DiCaprio delivers remarks on the second day of the 'Our Ocean' Conference at the State Department in Washington, DC, USA, 17 June 2014. © EPA/JIM LO SCALZO/LANDOV

The Reference Shelf, 2014, published by Grey House Publishing, Inc., Amenia, NY, under exclusive license from EBSCO Information Services, Inc.

Printed in Canada

Contents

3

The Ocean

4

Embracing New Paradigms in Education

Preface

Representative Speeches

Speeches inform people of important facts, persuade them to adopt a particular point of view, and motivate them to take action. Speeches are used in a variety of contexts: more than two thousand years ago, religious sermons propelled the growth of Christianity, then a brand new religion. Throughout the nineteenth century, political candidates running for president of the United States and other national offices spent months traveling the continent, delivering speeches to persuade voters across increasingly far-flung states and territories; strong orators often had a significant advantage at the polls. World War II was fought with both weapons and words, as Nazi propaganda was delivered to the German masses through powerful speeches delivered at rallies, and President Franklin D. Roosevelt used his "fireside chat" radio addresses to motivate Americans to sacrifice personal comforts in support of the war effort.

Speeches continue to be a powerful means to deliver a message. Presentations at large-scale political conventions still hold significant weight for many people assessing which candidates to vote for. The popular TED Talk series presents speeches on an enormous variety of topics, many of which are available freely to the public online. And motivational speeches delivered at university commencements increasingly "go viral" online and inspire people far beyond the group of graduates to whom they were originally delivered.

In 2013 and 2014, the United States faced many diverse issues. These included implementing healthcare reform and the federal Affordable Care Act (ACA); gender issues such as the underrepresentation of women in the workforce, especially in the science, technology, engineering, and mathematics (STEM) fields; wealth inequality and its impact on national and global economic stability; education reform; and the need to protect and secure the world's oceans from environmental and security threats. Throughout the year, government officials, nonprofit and civic organizations, corporate leaders, scientists, and entertainers delivered many speeches touching on these topics. Some informed the public about important issues or clarified facts about a complex situation, while others sought to persuade the audience of a particular point of view or motivate listeners to take action.

Informing the Public

Speeches can efficiently and effectively provide factual information to the public. This is especially helpful for complex topics such as healthcare reform, because it allows experts to provide additional information and answer specific questions about how a new law or policy will affect people's lives. A lack of comprehensible information can cause panic and misunderstanding, which in turn can lead to swift implementation of poor policies; thus, these speeches often address explicitly the challenges of communicating the details of healthcare, medicine, and related policy matters to the general public.

For example, in his speech at Town Hall Los Angeles, Drew Altman of the Henry J. Kaiser Family Foundation addresses the Affordable Care Act (ACA)—commonly called "Obamacare"—and its challenges. He observes that many Americans do not understand the law or how it might affect their families, and that the media has not been helpful in resolving the confusion. He believes that the problems with the ACA, and the difficulties communicating its provisions to the public, are symptoms of much greater issues in the US political system. The heavily politicized approach, combined with oversimplification in the media, leads to rash judgments about whether the ACA is "good" or "bad"—a determination that is extremely difficult to make about a highly nuanced law—and does not foster helpful dialog about how to improve the ACA. To help the audience better understand how the law operates, Altman describes the large number of "risk pools" that spread the insurance cost across the United States, and explains why this complicates making accurate nationwide statements about insurance costs, premium increases, and other significant aspects of the ACA's implementation.

In another example from Town Hall Los Angeles, Keith L. Black explains the growing concern about Alzheimer's disease as the American population ages, and the challenges faced by researchers hoping to cure the disease. He cites statistics on how many individuals might experience Alzheimer's disease, and estimates of the costs of the long-term care these individuals will need. He then explains a significant challenge of Alzheimer's research: as of 2014, patients are not typically diagnosed until the disease has reached a very late stage. As a result, researchers must figure out how to regenerate brain cells in order to help patients regain cognitive functions, which is extremely difficult. Black describes his team's cutting-edge research, which explores new ways to diagnose Alzheimer's disease early enough to halt its progress before the patient experiences significant cognitive impairments.

In both of these speeches, experts educate the public on the scientific initiatives being pursued to address serious and growing public health problems. They strive to balance the need for specific, technically correct information with the understanding that a nontechnical audience might not understand all the details of complex topics such as insurance risk pools or neurology research. If successful, the result is a well-informed and empowered public.

Motivating the Masses

Another important role of speeches is to motivate. Dynamic public speakers stir their audience's emotions through their delivery style and their message. The speeches on gender issues in the workforce in this collection illustrate how different approaches effectively motivate different audiences. Research shows that greater female participation in the workforce leads to stronger economies in developed countries, so experts want to understand how to motivate women to join the workforce, and how public and private organizations can provide support to help them remain active participants.

At the launch of the World Bank's *Gender at Work* report, Catherine M. Russell discusses the role of women in the workforce and the economy worldwide. Her speech is a call to action to governments across the globe to encourage women to enter the workforce and protect their rights adequately once they arrive. Russell wants to motivate world leaders to remove the legal, social, financial, and educational barriers women face when seeking to enter the workforce. To support this, she cites studies demonstrating that many of the world's developed economies experienced significant growth during the second half of the twentieth century as a result of women entering the workforce. These arguments are calculated to persuade government leaders, for whom the economic stability of their constituency is a significant concern.

By contrast, in her speech at the International Women in Aviation Conference, Deborah A. P. Hersman addresses a group of women and men who work in the aviation industry, including astronauts, pilots, maintenance technicians, air traffic controllers, aviation safety officials, airport managers, and related business owners. Throughout her speech, Hersman reminds the audience of women's significant contributions to aviation, and motivates the audience to consider how to encourage more women to pursue STEM-related careers. She concludes by imploring audience members not to be content with small victories, but instead to be ambitious with their vision.

While the messages are similar, Hersman's approach to motivating her audience is different from Russell's: rather than speaking to government officials, Hersman is addressing individuals—including many women—who are already working in the STEM-related field of aviation. Policy-based arguments about global economic stability are less likely to motivate this audience than a rousing reminder of the significant achievements of women in aviation and related fields.

Speaking to the Audience

To achieve maximum effectiveness, speeches must appeal to the audience to which they will be delivered. Examples of this appear in the collection of speeches regarding wealth inequality, most of which address one of two groups with a significant stake in the issue: those who have a lot of money or influence in the government or corporate world, and those who are workers, wage-earners, and small business owners. Even when the underlying message is the same, speakers address these audiences in different ways, based on the audience's background, knowledge, and experiences.

For example, President Barack Obama delivered a speech in Kansas City, Missouri, where he addressed key economic issues affecting the working population. Many people had written him letters describing their personal financial situations, and Obama arranged to speak with several of them privately before delivering a wider address. Then in his speech, the president cites some of the specific concerns voiced to him by the community members. He also mentions his desire to see people make more than the current federal minimum wage, the need for people to have secure retirements, and the significance of attending college without undertaking unmanageable amounts of debt. He discusses some of the federal government initiatives such as the Affordable Care Act, and notes that wages improved and unemployment decreased in many areas around the country. Finally, he criticizes Congress for blocking additional initiatives that he believes would help individuals provide for themselves and their families. In this case, the president's casual delivery style and the content of the speech is very much tailored to his audience.

By contrast, Christine Lagarde, managing director of the International Monetary Fund, begins her speech on economic inclusion and financial integrity by defining the idea of "inclusive capitalism" and reflecting on the origins of capitalism as a broader concept. Her tone is quite different from President Obama's address because she is speaking to a group of financial professionals and world leaders at the international Conference on Inclusive Capitalism. But her message is similar: she notes that excess risk-taking by leaders and financial institutions have damaged the public's trust, and led to high unemployment and rising social tension. Like Obama, Lagarde's speech stresses the importance of involving the average worker in the economy and keeping employment rates high. But Lagarde's arguments focus on studies that support the notion that more even wealth distribution leads to more stable economic growth, whereas Obama's speech addresses the direct, personal impact that initiatives such as increased minimum wage would have on the individuals and families in his audience. These varied approaches are necessary to reach effectively the specific audience to which the speech is addressed.

Achieving a Goal

Achieving a goal that is both large-scale and specific requires motivating a vast array of people and organizations, which in turn requires multiple speeches combining all of these elements. For example, addressing the environmental damage and security threats to the world's oceans requires international cooperation from government and civic organizations, private companies, scientists, and individuals. Each of these groups has a different level of expertise in the issue, requires a different amount and type of information, and is motivated by different considerations.

US Consul General Jennifer McIntyre's speech at the Maritime Trade and Security Conference in Chennai, India, addresses the subject of security in international waters. Speaking to an audience of government officials and large corporate interests, McIntyre addresses the economic impact of this issue. She cites statistics about trade in India and Southeast Asia, and notes the significant impact on the United States of trade in this region—which includes more than $500 billion in exports, and supports approximately 2.8 million American jobs. She observes that securing waterways from piracy and other attacks requires the cooperation of both government and private interests, and uses economic impact to motivate the audience to care about the potential consequences of ignoring this key issue.

On the other hand, in his speech at the Google Workshop for Maritime Domain Awareness, Icelandic president Ólafur Ragnar Grímsson details the steps Iceland has taken to preserve its waterways, both environmentally and economically. As an island nation, much of Iceland's economy is based on fishing; as a result, the economic health of the country is closely tied to the health of the oceans. Grímsson explains that, to prevent overfishing, the Icelandic government and local community leaders work closely with the Marine Research Institute to understand and limit the impact of fishing on the environment. He credits this careful management with helping Iceland recover quickly and effectively from its financial crisis in 2008, and notes the wider benefits of the engineering and information technology advances made in order to help the fishing industry.

Grímsson's speech outlining Iceland's approach to ocean resource preservation underscores the importance of bringing together multiple interest groups to achieve a common goal. The collection of speeches presented here illustrates the wide variety of groups that must be reached to achieve significant and lasting change in any area affecting the United States and the world today—as well as the equally wide variety of approaches leaders must take to motivate these groups to act.

—Tracey DiLascio

1

A Year in Review

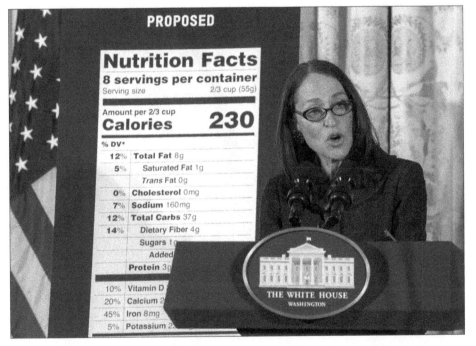

FDA Commissioner Peggy Hamburg makes remarks as proposed changes to the Nutrition Facts labels of foods are announced during an event in the East Room of the White House in Washington, DC, on February 27, 2014. The changes highlight the calorie count and add detail on added sugars in all foods to make the information easier for the consumer to understand.

Will Obamacare Succeed?

By Drew Altman

In this speech, Drew Altman, president and chief executive officer of the Henry J. Kaiser Family Foundation, delivers an address on the Affordable Care Act (ACA), also known as Obamacare, to a group gathered for Town Hall Los Angeles on April 24, 2014. The Kaiser Family Foundation is a nonprofit organization that produces surveys and policy analysis for the media and policy makers, providing research-based studies of public opinion and the function of various policy initiatives. Altman describes the ACA from two perspectives. First, he explains why the law has been unpopular with citizens, media, and legislators. Then he discusses the benefits of the ACA, including reducing the number of uninsured, addressing the issue of insurance restrictions for those with preexisting conditions, and addressing the issue of the lifetime cap. Altman argues that the national debate surrounding the ACA's success is largely misinformed because it fails to recognize the fact that the success of the program will differ from state to state, especially given the Supreme Court's ruling for state discretion on the expansion of Medicaid. On this point, he criticizes the twenty-four states that have failed to expand Medicaid for contributing to the middle-class insurance problem. Discussing efforts to judge the success of the ACA based on surveys, he then reports that the Kaiser Family Foundation does not find any of the current surveys sufficient to judge the overall success of the program. Altman joined the Kaiser Family Foundation in the early 1990s, significantly changing the focus and function of the organization.

Thank you so much, Kim. I've come to talk about the ACA, and about health reform. There are many days now——I'm sure you may feel this way too, maybe most days—when the debate about the ACA is kind of a through-the-looking-glass experience for me. It's kind of, I don't know, a fantasy world where the focus is on the wrong things and it's on the wrong numbers, and there is misperception, and there is also sometimes deliberate misrepresentation. And maybe it's a little bit more on one side than on the other side, but it is both, it is on all sides. And our monthly tracking polls, which I think some of you see, show that the public is still more than a little bit confused about the ACA, and the media, which tries very hard and is our best protection against a broken political system, just seems still incapable of giving the American people the information they need to come to an informed judgment about this law. And most importantly—we were talking about this: helping people answer what is really the question they have about this law—which is, what does this mean for me and my family? They are really just trying to figure out that one

Delivered April 24, 2014, at a meeting of Town Hall Los Angeles at the Millennium Biltmore Hotel, Los Angeles, California.
Drew Altman,"Will Obamacare Succeed?," The Henry J. Kaiser Family Foundation, April 24, 2014.

question. If we work on anything in our organization, it is trying to help people answer that one very basic question—and employers have that question, too, what does it mean for us?

This is a little bit of an academic point, but I was once an academic—I have come to the view that the debate we've had about the ACA maybe tells us more about ourselves and the problems with our political system and our media and our ability to have an informed debate about any big issue, but also about this issue, than it does about the good or the bad in the ACA itself. So one way of looking at this is, maybe we got the health reform law, or if not the health reform law, the debate about the health reform law, that we deserve until we deal with some of the more underlying problems in our political system. I've spent a lot of time in Washington, so I actually feel that very tangibly. And so, what I want to do today is focus on what I see as the real challenges facing the ACA. I'll be very practical, and mostly focus on the year ahead for you, and also on what I see as the challenges to having a better debate, a real debate, a more informed and rational debate about this law.

But before I get into this, I do often find that a little explanation about us is helpful when I'm speaking to California audiences. It's somewhat ironic, because we're a California-based organization based in Menlo Park, but there was a headline about us in a California newspaper that said, nationally very well-known but not so much in California, and that's absolutely true. So just very quickly, I did start the modern day Kaiser Family Foundation. That was in the early '90s, and it was in the middle of a very different health reform debate with the two Clintons, with Bill and Hillary Clinton. And many of you will remember that debate, and it was because I believed there needed to be an independent voice and source of information and research on all these big, hotly contested national health policy issues—not so much because I'm obsessed with research, which I may be—but because I felt there needed to be a counterweight to all of the money and politics and vested interests which so dominate everything that happens in our system. And we do that at our organization by producing basic facts, we do it by producing heavy-duty policy analysis which is sometimes interesting and sometimes will make your eyes glaze over. We do that by producing lots of polling and survey research. You may have seen our poll in *The New York Times* today. We do a lot of our polls with news organizations and we do that through journalism. We've launched the first national nonprofit health policy news service with the goal of producing in-depth coverage of these complicated issues. We actually have three journalists right now based in LA. We're defined a little bit by what we're not, which is kind of frustrating, but we are. As Kim mentioned, we're called Kaiser, but we have no connection with that giant HMO which is so much better known in California, except I get lots of angry letters from their enrollees who want to know why we wasted their premium dollars on this study or that study.

We are called a foundation, but we're actually legally not a foundation. We are a different—it's called a public charity, but I know that sounds like we're sitting on the street corner with a tin cup. The important thing for you to know is we do not make grants. We operate the programs that we run. We were called the think tank of the year, this year, by *The Washington Post*. Happy to have the recognition, but I refute it. Please do not have an image of us sitting up in Menlo Park in togas, eating grapes. We actually try and do things. We just believe deeply that there needs to be an independent voice and source of information in the hyper-partisan world of health policy, and that there actually are facts, and we try and—you know, we're under new illusions, I am, that objective is neutral in the hyper-partisan world of health policy, but we think there is a need for that. Our benefactor, Henry Kaiser, had a motto, which was find a need and fill it. We actually try and do that, and we try and do it to the best of our ability. We don't always get it right, we're not perfect.

Ok, the ACA. Let me give you two views of the Affordable Care Act. See if you recognize one or both of them. Here's one view: this is a law with few friends. Republicans hate it and Republican politicians rail against it while Democratic politicians give it only lukewarm support. Media stories criticize it, I would say, with a kind of reflexive negativity. It's not very popular with the American people and it's become a lightning rod for all that ails the American healthcare system. This is the—remember Colin Powell's Pottery Barn rule about Iraq, you break it, you own it? It kind of applies also to the ACA. It has an individual mandate that Americans don't like, and narrow networks which we were talking about, which people don't really like either, and some people in the individual market don't like it because they have to pay more. So, sick people can get coverage and pay less, and nobody exactly told them when this started that it was going to work out that way, and there were tradeoffs involved to fix the utterly broken individual market. And so, it's an overreach. It's too big a role for the federal government. I won't ask you if that's your view, but I'm sure you recognize the view.

Here's another view. The ACA has survived an election, a Supreme Court challenge, a government shutdown, a website meltdown, far exceeding year one enrollment expectations. It has more lives than, I don't know, Arnold Schwarzenegger in "The Terminator" or Bill Clinton in a presidential election campaign. It will cover 25 to maybe 30 million of the uninsured, and in so doing address a national shame—our roughly 50 million uninsured people in our country. It will also eliminate the worst abuses in our health insurance system—the most famous one is not covering people with preexisting conditions, but there are many, many others, like the lifetime caps which can bankrupt many families, including someone in my family who is quite sick right now. It does that. We can debate whether it will control costs, and maybe we'll do that in the Q&A, but it absolutely does that while paying for itself, which the Congressional Budget Office has determined and so have we. It passed without any bipartisan support because it had to. The lack of bipartisan support is a defining characteristic of this law, but it passed without any bipartisan support because it had to. Republicans were not going to support a health reform law brought to them by President Obama. So, it's the best that could be done, it's the right thing to do, and maybe now it has turned a corner. That's another view.

So, I won't ask you which view you hold, or if those are your views, but which of those views is right? Do any of you remember, I don't know if any of you saw this, but I thought it was amazing, *The Daily Show* segment when Jon Stewart ridiculed

CNN for reducing Obamacare and a few other issues to a single judgment, which was, was it good or was it bad? And I'm sure that some producer came up with that largely to drive ratings, but in the middle of every discussion, every CNN anchor had to interrupt the guest and just say, but is it good or is it bad? There was no context, there was no nuance, there was no complexity. It was an analysis of the ACA that you were intended to be able to grasp if you were getting dressed in a hotel room or running through an airport. It may be that what happens with CNN viewers is you actually go to the airport in order to watch CNN. I'm not sure how it works.

My answer to this is that neither of these good or bad views is right because the ACA is going to play out differently in every state, in every insurance market, for people at different income levels and depending on where they live and where they work and what kind of employer they work for. And so, while this will frustrate the American desire for a winner or a loser—you are either Rocky or the Russian, if you saw the movie—it will vary tremendously across the country. We just finished the first year of open enrollment in the ACA, and if you followed the national narrative for the first year, here's what you heard. If the ACA enrolled 7 million people in new marketplaces and enough of them are young adults, then the ACA was a success, and if it didn't, it was a failure. It was as simple as that, and there were two metrics—7 million, which was actually reduced by the CBO to 6 million, but let's call it 7 million, and young adults. The problem is, as I wrote in a column not too long ago, actually virtually nothing about that narrative is right because the 7 million is a number that was made up for different purposes, as I'll discuss in a minute, and because risk is pooled at the state level, and premiums are actually set in little local marketplaces depending on how much, largely on how much competition there is between insurers in those marketplaces.

So now, let me begin to get into some of the substance of the ACA and break this down for you. First of all: the 7 million. The CBO, the Congressional Budget Office, invented that number. The CBO developed that number for one purpose only—this is all the CBO does—to estimate the potential impact of the ACA on the federal budget. That is why the CBO exists. They were making no judgment about how many people should enroll in the ACA in the first year, how many people might be needed to have a healthy risk pool, what the goal should be for the ACA for the first year. Their only purpose in life was to come up with a likely number of people who might enroll in order to estimate the potential impact of the ACA on the federal budget. Nevertheless, that number, 7 million, became a magic number. It became a litmus test which the ACA, by the way, and the administration passed with flying colors, ultimately enrolling 8 million people. And I think they deserved the victory lap after the website problems. But it actually has little or nothing, almost nothing to do with what the real impact, as I'll describe in a second, of the ACA will be on people, on employers, in the country.

Second: young adults, that was the other big number. We put out a number, CBO put out the same number, that 40 percent of the potential market are young adults. And then magically, everyone latched onto that number as the goal. And you would hear media story after media story that unless Obamacare enrolls 40 percent of young adults, it's all over, and there will be a death spiral, and the goal is 40 percent of young adults, just like the 7 million. Well, it turns out that if they enroll just half of that number, 20 percent turn out to be young adults, the premiums will go up by about 2 percent. So yes, young adults are very important because they're healthier and the more the better, but never were young adults a make it or break it issue for the risk pool. What really matters are healthy people, not young people. So to put it as simply as I can, a healthy 50-year-old matters much more than a 27-year-old, and 60-year-old gym rat is worth his or her weight in gold, actuarially. What they did was, they transferred electoral politics—the young adults really mattered for the election of the president—to risk pools. It doesn't really work.

Third: they're talking about the 7 million and the make-up of the 7 million and how many are young adults. But there's actually no national risk pool at all. Under the law, risk is pooled at the state level. So, that means, some states are going to have good risk pools and some states are going to have bad risk pools. We don't know yet what those risk pools are going to look like. And that's going to vary a lot around the country.

Fourth: and this is my personal favorite ACA number, the premiums for the ACAs are set in what are called local rating markets. And guess what, there are 501—that's my favorite number—501 local rating areas under the ACA. Some states have one, California has 19, Florida has 67 because they're very inclusive in Florida—it's each county in Florida. So, the way to think about it is, if you're thinking about the premiums for the ACA, there are 501 ACAs running around out there. You can go adopt your own, whichever one you like.

And finally fifth: what matters most, even more than any of that, are the bets that insurance companies made about what their risk pools would look like in those markets. So, if they made good bets about how healthy or sick the people would be in their risk pools, their premiums are not going to go up very much this year. And if they bet wrong—there's more to this, I'm oversimplifying—but if they bet wrong, then the premiums could really go up a lot, and that again has nothing to do with how many young adults are in this 7 million, or whether it's 7 million or 6 million or 10 million or 15 million. So, the numbers to have in your heads are not 7 million or the percentage of young adults at all. It's 50 states, it's 501 rating areas, and what it means is, there will be tremendous variation by local market and state, and how the ACA plays out around the country is really going to be very different. You cannot look at a few national numbers and answer Wolf Blitzer's is it good or is it bad question. And so my metaphor for that is, it's like trying to predict the local weather from national averages. And that wouldn't matter, except for people it's the local weather that matters. It's, what's my premium, how much is my premium going to go up, and can I afford this?

So then, the issues we were talking about at our table, what are the real questions that we should be asking about the Affordable Care Act now? Probably the biggest one, I think it's the biggest one, is will the people who get coverage think it's affordable, will they think it's a good deal or not a good deal in this first year? I think much of the verdict on the law will turn on this. Everybody including the press is watching a relatively small number of people. First thing I will say about that is, it will take time for people to know, because it isn't just about the premium, it's also about the cost sharing and the deductibles, and you have to use health services in order to actually pay your cost sharing and your deductibles. So, we will not know the answer to that, people will not know the answer to that overnight. The deductibles in the ACA are very large, so we really do need to wait to see how people feel about them. In a typical silver plan, they can be $2,000–$4,000 for an individual policy, $5,000–$10,000 for a family policy. Let me put that in a political context for you. Conservatives hate this law, they whine about this law, but you could actually say that in a fundamental sense they're winning, because it is the conservative vision of what health insurance should look like with lots of skin in the game, which is now being promoted as a matter of national policy by Obamacare. Kind of a funny thing to think about, but it's absolutely true.

There will be winners and there will be losers. There probably will be far more winners than losers because 82 percent of the people who buy policies in the exchanges—or now we're supposed to call them marketplaces—get a subsidy tax credit. And some of them get a pretty big subsidy. But I would add to that, that one of the things we learned in—you remember that debate about the people whose plans were cancelled—one of the things we learned in that debate is it is not what us experts think about someone's policy, whether we think it's a good policy or a bad policy, or what an actuary thinks. It's what they think. So, a lot of people had their policy cancelled, far fewer than critics allege, but a lot of people had their policy cancelled. And we looked at it and said, what's your problem, that's a really terrible policy? And they said I picked that policy, I like that policy. I don't care about maternity care, or whatever it was. So, fundamentally, it is their perception of whether the policy is a good policy or a bad policy, not my perception as a health policy expert of whether they should like that policy or they shouldn't like that policy. And finally on this point, never have so few people meant so much to a policy debate. You know there are only 11 million people in this entire individual insurance market, but we will all be watching like hawks, and what they feel about their coverage.

A second big issue is what'll happen to the premiums in this second year and will they spike or not. Again, that will play out differently in each of—I hope my big discovery for you today—501 little ACAs around the country, and there will be great variation, and they will go up based on a mind boggling array of factors, including the trend in underlying healthcare costs, which is starting to go up. Including there were shock absorbers built into the ACA to cushion insurance companies against bad bets about what their risk pools would be. Those are beginning to phase out, including a new health insurance tax that is kicking in that will increase the cost of people's premiums, including the risk pools. Will it be a good risk pool or a bad risk pool? Including fundamentally the degree of competition in these little rating areas. More competition, lower premiums, less competition, higher premiums—it absolutely works. And finally, in some states they have very aggressive rate review. They regulate. In some states, they don't have any rate review. Put all these factors into the mix and the question is, how high will these premiums go? And so in some of these 501 rating areas, there'll be single-digit increases and in some there could be 30 percent premium increases. And what the average will be, will be very important. It will also be hard to know how much of that was caused by the ACA and how much of it was something else that is blamed on the ACA, back to the Pottery Barn rule.

Another big question that I was asked earlier today is how much is the ACA then reducing at the end of the day the ranks of the uninsured? It is a very fair question. It's the fundamental purpose of this law. If it doesn't do that, it failed—I mean, just flat out. But it's going to be hard to know anytime soon with any precision. There are a bunch of private surveys out there—the biggest one is Gallup, and you may read this. They have a lot of uninsured people in their giant sample, but if you look at— so, they should be able to tell—but if you look at their survey results over time, there just are a lot of unusual patterns in it. So, we're not completely confident about that. RAND has one, but it's a small survey. Urban Institute has one. We usually rely on federal surveys for this, but they've changed how they've asked their questions and so we won't be able to compare what happens now with how many uninsured we had before, which complicates things tremendously. All I can tell you is, the direction is very clear. It's reducing the number of uninsured. We will not have a reliable number for quite some time. We have our same numbers at Kaiser. We're not actually putting them out because we don't want to play, look at our bad number, too. And so we just aren't going to have a perfect answer to that question. It's not my fault, but I apologize for it on behalf of all of us in the policy analysis business.

An issue that I especially care about, which is a big California issue, is can they reach the long-term uninsured, the people who really need the insurance most? So, during the website debacle—I think everyone, a pernicious side effect of the whole website mess was—that it gave everyone the feeling that ok, if they fix the website it's all fine because it's Travelocity and it's Amazon.com. But did you know that 50 percent of the uninsured in California have been uninsured for two years or more or have never had insurance? And 20–25 percent of the uninsured have no Internet access and don't have a computer. I don't know how many of you saw those Twitter pictures of the long lines of people waiting to enroll in the last days of the open enrollment period. And sure, they showed that there was a late surge of interest in enrollment in Obamacare, but they showed something else as well. They showed that for a lot of those people, they weren't going on a website. They wanted to go talk to a real human being and get some help enrolling and making choices about complicated health insurance arrangements. So, the way I like to describe this is yes, there's an actuarial mission, getting a healthy risk pool. There's a social mission here too, which is the more important mission, which is reaching the people who need the insurance most. And for that, outreach is key, community-based enrollment services are key. It is underfunded in the federal exchange states for complicated political reasons. It is very well-funded in California. California has more money for outreach than all of the federal exchange states combined, but yet we are still struggling in California to reach the Latino population and to reach the long-term uninsured.

I'll tell you a little story, and I may cut some things short just to tell you this story, but when I was Commissioner of Human Services in New Jersey, I developed a really big school-based services program I was very proud of, hundreds of sites. But in developing it, I was traveling around the state and I went to the poorest part of the state, which by the way is not Camden or Newark. It's a rural part of the state which is—do you know there's a part of New Jersey below the Mason-Dixon Line? There is. So, I was being the technocrat, and I was visiting with these young people and asking them, what do you want? Do you want midnight basketball, do you want a doctor, do you want a nurse, do you want a pool table? What do you want in your school-based services program? And one kid, he was really small. He looked up at me and he said—it was an interesting thing to say to a cabinet officer—he said, Commissioner, you're just an idiot. And I thought that was great. And he said, I don't want any of that. What I want is somebody I can talk to who I trust. And of course, I was an idiot and he was totally right. But, it's really the same point here. I mean, for many people they really do want to talk to a human being when they need some help. And to make a broader political point about this, this is at the end of the day a largely low-income program. And for a lot of complicated political reasons everyone's always wanted to talk about it as mainly only a middle-class program, but at most it's both and it has implications for how you reach people. Another very big question is, can they bring the red states in? I think you've followed a little bit of this, but you probably know that there are 24 states who've decided to sit on the sidelines and not opt for the Medicaid expansion since the Supreme Court ruled the law was constitutional but made the Medicaid expansion a state option. The degree to which the Supreme Court fundamentally rewrote the law is really underappreciated.

Why is it critical? It's critical first of all because it leaves 4.8 million people without coverage who make too much money to be eligible for their state's Medicaid program but not enough money to be eligible for the tax credits in their state. It creates a crazy situation in these states where you've got these 4.8 million people who fall in the gap and don't get coverage, but you've got 10 million people who make more money than they do—it could be people in the same family—and they get tax credits to help them buy private coverage on the insurance exchanges. So as far as I'm concerned, you can hate Obamacare, you can love Obamacare, I don't care, but that's nuts. That's not a rational insurance system for the lower-income population.

But this is important in another way which I think is even more fundamental, which is if the red states come in, then there is a way to build a bipartisan constituency for the law over time which cannot be done in Washington for the foreseeable future. It is not that these states will come in cheering for Obamacare, but now they will have a stake in the law as well. What will it take? They want to expand on their own terms so they are not embracing Obamacare and get the federal money. They want to do that through what's called a private option, where they take the federal money and use it to help beneficiaries buy private policies instead of expanding the traditional Medicaid program. The key is to work that out in a way that protects low-income people, because the cost sharing can be too high for low-income people. I once got a federal waiver, a big one, a very controversial one, at 3:00 AM in the morning amidst very heated politics in the Reagan White House. So, the one thing I will tell you is, this stuff is negotiable. This is not a sterile technical process. If it were me, I would make this an absolute top priority, bringing in these red states, trying to be practical about it, and doing what it takes. Texas will be the toughest nut to crack. I think you know why—the governor's very opposed to all this. But New Hampshire, Utah, Pennsylvania are moving forward. It may be that the log jam is starting to break.

And now, just one final question, which is can the Congress learn and make improvements in the law? Kind of a political science point, but I think really quite important. Imagine a different world for just one second, one where both Republicans and Democrats had a stake in the ACA, we had a functional Congress rather than the polarized and paralyzed Congress we have today. And then, what would the ACA be? It would be a giant experiment where you could look and you could see what's working and what's not working, and what's not working would not be a daily attack line and headline, developing story, breaking news on CNN. We could actually learn from that and make improvements in the law, which every poll we do, including the one today in *The New York Times* in southern states shows is what the American people want to happen. We do not live in that world, right? That's just not the world we're living in right now. Our polarized and paralyzed Congress can't do that. States, on the other hand, can. States watch other states very closely. I can tell you as a former state official that stealing and borrowing the best ideas from other states is actually a virtue in state government. Maryland, which embraced the law and has a totally broken website, is now borrowing Connecticut's website. So, I think there is hope in that.

As we seek answers to these questions, and average people try and figure out what the ACA means for them, I do think the ACA will remain the poster child of hyper-partisanship, at least through 2016, after which I guess we can't call it Obamacare any longer, and a confused and heavily-spun public will remain largely dependent on the news media for information. People tell us overwhelmingly in our surveys that they get their information on the ACA from the national news media, which is actually different from how they get most of their health information, which is from local TV news. And that's actually why I began with, is this good or bad, from CNN.

And so, I caution some patients when it comes to judging a complex law like the Affordable Care Act and I do feel that in looking at the ACA debate we need to look in the mirror as well as at the law itself because the ACA has its issues. It also has its great virtues, but it is also a reflection of where we are right now in the country and where our political system is as well. Thank you very much. And remember, 501 rating areas.

Remarks on the Proposed Updates to the Nutrition Facts Label

By Margaret A. Hamburg

In this speech, delivered on February 27, 2014, Margaret A. Hamburg, commissioner of food and drugs for the US Food and Drug Administration (FDA), speaks about the proposed updates to the nutrition facts labels mandated on food products sold in the United States. This announcement was part of a conference organized to mark the fourth anniversary of First Lady Michelle Obama's "Let's Move!" campaign to combat childhood obesity. Commissioner Hamburg begins by describing the history of the FDA's nutrition facts labels, which began in 1994 as an effort to provide American consumers with nutritional information about the contents of food. In redesigning labels, Hamburg says, the FDA consulted with the Institute of Medicine and other sources to address information gained in the twenty years since the labels were introduced. Hamburg says that the new labels will require "added sugar," a primary cause for obesity, to be listed separately on a label. The new labels will also require foods to list the calories "per serving" and "per package." Vitamin D and potassium will also be added to the nutrients that are listed. Hamburg also says that the new labels will have an updated design, in hopes of making the labels easier for consumers to read and interpret. Margaret Hamburg is an American physician who has served as commissioner of the US Food and Drug Administration since 2009. Before joining the FDA, Hamburg was on the board of directors for Henry Schein, Inc., a corporation that supplies physicians, dentists, and veterinarians with health care supplies.

I am delighted to be joining you all for today's Let's Move announcement in which the FDA is unveiling our proposed changes for a new and improved—and user-friendly—version of the iconic Nutrition Facts label. Before I walk through our proposed changes, I also want to take a moment to thank First Lady Michelle Obama for her continued commitment to encouraging Americans to live healthier lifestyles—and to recognize the four-year anniversary of the Let's Move! initiative.

For 20 years, we have relied on the iconic Nutrition Facts label to help us make healthy choices when deciding what to eat. When it was first introduced back in 1994, this landmark label provided the American consumer with uniform information about the nutritional content of foods.

Since that time, we have gained a better understanding of the relationship between what we eat and many of the chronic diseases affecting millions of Americans. For example, we know that eating more calories than needed to maintain our

Delivered February 27, 2014, during a celebration of the fourth anniversary of the "Let's Move!" initiative, Washington, DC, by Margaret A. Hamburg.

body weight, coupled with a lack of physical activity, is a primary risk factor for obesity in the general population.

FDA experts relied on data from a variety of sources, including the Institute of Medicine to design this new label.

Let me highlight some of the proposed changes for you.

We know that as a nation we eat too much added sugar. While some of those sugars occur naturally in foods, much of it is added. The new label would provide more information about sugars in food by now indicating when a food has "added sugar."

Added sugars contribute to a substantial portion of Americans calories, but don't really provide much else in the way of nutrients. This has major implications in maintaining healthy body weight. We believe that requiring added sugars to be listed separately on the Nutrition Facts label will better allow consumers to identify and compare products with added sugar and enable them to make better choices.

We also hope this change will motivate the food industry to reformulate its products. As many of you may know, this occurred back in 2006 when we required food producers to add information about trans fats in the label. When Americans have better options, they can make healthier choices—and we all win.

Now let's talk about how much we eat. In many cases, people are now eating amounts that are different from the serving sizes that the FDA first put in place in 1994.

I should note that our official definition for serving size is a reference amount. It reflects how much we actually eat when serving ourselves. And for this reference amount to be useful to the consumer, it has to be close to what the average person would typically eat. So, contrary to what many may think, serving sizes on food packages are not recommended portions.

We also know that package size affects what people eat, and that people are likely to eat or drink all of the contents of certain packaged foods in one sitting. For packaged foods and beverages that are typically consumed in one sitting, we propose labeling all of them as a single serving and declaring calorie and nutrient information for the entire package. For example, a can of ready-to-serve soup is usually consumed as a single serving.

For packages that are larger and could be consumed as either single or multiple servings, manufacturers would have to provide a "dual column" label to indicate both "per serving" and "per package" calorie and nutrient information. This way, people will know how many calories and nutrients they are consuming if they eat or drink the entire amount at one time.

It might be surprising to learn that, in this day and age, there are still nutrients that some people aren't getting enough of. We have known for some time that potassium and Vitamin D are important nutrients for health, significant for maintaining a healthy lifestyle.

Potassium can help lower blood pressure, while Vitamin D is a key nutrient for helping to promote healthy bone development and general health. But what's new is that current data show that certain population groups are not getting enough of them.

Therefore, we are proposing that these nutrients be required elements that are listed on the Nutrition Facts label, along with calcium and iron, which have been required for some time. Vitamins A and C, which are currently required, could be listed voluntarily.

Finally, we are proposing changes to some Daily Values, which are intended to be a guide for how much of a particular nutrient a person should consume each day—or, in the case of things like sodium, an upper limit for the day.

The Daily Values are used to determine the Percent Daily Value that you see on the label. The Percent Daily Value helps you see how much of the Daily Value one serving of a particular packaged food contributes.

We've determined through our scientific research that some of these numbers should change. While the upper limit for sodium will decrease slightly to be in line with recent expert recommendations, data show that the daily targets for dietary fiber and calcium should increase somewhat.

Finally, let's see what's changed in the layout of the Nutrition Facts label itself.

You will see that information about calories and serving sizes jumps out at you. On the other hand, we've actually removed certain information, such as "calories from fat." That's because we've learned that total fat is less important than the type of fat.

These are important changes and our goal here is to design a label that is easier to read and one that consumers can understand.

This proposal is the culmination of years of research, study, and requests for public input. We have welcomed the comments we have received from experts and consumers alike to guide us toward a label we feel will provide people with the information they want and need. It's clear that the benefits will far outweigh the costs.

We believe these proposed updates to the Nutrition Facts label will help in improving public health, incorporating the latest nutrition recommendations to reduce the risk of chronic diseases such as cardiovascular disease, obesity, high blood pressure and stroke.

We realize that the label alone won't magically change how America eats, but we hope that once consumers decide to implement changes to their diet and lead a healthier lifestyle, it will provide them with the tools to be successful.

Thank you.

A Healthcare Tsunami: Decline of Cognitive Function with Aging

By Keith L. Black

In this speech, delivered to Town Hall Los Angeles in February 2014, Dr. Keith L. Black, of the Department of Neurosurgery at Cedars-Sinai Medical Center, discusses the significance of Alzheimer's disease research. Black begins with a personal account of his mother's diagnosis with Alzheimer's disease twelve years prior, and his subsequent efforts to learn about the disease. Explaining the depth of the Alzheimer's disease problem, he asserts that 50 percent of people eighty-five and older will develop Alzheimer's disease; the disease will become more common because, as the baby boom generation reaches retirement age, a larger proportion of the population will be elderly. According to Black, one of the most pressing difficulties in addressing Alzheimer's disease is the lack of reliable methods for diagnosing the disease before it reaches its final stages. He recommends reallocating funds to develop new diagnostic methods and describes research conducted in his lab—in collaboration with scientists from the Weizmann Institute in Israel—that resulted in a promising new diagnostic technique to detect signs of Alzheimer's disease in the retinal tissues of the eye. Black also emphasizes the use of vitamins, nutrition, and exercise as methods for decreasing the risk of Alzheimer's disease during one's lifetime. In conclusion, he talks about recent advancements in the ongoing search for medications to treat Alzheimer's disease, mentioning several insulin-based treatments currently considered promising within the neurological medicine community. Black has been with Cedars-Sinai Medical Center since 1997, and serves as chairman of the Department of Neurosurgery and director of the hospital's Neurosurgical Institute.

Thank you, Kim, and thank you Carl for inviting me here to Town Hall Los Angeles. My first Town Hall presentation and it's great to see all the networking. But I realize with a friend like Carl Dickerson, I can just call him and get to probably most people that I need to. So, it's nice to have good friends.

I'm a brain surgeon and usually brain surgeons do not deal with Alzheimer's disease. Alzheimer's is a disease that's mostly dealt with nonsurgically, and is taken care of primarily by neurologists or geriatricians. For me, this really became personal because my mother was diagnosed with Alzheimer's disease about 12 years ago. And so I realized firsthand how devastating this disease can be and that we really need to accelerate trying to come up with a solution for it. As Carl said, some people think I'm a fairly decent brain surgeon, but it was very difficult for me to accept the fact

Delivered February 26, 2014, at a meeting of Town Hall Los Angeles at the Millennium Biltmore Hotel, Los Angeles, California, by Keith L. Black.

that I've received all these awards and all these accolades, the cover of *Time* maga-zine and so forth, but when my mother developed a neurological disease, there was not much I could do. I've done a lot of research on things that neurosurgeons typi-cally focus on, like brain tumors and brain cancer. And brain cancer is really hard, because with brain cancer, you actually have to kill every single brain cancer cell. And we've done a lot of out of the box thinking on trying to come up with strategies, and we've developed things like a therapeutic vaccine for brain cancer—so that we've taken the most aggressive form of brain cancer called a glioblastoma multiforme, which with best standard of care includes surgery, radiation, and chemotherapy, the five-year survival is only about 5–10 percent. And with the latest generation of the vaccine that we developed at Cedars-Sinai, at least in a Phase 1 small single-institu-tion study, 50 percent of the patients were alive with no evidence of cancer out past five years. So, I know that we can solve really tough problems. And when my mother developed Alzheimer's, I really began to try to focus on the problem of Alzheimer's dementia.

The first thing I had to do, I had to educate myself about the disease. Even being a neurosurgeon, the significance of this problem wasn't readily apparent to me. And I know that we have the president of the Alzheimer's Association here and they know these facts very well. And one of the things that you realized is that the incidents of Alzheimer's actually are just a proportion of how old the population is. Our bodies are designed to really outlast our brains. And so, as we achieve the ability to get a longer and longer life span, our bodies are able to survive longer and healthier, but currently our brains are not. So if you actually don't expect to live very long, you can just enjoy the rest of your coffee and whatever and you don't need to listen to what I have to say. But if you actually hope to live a nice long life this really becomes a sig-nificant problem because by the time we actually get to be 65 and older in this popu-lation, 10 percent of us will have Alzheimer's disease. Imagine that, 65 and older.

How many people in the audience, just the guys, not the women, are 65 and older? In our parents' generation, this was really not an issue, because they had a life expectancy of 62. That's why we started Medicare at 65. Their parents' generation was maybe about 50, 55. But our life expectancy is about 78– 2, and a child that's born today has a one out of three chance of living to 100. By the time we get to be 85 and older, we're biologically programmed so that 50 percent of us 85 and older will have Alzheimer's disease. By the time we reach 90 and 90-plus, that incidence goes well over 80 percent. So, this is a real problem and that was really the first eye-opener to me because I didn't realize the magnitude of the problem. And with the aging population, not just in the US but globally, increasing year by year, this really becomes a healthcare tsunami, because we cannot afford not to find a solution to this problem.

Currently, we spend just in the United States about $200 billion a year on Al-zheimer's disease. To put that in some perspective, we spend about $54 billion a year on cancer and we spend about $150 billion on cardiovascular heart disease. That $200 billion is projected over the next few decades to go to $1 trillion with the increase in life expectancy. And as we get better and better at caring for people with Alzheimer's disease . . . you don't just live with, I mean, Alzheimer's doesn't necessarily kill you. It takes away your brain, the very essence of who you are. It takes away your memory, your personality, your language, your ability to interact with your family and your loved ones, but it doesn't really kill you. What kills you is the pneumonia or the blood clot to your lung or something you get from just being in bed a long time. And as we get better and better at that basic health care, people can live a very long time with Alzheimer's disease. So, it's not like brain cancer, where the bad time may be three months or four months. You can live 10 years with no memory, needing 24/7 care. Now, that's really expensive, and I happen to be fortunate enough to pay for people to do that for my mother, but most of us cannot do that. So what happens is that usually it's a daughter in the family who has to quit her job and care for the person. And the financial and emotional stress on the family and the loved ones that deal with this disease——because it also has a behavioral component to it where the person gets aggressive and belligerent and it's part of the disease and you don't quite understand it——and being the daughter trying to take care of the person——Why is grandpa yelling and screaming and not really doing these basic things?——their health becomes at risk. Their probability of getting illness is increased because of the stress of caring for this.

This is really a big issue, and we can talk about the Affordable Care Act and we can talk about the cost of Medicare, but I will tell you that one thing is absolutely clear. Unless we stop living longer, this will bankrupt the healthcare system. So, that's problem Number 1.

Problem Number 2 is that we really don't have a good way of diagnosing Alzheimer's disease. The way that we currently diagnose Alzheimer's disease is when the patient comes and they have memory loss. Usually it's your family doctor; maybe we refer the patient to a neurologist. The neurologist does a cognitive test, a memory test, and says the memory impairment you have in these various domains tend to fit with Alzheimer's disease. We think you have Alzheimer's disease. That's the way that 99 percent of patients with Alzheimer's disease are currently diagnosed in state-of-the-art health care in wealthy west downtown Los Angeles. The problem is that the disease actually started about 20 years before you got memory loss, and by the time you actually get memory loss, you've lost half of your brain weight and half of your brain cells. The disease is already in full bloom and is moving down a course in inflammatory pathological cascade that at that point, with 20 years of development, is very hard to reverse. So, it's as if someone has had untreated diabetes for 20 years and now they have end-stage heart disease, kidney failure, diabetic retinopathy, and they go to their doctor and he says, your glucose is 400, we need to treat it. That's going to do a little good, but it's not going to stop your end-stage heart disease and your blindness, right? The only way to have done that would have been to control the diabetes 20 years before, and prevent those end-stage organ failures from occurring. So, that's where we are right now with Alzheimer's disease. We're diagnosing it at the advanced stage.

Pharmaceutical companies are literally spending billions of dollars trying to develop drugs to treat a disease at the end-stage, which means they're trying to treat something where they actually have to reverse brain cell death, have to regenerate brain cells and remake all those connections, which is almost impossible to do. And that's why we essentially see drug failure after drug failure after drug failure, after billions and billions of dollars of medical research. Until we have the ability to have an early way of intervening 20 years before the person actually develops the disease, we're not going to solve the problem. So, that was problem Number 1.

We actually in our lab—and once my mother got Alzheimer's disease, I was in a very unique position, being head of the neurosurgical research institute at Cedars-Sinai, overseeing both clinical neurological care as well as a huge research portfolio that was primarily focused on brain tumors and stroke and things like that—I had the ability to actually deploy some of those resources and recruit some of the best scientific minds that I could find around the planet working on innovative ways of trying to solve the problem of Alzheimer's. So, I recruited a team of scientists actually from the Weizmann Institute in Israel. And one of the questions they ask is, wait a minute, it's really difficult to diagnose Alzheimer's. The first thing that occurs in the disease is the build-up of these toxic plaques made up of a misfolded very toxic protein called amyloid that occurs in the brain. And we know those plaques are the earliest change, and those plaques occur about 20 years before you actually become symptomatic and about 10 years before you get any other changes we know about. And a lot of people have tried to find these plaques. You cannot see them on a CT scan, you cannot see them on an MRI scanner. You can do a brain biopsy, but most people don't want to do a brain biopsy if they don't have any memory loss. Even as a neurosurgeon, I wouldn't subject myself to that. We've tried to develop PET scans to detect this amyloid, but PET scans are radioactive, it costs about $8,000 or $9,000 a scan, a limited number of centers around the country, and insurance won't pay for it. So, we asked the question, is there an easier way? And it turns out that when you look through the eye, you're really looking at brain tissue. The back of the eye is your retina and the retina is an embryonic outgrowth of the brain. So, whatever is occurring in the brain, maybe it also occurs in the retina, is the question they posed. And since we knew these toxic amyloid plaques occurred 20 years in the brain before the person became symptomatic, we asked the question, if we could find those plaques in the retina, could we have an easy test by just looking through the eye of actually seeing the plaques and making the diagnosis of Alzheimer's before it becomes symptomatic. So long answer short, the answer's yes.

We have these rat models that are genetically engineered to develop Alzheimer's disease. We actually fed the rats curcumin. Curcumin is the active ingredient in the Indian spice curry, turmeric acid. Curcumin has a couple of unique properties. One property is that they bind to these plaques which are the hallmark of Alzheimer's, but they also give off a natural fluorescence. If we could see the fluorescence, if they attached to these plaques, potentially we could look in the back of the eye and see them. So, they developed a technique where they modified some filters on a retinal scanner, looked in the rat's eye with the Alzheimer's disease, and we could actually see the individual plaques. Now, that concept was so revolutionary to the Alzheimer's scientific community that when we tried to report the finding, no one believed it, and we couldn't get the finding published. All the experts said, those cannot be plaques in the back of the eye, they just cannot exist.

So then, we actually ended up collaborating with the neuropathologist that for whatever reason had this bank of brains from Alzheimer's patients and had also saved the eyes. And we went back and looked at the brains pathologically and saw the plaques in the brain and we saw the plaques in the retina. And there was a direct correlation with the plaques in the brain and the plaques in the retina. That actually confirmed the plaques existed. And then we asked the question, could we actually see the plaques in a living person, not just an autopsy? So, we actually spun out the technology from Cedars-Sinai, developed a small startup, and actually developed a retinal imaging scanner very similar to what you would see at your optometrist or ophthalmologist's office when they look in the back of the eye, looking for diabetic retinopathy or macular degeneration. And we put the filters on to detect this fluorescence of the curcumin. We gave patients oral curcumin, and after a few days, we could look in their eyes and see the plaques. And we did that here in Los Angeles and we were able to with 100 percent accuracy detect patients with Alzheimer's disease, and show the ones that had Alzheimer's and show patients that didn't have Alzheimer's.

That was good, but the question is, how early can you detect it? Then we went into several other studies, and it turned out there's a very unique group of patients in Australia that the Australian government has funded to try to actually develop an early biomarker for Alzheimer's, because people realize this is a problem. They've taken about 1,000 patients, some people that are normal volunteers with no memory loss, no Alzheimer's disease, people with early mild cognitive impairment, not quite Alzheimer's, and Alzheimer's patients. And they've done a complete workup on these patients, everything from physical exam, blood test, MRI scans, PET scans looking for amyloid; they've done spinal taps looking for it in their fluid. This is a well-characterized group. And we put our retinal test, our 10-minute retinal test in that, and it turns out that it's better than any of these biomarkers they have, including spinal tap and PET. It has about 1,000 times the resolution of a PET scanner, and it doesn't require you to get a spinal puncture and it's not radioactive, and it probably can be done for a few hundred bucks noninvasively in about 10 minutes in your eye doctor's office. We believe this is a test that can basically transform the field of Alzheimer's disease because it can essentially be used as a screening test for people in their 50s who may be at risk of developing Alzheimer's 10–20 years later. That is really the first important breakthrough, we believe, in solving the problem, because we have to be able to treat the patients early. And the drug companies have to be able to test their new compounds on patients before they actually become symptomatic and before they lose half their brain cells.

When I talk to people about this, everyone really except for Carl—Carl said I'm going to take the test anyway. Most people then say, Dr. Black, that's really interesting, but you're going to tell me that I'm going to develop Alzheimer's disease 10 or 20 years from now and there's nothing I can really do about it? I don't know that I want to know. I'm just going to be the ostrich and bury my head in the sand and just forget about it, and when it comes, it comes. That's the response of most people. I'm just curious, how many people in this room would take the test if that test was available now? All right, you guys are really a selective group. This is a group that actually came to the talk. So, your assignment tonight is to actually go home and ask your friends if they would take the test, who didn't come to the talk.

Then the question becomes, what do you do about it? For me, I thought about this for a long time. When my mother developed Alzheimer's I said, obviously we're going to look for the drug that's going to be very effective, but before we get the drug, what do we know now that can actually make a difference in the course of this disease? Because this is a disease that goes over decades, so you slowly lose cognitive function over time. In fact, I have another bit of depressing information—I'm giving you a lot of depressing information today. You actually start losing cognitive ability about the age 30. That's why you see that most people that win the Nobel Prize in physics, they've always made their discovery before 30. Any physicists out there that are waiting on the Nobel Prize, hopefully you've made your discovery already. But, even when we get Alzheimer's, it's a slow progression. So, if you're developing the disease at 50 and you're going to get symptomatic at 70, we need to change the slope of that deterioration so you don't get symptomatic at 70, you get symptomatic at 95. So you can live out most of your life without symptomatic disease. And that's something that I think is readily achievable.

And so I began researching and we actually put together a team of neuroscientists. There are about 100 different things that are out there that people say this can help, that can help. But we actually looked at things that had scientific evidence. One of the best things you can do is to exercise. Exercise is probably one of the most important things you can do overall for heart health, health in general, but also it's good for brain health. If you exercise rats they actually generate more brain cells, they generate more synaptic connections. And it keeps your brain healthy more than just the cardiovascular effect. Exercise is critical. The other obvious thing is to keep your brain engaged. People that have high academic achievement, high educational levels actually have more brain reserve, more synaptic connections. That reserve allows you to cushion the brain cell loss over time and delay the symptomatic aspect of the disease. And the more you keep your brain active, the more of those connections you make throughout life, the more you actually regenerate those brain cells. So, that's really important. People ask me about Lumosity. It's not really doing crosswords, things that are repetitive. You have to do things that are challenging. You've got to learn, for example, how to—if you're terrible at music, try to learn how to play the piano. Me, I'm terrible at foreign languages; I need to learn how to speak French or something. So, learn how to fly a helicopter, but things that you are not comfortable with doing. If you're a great mathematician, doing more math problems isn't going to help. You have to get outside your comfort zone, which really drives those areas of connectivity within the brain. That's critical.

And then the third, we began to look at nutrients and vitamins and things like that. The first thing that will happen if you go to a neurologist with dementia is that they're going to test your Vitamin B levels, they're going to test your thyroid levels, make sure all of those things are fine. But it turns out that there are some things where the scientific weight of the evidence suggests they can be beneficial. And we don't have randomized, placebo-controlled clinical trials, but some things are very compelling. One of those things is curcumin. Curcumin is again what we use to detect the plaques in the retina, but it also binds to the plaques and helps the brain clear the plaques and decreases the inflammation which may be damaging in Alzheimer's disease. Asian Indians have one-fourth the incidents of Alzheimer's disease as the western population, the non-Asian population—because they're eating curry all of their lives, which is curcumin. Some people doubt those studies, but again, the evidence suggests in animal studies and uncontrolled patient studies that curcumin could have a very beneficial effect. Most of the curcumin you get from the vitamin store will not get absorbed out of your stomach—less than 1 percent does—so you have to have a special form that actually gets absorbed. Other things like green tea extract and DHA and phenacetin are all things that can appear helpful. So as Carl said, I started taking these vitamins myself because I felt the downside was low and the upside was there as a possibility. And then, we actually developed some bars that he gave you the website for if you're interested—actually taste pretty good—that contain about the level of vitamins that I was taking myself and that I still take myself, over the past few years. So, it's kind of an easy thing that you can do.

What's coming down the pike that we're excited about, that's actually interesting? There are a number of things, but I'm going to tell you about one that we're excited about and really trying to move into a Phase 1 trial, so that when you get the retinal test we can say here are some clinical trials that we have that you might be interested in participating in, here are lifestyle things you can do. And the beauty of that retinal test is that in our rat models, when we give things that actually work, we can see those plaques melt away in the retina, just like they would in the brain. So, we can actually see individual plaques and use that as a response to therapy, which is very exciting. It turns out there is an association between Alzheimer's and diabetes, but independent of the association between Alzheimer's and diabetes, one of the researchers that we recruited has a very interesting model, research model. And that model is that patients with Alzheimer's disease, they agree to donate their brains at death for Alzheimer's research. He's able to get the brains within six hours of death and he takes slices of the brain where the brain cells are still alive. And what he's found is that 80 percent of the brain cells in patients with Alzheimer's disease have insulin resistance. Now, insulin resistance is what causes diabetes in the periphery outside of the brain, because you need insulin to get sugar into the cells. Brain cells don't really need insulin to get sugar in, but they do need insulin to survive. So, when the brain cells become resistant to insulin, they are programmed to die. And we believe that may be why the brain cells are dying in Alzheimer's. They become resistant to the insulin and then they get a signal to die, and that's why we lose the brain cells.

The interesting thing about his research is that when he gives a drug to reverse the insulin resistance, the brain cells live. Now, why is that interesting? Because in the treatment of diabetes, we have drugs that are already FDA approved, that have a very reasonable safety profile, that can reverse insulin resistance—things like glucagon-like peptide-1 analogues, GLP-1 analogues that can be given either orally or an injection once a week. So, there was a pilot study in patients in Europe with Parkinson's disease that also has dementia. And when they gave these drugs to this small group of Parkinson's patients, within three months they saw an improvement in the cognitive function. And now, we're very excited about testing this hypothesis in a pilot study at Cedars with Alzheimer's disease, because if that's right, what that could mean is that we have drugs that are already FDA approved, so that we don't need to spend billions of dollars and 10 years of research to get a drug. We can just take a drug that's already approved, we can use a retinal test to tell if you're developing the disease years before you get it that is causing your brain cells to die, we can treat you with this drug prophylactically, monitor your eyes to make sure it's working, and essentially prevent Alzheimer's.

Those are the kind of moon shots that we're trying to put on goal at our research institute and we hope that they will ultimately be effective. We have a number of other candidates that we're trying, but those are the kinds of things that I think have real high potential, because if we don't solve this problem, God bless us all. So thank you.

Keynote Remarks at the Launch of the World Bank's *Gender at Work* Report

By Catherine M. Russell

Catherine M. Russell, US ambassador-at-large for global women's issues, gives the keynote lecture at the launch of the World Bank's Gender at Work *report, discussing the need to address gender imbalances in the workforce. The* Gender at Work *report is a comprehensive biannual review of World Bank programs aimed at promoting gender equality; it also presents research from a variety of sources measuring gender gaps and achievements around the world. Russell begins by addressing the purpose of the report, which is to provide analysis and recommendations to legislators and policymakers for use in advocating for gender equality programs. The data she presents indicates that there has been a global growth in female income and workplace participation, and that women now constitute 50 percent of the workforce in the United States. Reports also show, she adds, that addressing gender gaps could increase gross domestic product (GDP) globally and could have a significant impact on hunger and poverty. In terms of solutions to workplace inequity, Russell asserts that collaboration between public and private organizations is key to successfully integrating women into the workplace and cites examples of programs that have been supported by the US Department of State to create and support entrepreneurial opportunities for women worldwide. She then highlights some innovative programs—such as the Tech Girls program, which provides technological training to women in the Middle East—that support women in the workplace. Russell was chief of staff to Second Lady Jill Biden before she was appointed to serve as the US ambassador-at-large for global women's issues in 2013.*

Thank you, Kyle, and good afternoon everyone. I am grateful for the opportunity to be here. It's wonderful to see so many friends in the audience. This event—and your being here to launch the *Gender at Work* report—underscores the importance of taking action towards achieving gender equality.

Before I begin, I'd like to recognize the great work the World Bank has done in this area. Gender equality has become integrated into so much of the Bank's work—from a renewed IDA strategy for gender equality with more ambitious targets throughout the project lifecycle, to assisting in developing gender specialists in regional offices—and the leadership of the Bank and President Kim have made that possible.

I'd also like to recognize the experts who contributed to this valuable report. To Kyle Peters, Sri Mulyani, Jeni Klugman, Jesko Hentschell, and Matthew

Delivered February 20, 2014, at the launch of the World Bank's *Gender at Work* report, Washington, DC, by Catherine M. Russell.

Morton—congratulations on this tremendous effort. My team and I look forward to continuing our close collaboration with you in the months and years ahead.

The *Gender at Work* report gets to the heart of so many of the issues that we as a community strive to address. It explores how to bolster the roles of both the public and private sectors. And, more importantly, discusses just how critical it is for us to close data gaps if we hope to achieve our goals.

But, of course, this is much more than a report: it is a call to action.

As you know, investing in women isn't just as the right thing to do, and isn't just the moral thing to do: it's the wise thing to do.

Secretary of State Kerry has made economic empowerment a centerpiece of American foreign policy. As he said last year, "The United States believes gender equality is critical to our shared goals of prosperity, stability, and peace, and [that is] why investing in women and girls worldwide is critical to advancing U.S. foreign policy."

But achieving shared global prosperity is only possible if—and this is a big "if"—if we make dramatic progress in reducing gender gaps in the world of work.

Our shared economic potential is bright—but in order to achieve it, we need to encourage, cultivate, and harness the untapped talent and productivity of women across the globe. It must happen in every country and on every continent.

Thankfully, *Gender at Work* lays out a comprehensive roadmap for how to do just that. It provides insightful analysis and key recommendations that policymakers and advocates can use to level the playing field for women around the world.

This information is essential to the team I lead as the Ambassador at Large for Global Women's Issues. I was very encouraged to learn that recommendations in each of the report's three key areas—the private sector's role, the public sector's role, and the need to close data gaps—are in sync with our office's direction and priority areas.

Since I started my job, one of my primary goals has been to continue the momentum on women's economic empowerment. We are focusing on this area because of the profound impact that economic empowerment—or a lack of it—can have not just on the lives of billions of women and girls around the world, but on families, communities and nations. And we see what a difference that makes on both the macro and micro levels.

I'd like to begin with how gender equality and equality of opportunity at work matters at the macro level. At the APEC Women and the Economy Summit in San Francisco in 2011, former Secretary of State Clinton said: "By increasing women's participation in the economy and enhancing their efficiency and productivity, we can bring about dramatic impact on the competitiveness and growth of our economies."

As was often the case, she couldn't have been more right. To demonstrate the enormous potential that the economic empowerment of women can have on growth, here are a few telling statistics:

In the second half of the 20th century, the entry of women into the workforce propelled substantial growth for most of the world's developed economies.

In the U.S., according to 2011 report by McKinsey & Company, women now make up nearly 50 percent of our workforce and own 30 percent of small businesses, which generate $1.2 trillion a year in sales.

In Europe, the OECD found that the narrowing gap between male and female employment has accounted for a quarter of the continent's annual GDP growth over the past two decades.

In Latin America and the Caribbean, growth in female income made a crucial contribution to both extreme and moderate poverty reduction between 2000 and 2010. According to the World Bank, if income remained flat during that decade and the labor market held constant, extreme poverty would have been 30 percent higher in 2010 had female contributions not been more.

Further, the OECD recently reported that closing gender gaps in the labor market in the MENA region, where the ILO also notes particularly acute gender wage gaps, could increase per capita GDP by more than 25 percent.

In November, Vice President Biden and I traveled to Japan, the world's third largest economy. I saw firsthand how Prime Minister Abe, is trying to remove constraints on women in the workforce to boost his nation's economic performance. Not only did he recognize such steps made common sense, he also saw they made good business sense.

According to the IMF, Japan could see an additional 9 percent growth in their GDP if they addressed barriers and took steps to raise female labor force participation to that of males. And the UN found that the Asia Pacific region loses upwards of 47 billion dollars in GDP per year due to restrictions on women's ability to fully participate in the economy.

If we shift from economic growth to global hunger and nutrition, the data is equally compelling. The Food and Agriculture Organization estimates that if developing countries removed constraints that prevent equal yields of land farmed by women and men—they could boost their agricultural output by enough to pull 100 to 150 million people out of hunger.

At the micro level, by virtually every global measure and in almost every country, women are more economically excluded than men. Gender gaps are persistent across all areas—from farmers, to entrepreneurs, to employees alike.

In some regions—notably Africa and the Middle East—labor force participation is as low as 21 percent. However, simply increasing the number of women in the global workforce won't be enough.

As the 2012 World Development Report indicates, some of the poorest regions in the world have the highest levels of women's representation in the workforce.

The challenge is that men are nearly twice as likely as women to have good, full-time jobs from an employer. And even though women represent 40 percent of the total global workforce, they represent nearly 60 percent of all unpaid work, and half of all employment in the informal sector.

This means they are less likely to be protected by existing labor law, to be able to organize or negotiate higher wages, and to benefit from social protection schemes.

Many women who are working are hindered by legal, social, financial, and educational barriers. As the Women, Business and the Law report indicates out of 143 economies surveyed, 128 have at least one legal differentiation that impacts women's ability to participate in the economy. Now that is something that we should take note of.

It is also important to note that not only can reducing gender gaps in the world of work bolster economic growth and improve health and food security, not doing so can substantially hinder it. In fact, when jobs are limited and standards of living are low, the overall safety and prosperity of a community and a country are at risk.

Corruption thrives, security is threatened, human rights are at risk, and economic growth can slow and in some cases, even reverse.

While job creation is important, the report notes the importance of providing women with decent jobs—jobs that respect their rights and help improve outcomes for themselves, their families, and communities, as well as the need to close the gender wage gap.

And when women can both work and have a level playing field on which to compete, their opportunities grow, their productivity increases, and their potential is unleashed. Growth in women's entrepreneurship boosts economies and a rise in the number of women leaders, in the boardroom as much as on the factory floor, and improves the health of societies and governments.

That's why we're here today—that's why gender equality at work matters. And that's why this report is so important.

It looks at ways to level the playing field through government action, and takes into account the lifecycle of a woman—from childhood, to productive age, to the elder years—in long-term policy planning. It examines ways to remove formal biases and discrimination, and link services to address multiple constraints.

It looks at steps the private sector can take through proactive leadership and innovation. With the private sector supplying the largest number of formal sector jobs in most countries, the importance of making gender equality, along with respect for the full range of rights at work, a priority throughout internal and external business operations is crucial.

And last, it looks for ways to close data gaps and invest in knowledge—with the goal of incorporating and using evidence-based policy making whenever possible.

Each of these components has become a core pillar of US foreign policy on advancing women's economic empowerment.

At the government level we have launched initiatives such as the Equal Futures Partnership, a multilateral initiative designed to drive action by member countries to empower women economically and politically. The platform engages country leadership at the highest levels, enables and promotes best practice exchange and accountability between member countries, and encourages the private sector and civil society to work together with member partners to realize success.

Launched in 2012 with 12 member countries, and expanded in 2013 to 25, we are now moving towards technical working groups that will leverage evidence-based data and policy recommendations to advance our common objectives.

This March, on the margins of Commission on the Status of Women, the Partnership will be one of our first partner efforts centered on best practices to address gender-based violence.

As this report highlights, gender-based violence is an epidemic problem that not only infringes upon the rights of women but dramatically undermines women's ability to participate in the economy, damages communities, and negatively impacts economic growth.

At the policy level, the success of the 2011 APEC Women and the Economy Summit, which elevated and integrated women's economic participation as a key economic growth strategy— is now being mirrored in other major trade, finance, and economic forums, such as the Summit of the Americas, the G8 Broader Middle East and Northern Africa Initiative, and the G20.

When it comes to looking at how best to invest in women and girls, we believe strongly that this needs to be done in collaboration with both the private sector and civil society.

The U.S. Department of State partners on initiatives that support women and girls' empowerment at all levels and stages of life, from programs such as:

- Tech Girls, which provides tech training to aspiring computer scientists in the Middle East,
- The Fortune Global Women's Mentoring Partnership for women business executives,

To programs that aim at improving conditions for women workers, from regional initiatives such as *Women Entrepreneurs in the Americas*, the *African Women's Entrepreneurship Program*, and programs in South and Central Asia to the over 170 small grants in 76 countries that the Secretary's office has awarded to support women and girls in rural and marginalized communities.

We know that we cannot do it alone, but together we can drive action.

For all of us who work in this area, there are days that remind us of the enormity of the challenges before us. But for every challenge that seems insurmountable, there is a story that restores our confidence in our ability to have a real and lasting impact.

Let me tell you the story of Shah Rukh, a woman business owner of an interior design company in Pakistan called SMARTEK. I first met Shah at a Clinton Global Initiative event last September and recently visited with her about a week ago during my trip to Pakistan. In 2011, Shah participated in the U.S. Department of State's program Propelling Women's Entrepreneurship in Pakistan, which was developed in partnership with the Goldman Sachs 10,000 Women initiative.

Before participating in the program, she had been in operation for six years, had 1 partner and 13 employees. Six months after graduating from the program, Shah's business experienced a 20 percent growth in sales. And as of July 2013, Shah had hired four additional full-time employees, built a team of over 12 part-time workers, and has mentored many other women, three of whom have started businesses of their own.

Not only has she grown her business and given back to other women entrepreneurs, she also participated in our South Asia Women's Entrepreneurship Symposium where she shared her hard-earned lessons with women entrepreneurs from across the region. Shah's story represents the hope and the reality that we are making real progress.

And, thanks to the hard work of the experts who compiled this report, we'll be able to make even greater progress in the journey ahead.

I am honored for the opportunity to be here. Thank you.

I Saw a Woman Today

By Deborah A. P. Hersman

In this speech, Deborah A. P. Hersman, then chair of the National Transportation Safety Board (NTSB), talks about women in science, technology, engineering, and mathematics (STEM) careers to a group assembled for the International Women in Aviation Conference in Lake Buena Vista, Florida, on March 7, 2014. Hersman begins by speaking about the theme of the conference, "Today's Vision, Tomorrow's Reality," which she then relates to the history of the NTSB, saying that the NTSB had a vision of a world without airline accidents, and that they have never been closer to this goal. To frame her remarks, Hersman mentions Virginia Woolf's book A Room of One's Own, *in which Woolf speculated that women would, within one hundred years, take part in all occupations that had been denied to them when the book was published in 1929. Hersman then cites statistics indicating that while 58 percent of those receiving advanced degrees are now women, few of these women obtain employment in the STEM fields. Hersman also cites statistics indicating that 86 percent of women in STEM fields say that a lack of effective mentoring is a contributing factor to the difficulty that women face getting into and remaining in STEM positions. She notes programs designed to combat this disparity, such as the Embry-Riddle Aeronautical University's STEM Academy program that promotes STEM involvement among women and minorities. Hersman imagines that Woolf, if she were alive today, would see women pushing beyond their traditional roles and taking a leading, important role in science and technology, especially in the field of aeronautics. Hersman was the twelfth chair of the National Transportation Safety Board, from 2009 to 2014. Following this position, she was appointed to the National Safety Council, serving as chief executive officer of the organization.*

Thank you, Peggy [Chabrian].

What a legacy your conference has created—supporting not only astronauts and pilots, but also maintenance technicians, air traffic controllers, business owners, airport managers, and, as in my case, aviation safety officials.

The Conference theme—"Today's Vision, Tomorrow's Reality"—should be etched into the mind of everyone here. I know it's foremost on mine.

I'd like to start by recognizing three groups in the audience—my NTSB colleagues, the individuals who serve in the military, and the men!

At the NTSB we investigate accidents in transportation. In every investigation we look for ways to prevent the next accident. Our guiding vision, constant as the northern star, is to one day prevent all of them. Today's vision. Tomorrow's reality.

Delivered March 7, 2014, at the International Women in Aviation Conference, Lake Buena Vista, Florida, by Deborah A. P. Hersman.

In addition to this 25th conference, there are some other "birthdays" we'll celebrate this year. 2014 also marks the 100th anniversary of commercial flight.

Years ago, flying became the safest way to travel. Now our vision is getting closer to reality: many countries have reached the point where years go by without a fatality in commercial aviation—even here in the US, with millions of flights per year.

What was yesterday's vision, that brought us to today's reality?

And there's another anniversary some of the pilots here might celebrate: The 85th birthday of The Ninety-Nines, the international organization of women pilots—of which Amelia Earhart was a charter member.

I would like to have met Amelia Earhart. She was a woman of action, but also an endless source of inspirational quotes. Long before Nike, she said:

"The most effective way to do it, is to do it."

She took the most direct route between today's vision and tomorrow's reality: She just did it.

I might also like to have met Anne Morrow Lindbergh. Yes, she was the wife of Charles Lindbergh. But she was also an aviator in her own right, America's first woman glider pilot, and a notable twentieth-century poet and author.

Mrs. Lindbergh tells us that

"Yesterday's fairy tale is today's fact."

Today's vision, tomorrow's reality.

We know that they met each other, and stayed together, a number of times. We know that they corresponded.

We know that Amelia apologized profusely to Anne that the press had labeled her "Lady Lindy" for her interest in aviation and her resemblance to Charles Lindbergh.

In 1929—the same year that Amelia helped start the Ninety-Nines—Anne and Amelia also discussed Virginia Woolf's latest book, *A Room of One's Own*.

A Room of One's Own came from a lecture series about "Women and Fiction" that Woolf was asked to give to the women's colleges at Cambridge. Her lectures were expanded to a book.

She covers much more than women's fiction, including the historical barriers against women, the comparative poverty of women's colleges, and the importance of financial independence and personal space.

She urges her all-woman audience, similar to the one here today, to make their own money and create the conditions in which a female Shakespeare might one day appear—and thrive.

So why were two aviators talking about an essay about women and fiction? Amelia and Anne, like so many others, realized that Woolf's ideas did not only apply to literature.

The vision of 85 years ago led to today's reality: according to the latest census, among young adults age 25–29, 58% of those with advanced degrees are women.

But women graduates in STEM fields are another story.

A recent study found that in the U.S., Brazil, China, and India, roughly one-third of women graduates in science, engineering, and technology feel "stalled." They say that within a year, they are likely to leave not only their jobs, but their whole field. In the U.S., 86% of women in those fields say they lack mentors.

So I was gratified to see today's vision at work recently—pointing to tomorrow's reality.

Female students at Embry-Riddle Aeronautical University have been given a one-year membership in Women In Aviation—let me hear from any of you here today.

This week I visited Embry-Riddle, and I learned more about their STEM Academy, designed to nurture women and minorities in technical fields even before the undergraduate level.

I was also excited to see the activities planned for the "Bring Your Daughter to the Conference" program here tomorrow.

That's exactly the kind of inheritance that Woolf talked about in 1929. But she limited her vision to literature. It took others to apply it to aviation and other STEM fields.

If you have any doubt that visions can be too limited, just listen to Woolf's words, from *A Room of One's Own*. Remember, these are the words of a feminist—in 1929:

> [I]n a hundred years . . . women . . . will take part in all the activities and exertions that were once denied them. The nursemaid will heave coal. The shopwoman will drive an engine.
>
> . . . [E]xpose them to the same exertions and activities, make them soldiers and sailors and engine-drivers and dock labourers, and will not women die off so much younger, so much quicker, than men, that one will say 'I saw a woman today', as one used to say 'I saw an aeroplane'.

Well, that didn't happen—we survived.

But she was half-right: Women are indeed soldiers and sailors—aviators and mechanics—in today's military. To those of you who are, thank you for your service. And thank you to the WASPs here today—that band of sisters who flew missions for the U.S. Army Air Forces during World War II.

And women are in every other occupation Woolf mentions, and it's not killing us. In the U.S., since 1929, life expectancy has increased by more than 20 years—and even more for women.

So how could she be so right in some ways, and so wrong in others?

She underestimated us and she underestimated technology. Heaving coal no longer depends on human exertion. Technology has advanced women. It's time for us to advance technology.

As women in aviation, it's also striking to read that only 85 years ago, airplanes were still a recent invention. People still remembered saying "I saw an airplane."

Today, there are millions of passenger flights every year.

If Virginia Woolf were alive today, she would see a lot more airplanes—and a lot more women. And she would not just say "I saw a woman today."

She'd say,

I saw a woman today who graduated from Embry-Riddle, got her PhD, and rose to become NTSB's Senior Human Performance Investigator, and her name is Katherine Wilson.

I saw a woman today who is a senior aircraft maintenance technician with Whirlpool Corporation, and her name is Lisa Pelate.

I saw a woman today who is president of Massachusetts-based Cape Air, and her name is Linda Markham.

I saw women today who are pushing beyond the air and into space, and their names are Joy Bryant and Barbara Barrett and Eileen Collins and Nagin Cox.

So who's afraid of Virginia Woolf? I have to admit that in some ways I am.

I'm afraid that just like aviation in 1929, we only seem to be at our full potential, and we'll settle for that. And I fear that we'll settle for small visions: Convincing women in STEM fields not to leave within the year. Doubling the proportion of female engineers— to 26%. Being satisfied that there is one more woman CEO.

Today's vision **is** tomorrow's reality. Make the vision as ambitious as you can.

Today, as in Woolf's day, you don't say "I saw an airplane," because airplanes are everywhere. You don't say "I saw a woman today"—we're over half the population!

Tomorrow, I don't want to hear anybody say "I saw a woman mechanic!"

Or "I saw an all-woman flight crew!"

Or "I saw a woman engineer!"

Or "I saw a woman CEO!"

Or "I saw a woman in space exploration!"

Not because there are none of us there, but because there are so many of us there!

Many of you are flying so high that you shatter glass ceilings. Now leave an inheritance—whether by funding scholarships, mentoring, or formal diversity programs in your workplace—so that other women cruise comfortably at that altitude tomorrow.

Or as Amelia said,

"Some of us have great runways already built for us. If you have one, take off. But if you don't have one, realize it is your responsibility to grab a shovel and build one for yourself and for those who will follow after you."

Make today's vision as broad as you want tomorrow's reality to be. Then find a way to pass that vision on.

Remarks for Central Intelligence Agency Director John O. Brennan as Prepared for Delivery at the Conference on the Ethos and Profession of Intelligence, Georgetown University

By John O. Brennan

In this speech, Director John O. Brennan of the Central Intelligence Agency speaks to a group assembled for a conference on the Ethos and Profession of Intelligence held at Georgetown University on June 11, 2014. The Ethos and Profession of Intelligence conference was open to public attendance and provided a forum for CIA officials to speak about their mission and national function to the public. Brennan begins by addressing the notion of "ethos" in intelligence work, describing those who work in intelligence as being guided by many principles, including service, integrity, courage, and teamwork. Brennan then describes how the US intelligence community now faces an increasing number of challenges, including the ongoing threat of terrorism and extremism, and the threat of cybercrime and "hacktivism" undermining national security. Brennan then describes the mission of the CIA, which is to work with and support US military, law enforcement, and diplomatic efforts around the world. Brennan goes on to say that the intelligence service is faced with the challenge of relevancy, and must adjust its methods to remain effective in the information age. He asserts that digital information is still no substitute for human intelligence gained through the activities of the CIA and other intelligence organizations. Brennan argues that the CIA must strive to utilize the informational capacity of modern technology while simultaneously mitigating the potential risks of data security for intelligence agents operating in cyberspace. John Brennan has been director of the CIA since 2013, and was previously the assistant to the president for homeland security and counterterrorism under President Barack Obama.

Thank you, Burton [*Gerber*], not only for your kind words but also for your 39 years of distinguished service as a CIA officer and for your invaluable contributions to the study of the intelligence profession. It is an honor and pleasure to have you with us here today.

And, of course, I want to thank President DeGioia and everyone at Georgetown University for co-sponsoring this conference. There is simply no institution better

Delivered June 11, 2014, at a conference on the Ethos and Profession of Intelligence at Georgetown University, Washington, DC, by John O. Brennan.

suited to host a discussion of the topics we are tackling today, and it is a privilege for me to be here among the students and faculty of this great school.

As you know, the Central Intelligence Agency does not hold a lot of public conferences. Our foreign counterparts tend to hold even fewer—as in zero.

But like any other part of the United States government, the agency and our intelligence community partners must have the trust and confidence of the American people in order to do our job. To that end, I believe we must engage our fellow citizens and, to the extent we can, explain the work we perform on their behalf and articulate our motives, values, and objectives.

Just as importantly, we need to listen to what the people have to say and to hear the views of outside experts. CIA is very much a learning organization, one that makes a deliberate effort to learn from the past, adapt to the times, and refine its methods. This event was envisioned as an open forum from which we all can learn and benefit.

Ethos of Intelligence

I want to take a moment to shed some light on the origin of our conference title, "The Ethos and Profession of Intelligence," and to offer some thoughts on the subject itself.

Too often, the intelligence community is treated as a monolithic, almost mechanical entity rather than what it really is: a constellation of very talented, very committed women and men guided by a professional ethos with many dimensions—service, integrity, excellence, courage, teamwork, and stewardship, among others.

Our identity as Americans decisively shapes how we approach our work. We are acutely aware of the extraordinary authorities with which our government—indeed, our fellow citizens—have entrusted us, and we feel a deep and abiding obligation to justify and earn that trust. Likewise, we readily accept that the bar is set higher for us in part because of the natural tension that has always existed between the secrecy our mission requires and the openness of the society we serve.

Intelligence has been critical to our national interests and security since George Washington personally directed espionage networks during the founding of our nation. In subsequent years, America's efforts were mostly tactical and long confined to the military realm, and it wasn't until 1947 that the United States finally did what every other great power had done: establish a civilian intelligence service for both peacetime and war. President Truman did so to counter the growing Soviet threat to the postwar environment and to gain better insight into political, social, economic, and military developments worldwide.

I joined that service, the Central Intelligence Agency, in 1980. I believed in its mission then, and I believe even more strongly in it today. We have had the great fortune over the past 67 years to play an important role in keeping this nation strong and its people safe from the constantly evolving array of overseas threats.

Today, and certainly not for the first time in our history, America's intelligence community is at a crossroads. The transformational impact of technology and enhanced scrutiny and skepticism of the value, legality, and appropriateness of our mission have prompted a reexamination of the work of intelligence agencies, understandably and rightly so.

Global Challenges

But this reexamination is taking place at a time when our nation faces an ever-growing list of national security challenges, one that in my view has few precedents in our history. To be sure, we have confronted grave threats before, some of them more serious than the ones before us today. But rarely have we encountered such a bewildering variety of challenges and threats all at once. Just consider the events that are playing out on the world stage.

We see a terrorist threat that is atomizing into a patchwork of extremist groups across several continents, undermining political stability and basic law and order, and presenting new dangers to American interests. We see determined efforts to acquire the means for producing weapons of mass destruction. We see the tragedy of human trafficking, and the ruthless tactics of drug cartels seeking to protect and expand their turf.

In far too many countries, we see civil strife and violent conflicts over religion, land, political ascendance, sectarianism, and access to food and water. We see the growth of ungoverned spaces where extremists can take root. And we see the rise of groups like Boko Haram that are preying on the innocent, kidnapping girls for simply going to school.

In the past year, territorial disputes between nation states—the cause of so much suffering in the last century—have returned to the fore, most notably in eastern and southern Ukraine and in the waters of the East and South China Sea.

At the same time, the world is grappling with a new breed of challenges enabled by advancing technology, with cyber attacks unfolding on a massive scale, as rival nations, criminal gangs, and "hacktivists" seek to exploit vulnerabilities in the digital domain.

In this dangerous and dynamic world, intelligence and corresponding analysis are key to identifying, understanding, and successfully addressing the myriad national security issues that confront policymakers.

The complexity of this task is hard to overstate. It is one thing to report on a crisis that has already happened: to identify the key players, to map out their support networks, and to describe their methods and motivations. It is something else to put all that information together in advance, before an event occurs, and to provide it to policymakers with enough time—and enough precision—for them to act.

This is the mission to which CIA officers dedicate their lives. While we do not have a crystal ball, we have an obligation as intelligence professionals to look beyond the next horizon—to not only highlight key events around the globe, but to explain the forces that are likely to shape them in the weeks, months, and years to come.

We do not always get it right. We have made mistakes, more than a few, and we have tried mightily to learn from them. But every day, CIA officers go to enormous lengths to anticipate future threats, and to thwart the plans of those who would threaten our freedom and security.

CIA's Essential Mission

Our contributions span the gamut of national security challenges. We work with our military, law enforcement, and diplomatic colleagues, as well as our allies and partners overseas, to prevent devastating terrorist attacks—whether they be aimed at our homeland or at targets on foreign soil. We help protect our nation and our fellow Americans from cyber attacks. We support efforts to interdict shipments of illicit arms, to dismantle drug cartels, and to break up syndicates engaged in human trafficking.

And we help build the capacity of foreign security and intelligence forces so they can address the threats arising inside their own borders. Increasingly, governments around the globe recognize that no matter how capable their military, security, and intelligence agencies might be, no nation can counter the plethora of 21st-century transnational threats on its own.

Over the past five years alone, there have been major developments that have altered the course of world history—chief among them the political upheavals associated with the so-called "Arab Spring." From day one, CIA has played a central role in helping our policymakers navigate this rapidly changing landscape.

The fact is, good intelligence—timely, accurate, and insightful—is the cornerstone of almost every aspect of national security policy today, from military action to diplomacy to international law enforcement.

With it, our policymakers see an issue in its entirety, with the risks, challenges, and opportunities clearly delineated. Without it, our government would have to make its way in the treacherous global arena nearly blind.

Most of our work supporting policymakers involves information—collecting it, analyzing it, and getting it to the people who need it. But we do more than that. When directed by the president, we also use our covert action authorities to help advance U.S. foreign-policy objectives.

For all these reasons, CIA is a truly indispensable agency. As former CIA director under President George Herbert Walker Bush put it in 1991: "Intelligence remains our basic national instrument for anticipating danger—military, political, and economic."

Those words are as true now as they were then. In fact, given the number of threats and foreign policy challenges facing our country—and how difficult they are to track—I would argue that CIA has never been more important to the strength and security of our republic.

The question facing us today is how to ensure that our contribution to national security remains as positive and as meaningful in the future as it has been in the past. This is the fundamental challenge facing our agency, as we confront not only sweeping technological change that affects every aspect of our daily lives but also evolving considerations, policies, and legal frameworks about the appropriate and necessary role of intelligence in an open society.

You have heard some very informed and insightful views this morning on technology and the private sector, and how they relate to our work. I would now like to offer some thoughts on the role of intelligence in the 21st-century and the need to strike a proper balance between secrecy and accountability.

Role of Intelligence in the 21st-Century

As we position our agency for the future, one of our main challenges is how to remain relevant in the digital information age.

Information technology has transformed the world since I first embarked on my intelligence career. Today's 24-hour news outlets and social media provide instant coverage and analysis of global developments. The near-monopoly our stations and bases overseas once enjoyed in covering fast-breaking developments for policymakers—particularly in remote areas—is long gone.

In the business world, we have seen once great corporations decline and collapse when they fail to keep up with the times. To avoid that fate, CIA and our community partners must continually adapt if we are to compete with the ever-growing, ever-accelerating supply of information and analysis.

As a former policymaker myself, I can assure you that CIA still provides information and analysis that social media, news organizations, and our foreign intelligence partners cannot. A key reason is the type of information our agency collects—not just intelligence, but human intelligence.

For all the technical wizardry that is currently available worldwide, nothing can replace the insight that comes from a well-connected human source. At their best, human sources go beyond the dry facts of an issue and help discern the intent of an adversary—precisely the edge that our policymakers are looking for. As former CIA Director Richard Helms once said: "Gadgets cannot divine man's intentions."

One of CIA's main challenges in the coming years, then, is to make to the most of this advantage. We must focus our efforts on uncovering secrets that only human sources can acquire, those that are typically locked inside the inner circle of an adversary. These are the hardest of hard targets, but they are ones that CIA is especially well equipped to pursue.

The Cyber Challenge

Looking ahead, another big challenge for CIA will be cyberspace—figuring out how to take advantage of the opportunities while mitigating the risks.

For the intelligence community, the cyber world is a double-edged sword. Digital footprints may enable us to track down a suspected terrorist, but they may leave our officers vulnerable as well. Websites and digital platforms can shed light on the practices of despotic regimes, but they can also be used to inspire violence against our citizens and interests. And while our networks allow us to communicate instantly around the globe, they can also be targeted by hackers seeking to disrupt our operations and steal our information.

The same is true for the private sector, where American businesses and institutions of all stripes are fending off repeated efforts to intercept their communications, shut down their networks, and harvest their know-how.

But for the intelligence community, the problem is about much more than cyber attacks per se. It is also about the technologies that make it possible to study bomb making on the Internet, to case a target remotely, and to coordinate among far-flung associates to carry out a sophisticated attack. Aided by the cyber domain, individuals and small groups—not only nation states—now have the power to sow enormous destruction, greatly expanding the number of threats that our government must monitor to keep our nation safe.

Indeed, there is hardly an intelligence problem today that is not affected to a large degree by the cyber realm. It is where so many of life's basic transactions are now taking place—social, financial, political, commercial, educational, and more. Yet it still remains our planet's new and relatively uncharted frontier. If we are to understand the world we cover, and to provide our policymakers with the intelligence they expect, we must immerse ourselves in that frontier, and adjust our tradecraft accordingly.

In developing powerful tools to meet this challenge, CIA and our community partners face a question that may be unprecedented in our history: If we possess an extraordinary technical capability—and are legally authorized to use it—should we necessarily do so?

If this were asked on September 12, 2001, we could be reasonably certain of the answer. From the vantage point of that terrible crisis, the fact that we are asking this question now would be seen as a remarkable change. But this question is made possible by the tremendous strides we have made over the past 13 years in strengthening our national security.

The question of foregoing a collection capability also reflects the complexity of our mission in a world that is becoming intensely interconnected. Boundaries between domestic and foreign communications are disappearing rapidly in a world vastly different from the one that existed at CIA's founding.

The Soviets were a closed society with a communications network largely segregated from that of the free world. The enormous collection effort fielded against their vast military complex carried little or no legal or moral ambiguity.

But the terrorists we face today routinely use the same channels everyone else does. And, of course, it is that distinction—confronting an enemy who seeks to operate within our own borders, who uses our own infrastructure, and who relies in part on the protections provided by our own laws and regulations—that lies at the heart of the thorniest issues under debate in this country and in free societies everywhere.

Conclusion: Striking a Delicate Balance

We all seek a common goal: to strike a balance between the need to protect civil liberties and the need to protect the lives of our citizens. And wherever that equilibrium may lie, we know it is a moving target.

It tends to swing back and forth between periods in which society is preoccupied by external threats, and those in which it is preoccupied by a sense that the government's response to those threats has strayed from principle or even the law.

Even as we move to achieve a balance that is responsive to what the times demand, we must be mindful that there are natural limits to how open any espionage service can afford to be. As intelligence officers, we at CIA have a solemn obligation to safeguard not only the nation we serve, but the sources and methods that enable us to do so. Stewardship is an essential element of our professional ethos, and we must honor it as surely as the oath we take to defend the Constitution.

As I have said, we in the intelligence community act on behalf of the American people. Every power we have—every authority with which we are entrusted—comes from them. And just as our tradecraft must keep pace with technology if we are to accomplish our mission, so too must our decisions faithfully reflect the will of the American people.

President Obama already has taken a number of steps to provide greater accountability and insight into the work of our community. These measures largely address the operations of our colleagues at the National Security Agency, but they set a clear direction for us all. CIA is committed to charting a way forward that, in the president's words, "secures the life of our nation while preserving the liberties that make our nation worth fighting for."

Ultimately, that is the ethos that guides our profession. While much of what we do must remain secret, our actions must conform—in every instance—to the values and principles upon which our nation was founded.

Thank you all very much.

The Ultimate Test of Ukraine

What Kind of Europe, What Kind of America, What Kind of World Will We Leave Behind?

By Barack Obama

In this speech, US president Barack Obama speaks to a group gathered in Brussels, Belgium, on March 26, 2014, about the Ukraine crisis of 2014 and the future legacy of the United States and the European Union. President Obama begins by addressing the ongoing effort to balance the advance of industry and technology with the ability to resolve differences through diplomacy, and how this evolutionary struggle has defined the twentieth century for nations around the world. He mentions the construction of the NATO alliance, the Cold War, and the civil rights movement in the United States as examples of challenges of the past that have shaped the present world, where there is less conflict and greater freedom than at any other time in history. Obama then states that Russia's actions in the Ukraine are challenging the twenty-first century belief in many nations that law, rather than force, should define the borders of Europe. Obama calls for the international community to condemn Russia's actions as a violation of international law and an affront to Ukraine's sovereignty. He further cites his belief that increased pressure from NATO and the international community, through trade sanctions and diplomacy, will eventually bring the conflict to a diplomatic end. Finally, Obama argues that the decision to resolve conflict through diplomatic intervention becomes part of the legacy that each nation leaves to its next generation of citizens. President Obama is the forty-fourth president of the United States, having been elected to office in 2008. Prior to becoming president, Obama was a United States senator representing the state of Illinois from 2005 to 2008.

Your Majesties, Mr. Prime Minister, and the people of Belgium, on behalf of the American people, we are grateful for your friendship. We stand together as inseparable allies. And I thank you for your wonderful hospitality. I have to admit it is easy to love a country famous for chocolate and beer.

Leaders and dignitaries of the European Union, representatives of our NATO alliance, distinguished guests, we meet here at a moment of testing for Europe and the United States and for the international order that we have worked for generations to build. Throughout human history, societies have grappled with fundamental questions of how to organize themselves, the proper relationship between the individual and the state, the best means to resolve the inevitable conflicts between states.

Delivered March 26, 2014, to a group gathered at the Palais des Beaux-Arts, Brussels, Belgium, by Barack Obama.

And it was here in Europe, through centuries of struggle, through war and enlightenment, repression and revolution, that a particular set of ideals began to emerge, the belief that through conscience and free will, each of us has the right to live as we choose, the belief that power is derived from the consent of the governed and that laws and institutions should be established to protect that understanding.

And those ideas eventually inspired a band of colonialists across an ocean, and they wrote them into the founding documents that still guide America today, including the simple truth that all men, and women, are created equal.

But those ideals have also been tested, here in Europe and around the world. Those ideals have often been threatened by an older, more traditional view of power. This alternative vision argues that ordinary men and women are too small-minded to govern their own affairs, that order and progress can only come when individuals surrender their rights to an all-powerful sovereign. Often this alternative vision roots itself in the notion that by virtue of race or faith or ethnicity, some are inherently superior to others and that individual identity must be defined by us versus them, or that national greatness must flow not by what people stand for, but what they are against.

In so many ways, the history of Europe in the 20th century represented the ongoing clash of these two sets of ideas, both within nations and among nations. The advance of industry and technology outpaced our ability to resolve our differences peacefully. And even—even among the most civilized of societies on the surface, we saw a descent into barbarism.

This morning at Flanders Field, I was reminded of how war between peoples sent a generation to their deaths in the trenches and gas of the first world war. And just two decades later, extreme nationalism plunged this continent into war once again, with populations enslaved and great cities reduced to rubble and tens of millions slaughtered, including those lost in the Holocaust.

It is in response to this tragic history that in the aftermath of World War II, America joined with Europe to reject the darker forces of the past and build a new architecture of peace. Workers and engineers gave life to the Marshall Plan. Sentinels stood vigilant in a NATO alliance that would become the strongest the world has ever known. And across the Atlantic, we embraced a shared vision of Europe, a vision based on representative democracy, individual rights, and a belief that nations can meet the interests of their citizens through trade and open markets, a social safety net, respect for those of different faiths and backgrounds.

For decades, this vision stood in sharp contrast to life on the other side of an Iron Curtain. For decades, a contest was waged, and ultimately, that contest was won, not by tanks or missiles, but because our ideals stirred the hearts of Hungarians, who sparked a revolution, Poles in their shipyards who stood in solidarity, Czechs who waged a Velvet Revolution without firing a shot, and East Berliners who marched past the guards and finally tore down that wall.

Today what would have seemed impossible in the trenches of Flanders, the rubble of Berlin, a dissident's prison cell—that reality is taken for granted: a Germany unified, the nations of Central and Eastern Europe welcomed into the family of democracies. Here in this country, once the battleground of Europe, we meet in the hub of a union that brings together age-old adversaries in peace and cooperation. The people of Europe, hundreds of millions of citizens, east, west, north, south, are more secure and more prosperous because we stood together for the ideals we shared.

And this story of human progress was by no means limited to Europe. Indeed, the ideals that came to define our alliance also inspired movements across the globe—among those very people, ironically, who had too often been denied their full rights by Western powers. After the second world war people from Africa to India threw off the yoke of colonialism to secure their independence. In the United States citizens took Freedom Rides and endured beatings to put an end to segregation and to secure their civil rights. As the Iron Curtain fell here in Europe, the iron fist of apartheid was unclenched and Nelson Mandela emerged upright, proud, from prison to lead a multiracial democracy; Latin American nations rejected dictatorship and built new democracies; and Asian nations showed that development and democracy could go hand in hand.

The young people in the audience today, young people like Laura, were born in a place and a time where there is less conflict, more prosperity and more freedom than any time in human history. But that's not because man's darkest impulses have vanished. Even here in Europe we've seen ethnic cleansing in the Balkans that shocked the conscience. The difficulties of integration and globalization, recently amplified by the worst economic crisis of our lifetimes, strained the European project and stirred the rise of a politics that too often targets immigrants or gays or those who seem somehow different.

While technology has opened up vast opportunities for trade and innovation and cultural understanding, it's also allowed terrorists to kill on a horrifying scale. Around the world sectarian warfare and ethnic conflicts continue to claim thousands of lives. And once again, we are confronted with the belief among some that bigger nations can bully smaller ones to get their way—that recycled maxim that might somehow makes right.

So I come here today to insist that we must never take for granted the progress that has been won here in Europe and advanced around the world, because the contest of ideas continues for your generation.

And that's what's at stake in Ukraine today. Russia's leadership is challenging truths that only a few weeks ago seemed self-evident, that in the 21st century, the borders of Europe cannot be redrawn with force, that international law matters, that people and nations can make their own decisions about their future.

To be honest, if we define our—our interests narrowly, if we applied a cold-hearted calculus, we might decide to look the other way. Our economy is not deeply integrated with Ukraine's. Our people and our homeland face no direct threat from the invasion of Crimea. Our own borders are not threatened by Russia's annexation. But that kind of casual indifference would ignore the lessons that are written in the cemeteries of this continent. It would allow the old way of doing things to regain a foothold in this young century. And that message would be heard, not just in Europe, but in Asia and the Americas, in Africa and the Middle East.

And the consequences that would arise from complacency are not abstractions. The impacts that they have on the lives of real people, men and women just like us, have to enter into our imaginations.

Just look at the young people of Ukraine, who were determined to take back their future from a government rotted by corruption; the portraits of the fallen shot by snipers; the visitors who pay their respects at the Maidan. There was the university student wrapped in the Ukrainian flag expressing her hope that every country should live by the law; a postgraduate student speaking for fellow protesters, saying, I want these people who are here to have dignity. Imagine that you are the young woman who said, there are some things that fear, police sticks and tear gas cannot destroy.

We've never met these people, but we know them. Their voices echo calls for human dignity that rang out in European streets and squares for generations. Their voices echo those around the world who at this very moment fight for their dignity. These Ukrainians rejected a government that was stealing from the people instead of serving them, and are reaching for the same ideals that allow us to be here today.

None of us can know for certain what the coming days will bring in Ukraine, but I am confident that eventually those voices, those voices for human dignity and opportunity and individual rights and rule of law, those voices ultimately will triumph.

I believe that over the long haul as nations that are free, as free people, the future is ours. I believe this not because I'm naive. And I believe this not because of the strength of our arms or the size of our economies. I believe this because these ideals that we affirm are true. These ideals are universal.

Yes, we believe in democracy, with elections that are free and fair, and independent judiciaries and opposition parties, civil society and uncensored information so that individuals can make their own choices. Yes, we believe in open economies based on free markets and innovation and individual initiative and entrepreneurship and trade and investment that creates a broader prosperity.

And yes, we believe in human dignity, that every person is created equal—no matter who you are or what you look like or who you love or where you come from. That is what we believe. That's what makes us strong. And our enduring strength is also reflected in our respect for an international system that protects the rights of both nations and people—a United Nations and a Universal Declaration of Human Rights, international law and the means to enforce those laws.

But we also know that those rules are not self-executing.

They depend on people and nations of good will continually affirming them.

And that's why Russia's violation of international law, its assault on Ukraine's sovereignty and territorial integrity, must be met with condemnation, not because we're trying to keep Russia down, but because the principles that have meant so much to Europe and the world must be lifted up.

Over the last several days, the United States, Europe and our partners around the world have been united in defense of these ideals and united in support of the Ukrainian people. Together, we've condemned Russia's invasion of Ukraine and rejected the legitimacy of the Crimean referendum. Together, we have isolated Russia politically, suspending it from the G-8 nations and downgrading our bilateral ties. Together, we are imposing costs through sanctions that have left a mark on Russia and those accountable for its actions.

And if the Russian leadership stays on its current course, together, we will ensure that this isolation deepens. Sanctions will expand, and the toll on Russia's economy, as well as its standing in the world, will only increase.

And meanwhile, the United States and our allies will continue to support the government of Ukraine as they chart a democratic course. Together, we are going to provide a significant package of assistance that can help stabilize the Ukrainian economy and meet the basic needs of the people.

Make no mistake, neither the United States nor Europe has any interest in controlling Ukraine.

We have sent no troops there. What we want is for the Ukrainian people to make their own decisions, just like other free people around the world.

Understand as well this is not another Cold War that we're entering into. After all, unlike the Soviet Union, Russia leads no bloc of nations, no global ideology. The United States and NATO do not seek any conflict with Russia. In fact, for more than 60 years we have come together in NATO not to claim other lands but to keep nations free.

What we will do always is uphold our solemn obligation, our Article 5 duty, to defend the sovereignty and territorial integrity of our allies. And in that promise we will never waver. NATO nations never stand alone.

Today NATO planes patrol the skies over the Baltics, and we've reinforced our presence in Poland, and we're prepared to do more.

Going forward, every NATO member state must step up and carry its share of the burden by showing the political will to invest in our collective defense and by developing the capabilities to serve as a source of international peace and security.

Of course Ukraine is not a member of NATO, in part because of its close and complex history with Russia. Nor will Russia be dislodged from Crimea or deterred from further escalation by military force.

But with time, so long as we remain united, the Russian people will recognize that they cannot achieve the security, prosperity and the status that they seek through brute force.

And that's why throughout this crisis we will combine our substantial pressure on Russia with an open door for diplomacy.

I believe that for both Ukraine and Russia, a stable peace will come through de-escalation, a direct dialogue between Russia and the government of Ukraine and the international community, monitors who can ensure that the rights of all Ukrainians are protected, a process of constitutional reform within Ukraine and free and fair elections this spring.

So far, Russia has resisted diplomatic overtures, annexing Crimea and massing large forces along Ukraine's border. Russia's justified these actions as an effort to prevent problems on its own borders and to protect ethnic Russians inside Ukraine.

Of course, there is no evidence, never has been, of systemic violence against ethnic Russians inside of Ukraine.

Moreover, many countries around the world face similar questions about their borders and ethnic minorities abroad, about sovereignty and self-determination. These are tensions that have led in other places to debate and democratic referendums, conflicts and uneasy co-existence. These are difficult issues and it is precisely because these questions are hard that they must be addressed through constitutional means and international laws, so that majorities cannot simply suppress minorities and big countries cannot simply bully the small.

In defending its actions, Russian leaders have further claimed Kosovo as a precedent, an example, they say, of the West interfering in the affairs of a smaller country, just as they're doing now. But NATO only intervened after the people of Kosovo were systematically brutalized and killed for years. And Kosovo only left Serbia after a referendum was organized not outside the boundaries of international law, but in careful cooperation with the United Nations and with Kosovo's neighbors. None of that even came close to happening in Crimea.

Moreover, Russia has pointed to America's decision to go into Iraq as an example of Western hypocrisy. Now, it is true that the Iraq war was a subject of vigorous debate, not just around the world but in the United States, as well. I participated in that debate, and I opposed our military intervention there.

But even in Iraq, America sought to work within the international system. We did not claim or annex Iraq's territory.

We did not grab its resources for our own gain. Instead, we ended our war and left Iraq to its people in a fully sovereign Iraqi state that can make decisions about its own future.

Of course, neither the United States nor Europe are perfect in adherence to our ideals. Nor do we claim to be the sole arbiter of what is right or wrong in the world.

We are human, after all, and we face difficult decisions about how to exercise our power.

But part of what makes us different is that we welcome criticism, just as we welcome the responsibilities that come with global leadership. We look to the east and the south and see nations poised to play a growing role on the world stage, and we consider that a good thing. It reflects the same diversity that makes us stronger as a nation and the forces of integration and cooperation that Europe has advanced for decades. And in a world of challenges that are increasingly global, all of us have an interest in nations stepping forward to play their part, to bear their share of the burden and to uphold international norms.

So our approach stands in stark contrast to the arguments coming out of Russia these days. It is absurd to suggest, as a steady drumbeat of Russian voices do that America is somehow conspiring with fascists inside of Ukraine but failing to respect the Russian people. My grandfather served in Patton's Army, just as many of your fathers and grandfathers fought against fascism. We Americans remember well the unimaginable sacrifices made by the Russian people in World War II, and we have honored those sacrifices. Since the end of the Cold War, we have worked with

Russia under successive administrations to build ties of culture and commerce and international community, not as a favor to Russia, but because it was in our national interests.

And together, we've secured nuclear materials from terrorists, we welcomed Russia into the G-8 and the World Trade Organization. From the reduction of nuclear arms to the elimination of Syria's chemical weapons, we believe the world has benefited when Russia chooses to cooperate on the basis of mutual interests and mutual respect.

So America and the world, and Europe, has an interest in a strong and responsible Russia, not a weak one. We want the Russian people to live in security, prosperity and dignity like everyone else, proud of their own history. But that does not mean that Russia can run roughshod over its neighbors. Just because Russia has a deep history with Ukraine does not mean it should be able to dictate Ukraine's future. No amount of propaganda can make right something that the world knows is wrong.

You know, in the end, every society must chart its own course. America's path or Europe's path is not the only ways to reach freedom and justice. But on the fundamental principle that is at stake here, the ability of nations and peoples to make their own choices, there can be no going back. It's not America that filled the Maidan with protesters. It was Ukrainians.

No foreign forces compelled the citizens of Tunis and Tripoli to rise up. They did so on their own. From the Burmese parliamentarian pursuing reform to the young leaders fighting corruption and intolerance in Africa, we see something irreducible that all of us share as human beings: a truth that will persevere in the face of violence and repression and will ultimately overcome.

For the young people here today, I know it may seem easy to see these events as removed from our lives, remote from our daily routines, distant from concerns closer to home. I recognize that both in the United States and in much of Europe, there's more than enough to worry about in the affairs of our own countries.

There will always be voices who say that what happens in the wider world is not our concern nor our responsibility. But we must never forget that we are heirs to a struggle for freedom. Our democracy, our individual opportunity only exist because those who came before us had the wisdom and the courage to recognize that ideals will only endure if we see our self-interest in the success of other peoples and other nations.

Now is not the time for bluster. The situation in Ukraine, like crises in many parts of the world, does not have easy answers nor a military solution.

But at this moment, we must meet the challenge to our ideals, to our very international order, with strength and conviction. And it is you, the young people of Europe, young people like Laura, who will help decide which way the currents of our history will flow.

Do not think for a moment that your own freedom, your own prosperity, that your own moral imagination is bound by the limits of your community, your ethnicity or even your country. You're bigger than that. You can help us to choose a better history. That's what Europe tells us. That's what the American experience is all about.

I say this as the president of a country that looked to Europe for the values that are written into our founding documents and which spilled blood to ensure that those values could endure on these shores. I also say this as the son of a Kenyan whose grandfather was a cook for the British, and as a person who once lived in Indonesia as it emerged from colonialism.

The ideals that unite us matter equally to the young people of Boston or Brussels or Jakarta or Nairobi or Krakow or Kiev.

In the end, the success of our ideals comes down to us, including the example of our own lives, our own societies. We know that there will always be intolerance, but instead of fearing the immigrant, we can welcome him. We can insist on policies that benefit the many, not just the few, that an age of globalization and dizzying change opens the door of opportunity to the marginalized, and not just a privileged few.

Instead of targeting our gay and lesbian brothers and sisters, we can use our laws to protect their rights. Instead of defining ourselves in opposition to others, we can affirm the aspirations that we hold in common. That's what will make America strong. That's what will make Europe strong. That's what makes us who we are.

And just as we meet our responsibilities as individuals, we must be prepared to meet them as nations because we live in a world in which our ideals are going to be challenged again and again by forces that would drag us back into conflict or corruption. We can't count on others to rise to meet those tests.

The policies of your government, the principles of your European Union will make a critical difference in whether or not the international order that so many generations before you have strived to create continues to move forward, or whether it retreats. And that's the question we all must answer: What kind of Europe, what kind of America, what kind of world will we leave behind?

And I believe that if we hold firm to our principles and are willing to back our beliefs with courage and resolve, then hope will ultimately overcome fear, and freedom will continue to triumph over tyranny, because that is what forever stirs in the human heart.

Thank you very much.

Commencement Address: University of Pennsylvania

Love Yourself, Love Your Work, Love the People around You

By John Legend

In this speech, Grammy Award–winning singer and alumnus John Legend gives the 2014 commencement address to the graduating class of the University of Pennsylvania (Penn), in Philadelphia. Legend gives a heartfelt account of his own life, beginning in a blue-collar community in Ohio where his parents' divorce and his mother's subsequent drug abuse left him unable to embrace love, except in his passion for music. His decision to turn his love of music into a career, he adds, was the key to his success, combined with his willingness to open himself up to deep relationships with others. Love in one's work and love for one's friends and family are, according to Legend, the keys to success. He also shares his belief that a more universal love for humanity should serve as the basis for social justice. What would the education system look like, he asks, if all people were committed to the idea of loving humanity and were dedicated to philanthropy? Legend credits Penn professors Marty Seligman and Adam Grant as proof of his belief that generosity and living a life based on the principle of love make up the path to success and happiness. In closing, he encourages the Penn graduates to approach their lives with love and compassion rather than apathy and cynicism. Along with producing several albums, Legend has become a dedicated philanthropist, supporting projects that include sustainable farming, disease research, and education programs.

Thank you. Thank you so much. Good morning. And congratulations!

Now I'll try to be brief this morning. As a musician, this is about 10 hours before I normally go to work, so I'm gonna need a nap soon. And you've got degrees to receive.

And I *also* have a feeling some of you are already tired of me. The thing about pop radio in America, somehow they've scientifically determined that the public is only capable of liking the *same 10 songs* at any given time, so they simply play those songs over and over and over until you're finally completely exasperated. Then they move on . . .

I've had a 10-year career as a solo artist and none of my songs has ever been one of those 10 songs. Until this moment. And now "all of you, are so over me; you're

Delivered May 19, 2014, at the University of Pennsylvania commencement, Philadelphia, Pennsylvania, by John Legend.

tired of hearing that I went to Penn. Why'd they bring him back again?" (sung to the tune of *All of Me* chorus)

That was my humblebrag way of saying I have the biggest song in the country. Very artful, wouldn't you say?

But, honestly, I am truly humbled and honored and grateful to be here at the commencement of one of the finest universities on the planet. I first visited this campus as a high school senior named John Stephens in 1995—19 years ago—and I would have never thought at that moment that I would be standing here as John Legend, speaking to you today.

The reason I'm here, the reason I've had such a wonderful journey so far, is that I've found love. Yes, love. We were all made to love. And I've found that we live our best lives, we are at our most successful, not simply because we're smarter than everyone else, or because we hustle harder. Not because we become millionaires more quickly. The key to success, the key to happiness, is opening your mind and your heart to love. Spending your time doing things you love and with people you love.

My life could have gone differently though. At first, I had a pretty good childhood. I grew up in a small blue-collar city called Springfield, Ohio. I was surrounded by family, including two loving parents who cared so much about our education that they home-schooled us for several years during grade school. And they took the time to teach us more than academics. They taught us about character, about what it meant to live a good life.

My father often talked to us about his definition of success. He told us that it wasn't measured in money and material things, but it was measured in love and joy and the lives you're able to touch—the lives you're able to help. And my parents walked the walk. They gave of themselves to our church. They took in foster kids and helped the homeless, even though we didn't have much money ourselves.

Growing up in the Stephens' house also meant you were immersed in art and music and encouraged to be creative. We had a piano and a drum kit in the house. I begged to take piano lessons when I was four. I started singing in the church choir and in school plays by the time I was seven. So I fell in love with music at a very young age.

My family was like a model family in our church and local community. My parents were leaders, raising intelligent, talented kids in a loving environment. We even had a little singing group called the "Stephens 5."

But things started to fall apart when I was 10. My maternal grandmother passed away that year when she was only 58 years old, and her death devastated my family. She was our church organist, and on Sundays after church, I would go to her house just to hang out with her. She would make chicken and collard greens and corn bread. And she would teach me how to play gospel piano. She was one of my favorite people on the planet.

She and my mother were also very close, and her death sent my mother into a deep depression that eventually tore our family apart. My world was shattered. My parents got divorced. My mother disappeared into over a decade of drugs and despair. And I was confused and disoriented.

After the initial shock of my family breaking apart, my outward response wasn't very emotional. I coped by being stoic and seemingly unaffected. I thought if I didn't expose myself to any more pain and vulnerability, I could never get hurt. If I didn't fall in love, no one could ever betray me like that again.

I busied myself with school work and lots of activities, and tried not to think too much about my family situation, tried to avoid pain whenever possible. A big reason I only applied to colleges on the east coast was to make sure I had no reminders of home in my daily life.

The only thing I allowed myself to really love without reservation was music. I put all of my passion into it. I spent so much of my spare time working on it, that I barely got any sleep. At night, I was doing community choir, show choir and musicals in high school; a cappella and a church choir in college. I wrote my own songs. Played in talent shows. I put a lot of energy into becoming a better artist, a better writer and a better performer. And in some ways, it made me a better student and a better leader. Because when you actually care about something, you want to lead. Apathy's not so cool any more.

When I graduated from Penn, I had many of the traditional opportunities in front of you now, and I took a job at the Boston Consulting Group. But I couldn't shake my passion for music. I had followed the path that the Penn graduate was supposed to take, but I didn't fall in love. I immediately started thinking about how I could leave BCG and become a full-time musician. I spent hours during the day preparing PowerPoint presentations and financial models. And I spent almost as many hours at night writing songs and performing at small gigs around New York and Philadelphia.

I always believed that my big break would come sooner rather than later. In fact, from 1998, while I was still at Penn, to early 2004, I spent each of those years always thinking that I would get that big record deal within the next few months. I always thought my moment was just around the corner. But I was rejected by all the major labels; some of them rejected me multiple times. I played for all the giants of the business—Clive Davis, L.A. Reid, Jimmy Iovine, you name it. And all of them turned me down.

But I did find a young producer from Chicago named Kanye West who believed in me. Kanye happened to be the cousin of my good friend DeVon Harris, a classmate and roommate of mine here at Penn. DeVon introduced me to Kanye in 2001, and we've been working together ever since. Our collaboration has been a huge part of my career, and it had a lot to do with me finally getting a major recording contract in 2004.

Now, Kanye and I have very different personalities, as you might have guessed. But what unites us is our true love for music and art. We love to create, and at no point in our creative process do we stress about what will sell or what's already popular. We think about making something beautiful, something special, something we can be proud of. We truly do this because we love it. We put all of ourselves into it.

And it turns out that love *requires* that level of commitment from you. Half-doing it is not doing it right. You have to go all in. And yes, your personal relationships require that too.

I know what it's like to be all ego in your 20s. I know what it's like to be selfish and just focus on your immediate wants and desires. I know what it's like to protect your heart from pain and disappointment. I know what it means to be all about the rat race and winning.

But years from now, when you look back on your time here on earth, your life and your happiness will be way more defined by the *quality* of your relationships, not the quantity. You'll get much more joy out of *depth*, not breadth. It's about finding and keeping the best relationships possible with the people around you. It's about immersing yourself in your friendships and your family. It's about being there for the people you care about, and knowing that they'll be there for you.

I know. It's not easy to go all in on love. I'm 35 and I'm married and I'm still learning how to do this completely. But I've found someone who makes me want to try, someone who makes me want to take that risk. And it's made all the difference.

Now, I've already talked about the power of love in your work and your personal lives. But I also want to talk about how love changes the world. There are seven billion other people out there. Seven billion strangers. I want you to consider what it means to love them too. What does it mean to love people we don't know, to see the value in every single person's life?

Think about that. It's a pretty radical notion. It means your daughter or son, your neighbor's daughter or son and the daughters and sons of people who live thousands of miles away, all deserve the right to life, liberty and the pursuit of happiness. It means we let go of fear and see each other's humanity. It means we don't see Trayvon Martin as a walking stereotype, a weaponized human. We see him as a boy who deserves the chance to grow into a man, even if he makes boyish mistakes along the way. It means American lives don't count more than Iraqi lives. It means we see a young Palestinian kid not as a future security threat or demographic challenge, but as a future father, mother and lover. It means that the nearly 300 kidnapped girls in Nigeria aren't just their problem. They're our girls too. It's actually quite a challenge to love humankind in this way.

Professor Cornel West gives us a word for what this kind of love looks like in public. That word is justice.

If you're committed to loving in public, it requires you opening your eyes to injustice, to see the world through the eyes of another. This is not a passive activity. You have to read. You have to travel to other neighborhoods, other parts of the world. You may have to get your hands dirty. You have to allow people to love you, and you have to love them back.

My team and I met a young girl named Rose from a small, impoverished village in Ghana. When you're working with development organizations and visiting the communities they work in, you're not really supposed to single out one child to fall in love with. You're supposed to stick to the program and focus on the interventions that lift the community as a whole. But we couldn't help it. We fell in love with Rose. Something about the spark in her eyes and her indomitable spirit made us want to go the extra mile to help her. So we decided to use our own funds to sponsor her tuition to secondary school.

We've stayed in touch with her over the past seven years, and we're so proud of what she's done individually. But we're also happy that she inspired us to formalize and expand our scholarship program to many girls in communities like hers throughout Africa, communities where the parents often invest in the boys' secondary education, but don't do the same for the girls.

In my travels around the world, I've looked in the eyes of many young girls and boys from Africa to Southeast Asia to Harlem, kids who had big dreams and needed someone to believe in them and invest in their future, in their education.

What would our schools look like if we were committed to love in public? If we cared about every kid in our school system, we would make sure they didn't go to school hungry. We would make sure they had proper health care and counseling. We would make sure they had excellent teachers in every classroom. We would make sure we weren't unfairly suspending them and criminalizing them for minor behavioral problems. We'd make sure all of them had the resources they need.

Every religion has this idea of philanthropy, love for mankind, at its core. But you shouldn't do this just to make sure you get into the "pearly gates." Look at the work of Marty Seligman here at Penn, who has literally written the book on happiness. Look at the work of Adam Grant, whom I hear is the most highly rated professor here: He has the data to show that giving works. There's an increasing body of research and knowledge that tells us that living a life of love and compassion is the true path to success and contentment.

So what's going to stop you? What's going to stand in your way? What's going to keep you from achieving your success? What will prevent you from going all in on love?

We're taught when we're young that the opposite of love is hate. But it's not. Hate is a byproduct. Hate is a result. Being a hater isn't cool. Nobody wants that. But hate comes from one thing: fear. And fear is the opposite of love. It's not a coincidence that when we talk about bigotry, we often talk in terms of fear: homophobia, xenophobia. Fear is what blinds us. Fear is corrosive. Fear makes us hold back. It whispers to us, tells us that we'll fail. It tells us that our differences are too much to overcome. Fear locks us in place. It starts fights. It causes wars.

And fear keeps us from loving. Even though we're made to love, we're often afraid to love. We're afraid of being hurt deeply. Afraid of feeling the pain I went through when my parents divorced. But you're never going to really love something or someone unless you put those fears aside. Don't hold back. Being in love means being ready to give freely and openly, and being ready to risk something. Risking pain and disappointment, conquering your fears and becoming anew.

Alice Walker once said, "The more I wonder, the more I love." Love calls you to open your eyes, to seek, to search, to wonder.

Love is all-consuming—it infiltrates your body, it's what allows you to experience bliss, joy and true friendship. You'll be more disappointed when something goes wrong. You might fall harder. But the only way you'll reach any height in life and in love is by taking the chance that you might fall.

You have to give your *all*.

Yes, I've been not-so-subtly working in my song lyrics. And some might think it's all a bit too much. Here I am, this R&B singer with an album called *Love in the Future*, who's recently married and wrote the biggest love song of the year, and what did I choose to talk about? *Love*. It's so *corny* isn't it. It's much cooler to be detached and apathetic, right? We all like a little snark and cynicism and irony, especially from our favorite artists and comedians and writers. I get it.

But that cool detachment only gets you so far. Passion gets you a lot further. It makes you a better entrepreneur, a better leader, a better philanthropist, a better friend, a better lover.

I want you to live the best life you can. You can be world-changers. When you leave here today, you're going to be looking for a lot of things: security, money, friendships, sex, all kinds of things. But the most important thing you'll find is love.

So love yourself, love your work, love the people around you. *Dare* to love those who are different from you, no matter where they're from, what they look like and who they love. Pursue this life of love with focus and passion and ambition and courage. Give it your all. And that will be your path to true success.

Congratulations to the Class of 2014 and thank you so much!

2

Wealth Inequality

The managing director of the International Monetary fund, Christine Lagarde addresses the Inclusive Capitalism Conference at the Mansion House in London, England, May 27, 2014.

Remarks by the President on Economic Mobility

By Barack Obama

In this speech, President Barack Obama addresses staff of the Center for American Progress (CAP) at the Town Hall Education Arts Recreation Campus (THEARC) in Washington, DC, discussing economic mobility in the United States. President Obama begins by looking into the history of the US government's efforts to care for the poor, unemployed, and disabled, and to provide opportunities for employment and education to disadvantaged groups. Obama then goes on to explain that the growth of the American economy, since the 1970s, has been marked by increasing inequality, with better than 90 percent increases in productivity translating to only 8 percent growth in the income of a typical family. Obama then discusses how inequality and a lack of economic mobility pose a combined threat to the American way of life, diminishing forward momentum for all sectors of the population. To combat this problem, Obama speaks about his federal and state initiatives designed to promote and support higher education for a larger share of the population, with a focus on innovation and technology, and to support unionization and workers' rights. Obama also mentions the goal to increase the minimum wage around the country, and the ongoing effort to address the situation faced by segments of the population hit hardest by the most recent economic recession. Elected to his first term in November 2008, Barack Obama is the forty-fourth president of the United States. Before becoming president, Obama was a United States senator representing the state of Illinois from 2005 to 2008 and, before that, was an elected member of the Illinois Senate.

Thank you. (Applause.) Thank you, everybody. Thank you so much. Please, please have a seat. Thank you so much. Well, thank you, Neera, for the wonderful introduction and sharing a story that resonated with me. There were a lot of parallels in my life and probably resonated with some of you.

Over the past 10 years, the Center for American Progress has done incredible work to shape the debate over expanding opportunity for all Americans. And I could not be more grateful to CAP not only for giving me a lot of good policy ideas, but also giving me a lot of staff. (Laughter.) My friend, John Podesta, ran my transition; my Chief of Staff, Denis McDonough, did a stint at CAP. So you guys are obviously doing a good job training folks.

I also want to thank all the members of Congress and my administration who are here today for the wonderful work that they do. I want to thank Mayor Gray and everyone here at THEARC for having me. This center, which I've been to quite a

Delivered December 4, 2013, at the Town Hall Education Arts Recreation Campus, Washington, DC, by Barack Obama.

bit, have had a chance to see some of the great work that's done here. And all the nonprofits that call THEARC home offer access to everything from education, to health care, to a safe shelter from the streets, which means that you're harnessing the power of community to expand opportunity for folks here in D.C. And your work reflects a tradition that runs through our history—a belief that we're greater together than we are on our own. And that's what I've come here to talk about today.

Over the last two months, Washington has been dominated by some pretty contentious debates—I think that's fair to say. And between a reckless shutdown by congressional Republicans in an effort to repeal the Affordable Care Act, and admittedly poor execution on my administration's part in implementing the latest stage of the new law, nobody has acquitted themselves very well these past few months. So it's not surprising that the American people's frustrations with Washington are at an all-time high.

But we know that people's frustrations run deeper than these most recent political battles. Their frustration is rooted in their own daily battles—to make ends meet, to pay for college, buy a home, save for retirement. It's rooted in the nagging sense that no matter how hard they work, the deck is stacked against them. And it's rooted in the fear that their kids won't be better off than they were. They may not follow the constant back-and-forth in Washington or all the policy details, but they experience in a very personal way the relentless, decades-long trend that I want to spend some time talking about today. And that is a dangerous and growing inequality and lack of upward mobility that has jeopardized middle-class America's basic bargain—that if you work hard, you have a chance to get ahead.

I believe this is the defining challenge of our time: Making sure our economy works for every working American. It's why I ran for President. It was at the center of last year's campaign. It drives everything I do in this office. And I know I've raised this issue before, and some will ask why I raise the issue again right now. I do it because the outcomes of the debates we're having right now—whether it's health care, or the budget, or reforming our housing and financial systems—all these things will have real, practical implications for every American. And I am convinced that the decisions we make on these issues over the next few years will determine whether or not our children will grow up in an America where opportunity is real.

Now, the premise that we're all created equal is the opening line in the American story. And while we don't promise equal outcomes, we have strived to deliver equal opportunity—the idea that success doesn't depend on being born into wealth or privilege, it depends on effort and merit. And with every chapter we've added to that story, we've worked hard to put those words into practice.

It was Abraham Lincoln, a self-described "poor man's son," who started a system of land grant colleges all over this country so that any poor man's son could go learn something new.

When farms gave way to factories, a rich man's son named Teddy Roosevelt fought for an eight-hour workday, protections for workers, and busted monopolies that kept prices high and wages low.

When millions lived in poverty, FDR fought for Social Security, and insurance for the unemployed, and a minimum wage.

When millions died without health insurance, LBJ fought for Medicare and Medicaid.

Together, we forged a New Deal, declared a War on Poverty in a great society. We built a ladder of opportunity to climb, and stretched out a safety net beneath so that if we fell, it wouldn't be too far, and we could bounce back. And as a result, America built the largest middle class the world has ever known. And for the three decades after World War II, it was the engine of our prosperity.

Now, we can't look at the past through rose-colored glasses. The economy didn't always work for everyone. Racial discrimination locked millions out of poverty—or out of opportunity. Women were too often confined to a handful of often poorly paid professions. And it was only through painstaking struggle that more women, and minorities, and Americans with disabilities began to win the right to more fairly and fully participate in the economy.

Nevertheless, during the post–World War II years, the economic ground felt stable and secure for most Americans, and the future looked brighter than the past. And for some, that meant following in your old man's footsteps at the local plant, and you knew that a blue-collar job would let you buy a home, and a car, maybe a vacation once in a while, health care, a reliable pension. For others, it meant going to college—in some cases, maybe the first in your family to go to college. And it meant graduating without taking on loads of debt, and being able to count on advancement through a vibrant job market.

Now, it's true that those at the top, even in those years, claimed a much larger share of income than the rest: The top 10 percent consistently took home about one-third of our national income. But that kind of inequality took place in a dynamic market economy where everyone's wages and incomes were growing. And because of upward mobility, the guy on the factory floor could picture his kid running the company some day.

But starting in the late '70s, this social compact began to unravel. Technology made it easier for companies to do more with less, eliminating certain job occupations. A more competitive world lets companies ship jobs anywhere. And as good manufacturing jobs automated or headed offshore, workers lost their leverage, jobs paid less and offered fewer benefits.

As values of community broke down, and competitive pressure increased, businesses lobbied Washington to weaken unions and the value of the minimum wage. As a trickle-down ideology became more prominent, taxes were slashed for the wealthiest, while investments in things that make us all richer, like schools and infrastructure, were allowed to wither. And for a certain period of time, we could ignore this weakening economic foundation, in part because more families were relying on two earners as women entered the workforce. We took on more debt financed by a juiced-up housing market. But when the music stopped, and the crisis hit, millions of families were stripped of whatever cushion they had left.

And the result is an economy that's become profoundly unequal, and families that are more insecure. I'll just give you a few statistics. Since 1979, when I graduated from high school, our productivity is up by more than 90 percent, but the income of the typical family has increased by less than 8 percent. Since 1979, our economy has more than doubled in size, but most of that growth has flowed to a fortunate few.

The top 10 percent no longer takes in one-third of our income—it now takes half. Whereas in the past, the average CEO made about 20 to 30 times the income of the average worker, today's CEO now makes 273 times more. And meanwhile, a family in the top 1 percent has a net worth 288 times higher than the typical family, which is a record for this country.

So the basic bargain at the heart of our economy has frayed. In fact, this trend towards growing inequality is not unique to America's market economy. Across the developed world, inequality has increased. Some of you may have seen just last week, the Pope himself spoke about this at eloquent length. "How can it be," he wrote, "that it is not a news item when an elderly homeless person dies of exposure, but it is news when the stock market loses two points?"

But this increasing inequality is most pronounced in our country, and it challenges the very essence of who we are as a people. Understand we've never begrudged success in America. We aspire to it. We admire folks who start new businesses, create jobs, and invent the products that enrich our lives. And we expect them to be rewarded handsomely for it. In fact, we've often accepted more income inequality than many other nations for one big reason—because we were convinced that America is a place where even if you're born with nothing, with a little hard work you can improve your own situation over time and build something better to leave your kids. As Lincoln once said, "While we do not propose any war upon capital, we do wish to allow the humblest man an equal chance to get rich with everybody else."

The problem is that alongside increased inequality, we've seen diminished levels of upward mobility in recent years. A child born in the top 20 percent has about a 2-in-3 chance of staying at or near the top. A child born into the bottom 20 percent has a less than 1-in-20 shot at making it to the top. He's 10 times likelier to stay where he is. In fact, statistics show not only that our levels of income inequality rank near countries like Jamaica and Argentina, but that it is harder today for a child born here in America to improve her station in life than it is for children in most of our wealthy allies—countries like Canada or Germany or France. They have greater mobility than we do, not less.

The idea that so many children are born into poverty in the wealthiest nation on Earth is heartbreaking enough. But the idea that a child may never be able to escape that poverty because she lacks a decent education or health care, or a community that views her future as their own, that should offend all of us and it should compel us to action. We are a better country than this.

So let me repeat: The combined trends of increased inequality and decreasing mobility pose a fundamental threat to the American Dream, our way of life, and what we stand for around the globe. And it is not simply a moral claim that I'm making here. There are practical consequences to rising inequality and reduced mobility.

For one thing, these trends are bad for our economy. One study finds that growth is more fragile and recessions are more frequent in countries with greater inequality. And that makes sense. When families have less to spend, that means businesses have fewer customers, and households rack up greater mortgage and credit card debt; meanwhile, concentrated wealth at the top is less likely to result in the kind of broadly based consumer spending that drives our economy, and together with lax regulation, may contribute to risky speculative bubbles.

And rising inequality and declining mobility are also bad for our families and social cohesion—not just because we tend to trust our institutions less, but studies show we actually tend to trust each other less when there's greater inequality. And greater inequality is associated with less mobility between generations. That means it's not just temporary; the effects last. It creates a vicious cycle. For example, by the time she turns three years old, a child born into a low-income home hears 30 million fewer words than a child from a well-off family, which means by the time she starts school she's already behind, and that deficit can compound itself over time.

And finally, rising inequality and declining mobility are bad for our democracy. Ordinary folks can't write massive campaign checks or hire high-priced lobbyists and lawyers to secure policies that tilt the playing field in their favor at everyone else's expense. And so people get the bad taste that the system is rigged, and that increases cynicism and polarization, and it decreases the political participation that is a requisite part of our system of self-government.

So this is an issue that we have to tackle head on. And if, in fact, the majority of Americans agree that our number-one priority is to restore opportunity and broad-based growth for all Americans, the question is why has Washington consistently failed to act? And I think a big reason is the myths that have developed around the issue of inequality.

First, there is the myth that this is a problem restricted to a small share of pre-dominantly minority poor—that this isn't a broad-based problem, this is a black problem or a Hispanic problem or a Native American problem. Now, it's true that the painful legacy of discrimination means that African Americans, Latinos, Native Americans are far more likely to suffer from a lack of opportunity—higher unem-ployment, higher poverty rates. It's also true that women still make 77 cents on the dollar compared to men. So we're going to need strong application of antidiscrimi-nation laws. We're going to need immigration reform that grows the economy and takes people out of the shadows. We're going to need targeted initiatives to close those gaps. (Applause.)

But here's an important point. The decades-long shifts in the economy have hurt all groups: poor and middle class; inner city and rural folks; men and women; and Americans of all races. And as a consequence, some of the social patterns that contribute to declining mobility that were once attributed to the urban poor—that's a particular problem for the inner city: single-parent households or drug abuse—it turns out now we're seeing that pop up everywhere.

A new study shows that disparities in education, mental health, obesity, absent fathers, isolation from church, isolation from community groups—these gaps are now as much about growing up rich or poor as they are about anything else. The gap in test scores between poor kids and wealthy kids is now nearly twice what it is between white kids and black kids. Kids with working-class parents are 10 times likelier than kids with middle- or upper-class parents to go through a time when their parents have no income. So the fact is this: The opportunity gap in America is now as much about class as it is about race, and that gap is growing.

So if we're going to take on growing inequality and try to improve upward mobility for all people, we've got to move beyond the false notion that this is an issue exclusively of minority concern. And we have to reject a politics that suggests any effort to address it in a meaningful way somehow pits the interests of a deserving middle class against those of an undeserving poor in search of handouts. (Applause.)

Second, we need to dispel the myth that the goals of growing the economy and reducing inequality are necessarily in conflict, when they should actually work in concert. We know from our history that our economy grows best from the middle out, when growth is more widely shared. And we know that beyond a certain level of inequality, growth actually slows altogether.

Third, we need to set aside the belief that government cannot do anything about reducing inequality. It's true that government cannot prevent all the downsides of the technological change and global competition that are out there right now, and some of those forces are also some of the things that are helping us grow. And it's also true that some programs in the past, like welfare before it was reformed, were sometimes poorly designed, created disincentives to work.

But we've also seen how government action time and again can make an enormous difference in increasing opportunity and bolstering ladders into the middle class. Investments in education, laws establishing collective bargaining, and a minimum wage—these all contributed to rising standards of living for massive numbers of Americans. (Applause.) Likewise, when previous generations declared that every citizen of this country deserved a basic measure of security—a floor through which they could not fall—we helped millions of Americans live in dignity, and gave millions more the confidence to aspire to something better, by taking a risk on a great idea.

Without Social Security, nearly half of seniors would be living in poverty—half. Today, fewer than 1 in 10 do. Before Medicare, only half of all seniors had some form of health insurance. Today, virtually all do. And because we've strengthened that safety net, and expanded pro-work and pro-family tax credits like the Earned Income Tax Credit, a recent study found that the poverty rate has fallen by 40 percent since the 1960s. And these endeavors didn't just make us a better country; they reaffirmed that we are a great country.

So we can make a difference on this. In fact, that's our generation's task—to rebuild America's economic and civic foundation to continue the expansion of opportunity for this generation and the next generation. (Applause.) And like Neera, I take this personally. I'm only here because this country educated my grandfather on the GI Bill. When my father left and my mom hit hard times trying to raise my sister and me while she was going to school, this country helped make sure we didn't go hungry. When Michelle, the daughter of a shift worker at a water plant and a secretary, wanted to go to college, just like me, this country helped us afford it until we could pay it back.

So what drives me as a grandson, a son, a father—as an American—is to make sure that every striving, hardworking, optimistic kid in America has the same incredible chance that this country gave me. (Applause.) It has been the driving force behind everything we've done these past five years. And over the course of the next year, and for the rest of my presidency, that's where you should expect my administration to focus all our efforts. (Applause.)

Now, you'll be pleased to know this is not a State of the Union Address. (Laughter.) And many of the ideas that can make the biggest difference in expanding opportunity I've presented before. But let me offer a few key principles, just a roadmap that I believe should guide us in both our legislative agenda and our administrative efforts.

To begin with, we have to continue to relentlessly push a growth agenda. It may be true that in today's economy, growth alone does not guarantee higher wages and incomes. We've seen that. But what's also true is we can't tackle inequality if the economic pie is shrinking or stagnant. The fact is if you're a progressive and you want to help the middle class and the working poor, you've still got to be concerned about competitiveness and productivity and business confidence that spurs private sector investment.

And that's why from day one we've worked to get the economy growing and help our businesses hire. And thanks to their resilience and innovation, they've created nearly 8 million new jobs over the past 44 months. And now we've got to grow the economy even faster. And we've got to keep working to make America a magnet for good, middle-class jobs to replace the ones that we've lost in recent decades—jobs in manufacturing and energy and infrastructure and technology.

And that means simplifying our corporate tax code in a way that closes wasteful loopholes and ends incentives to ship jobs overseas. (Applause.) And by broadening the base, we can actually lower rates to encourage more companies to hire here and use some of the money we save to create good jobs rebuilding our roads and our bridges and our airports, and all the infrastructure our businesses need.

It means a trade agenda that grows exports and works for the middle class. It means streamlining regulations that are outdated or unnecessary or too costly. And it means coming together around a responsible budget—one that grows our economy faster right now and shrinks our long-term deficits, one that unwinds the harmful sequester cuts that haven't made a lot of . . .sense (applause) and . . . then frees up resources to invest in things like the scientific research that's always unleashed new innovation and new industries.

When it comes to our budget, we should not be stuck in a stale debate from two years ago or three years ago. A relentlessly growing deficit of opportunity is a bigger threat to our future than our rapidly shrinking fiscal deficit. (Applause.)

So that's step one towards restoring mobility: making sure our economy is growing faster. Step two is making sure we empower more Americans with the skills and education they need to compete in a highly competitive global economy.

We know that education is the most important predictor of income today, so we launched a Race to the Top in our schools. We're supporting states that have raised standards for teaching and learning. We're pushing for redesigned high schools that graduate more kids with the technical training and apprenticeships, and in-demand, high-tech skills that can lead directly to a good job and a middle-class life.

We know it's harder to find a job today without some higher education, so we've helped more students go to college with grants and loans that go farther than before. We've made it more practical to repay those loans. And today, more students are graduating from college than ever before. We're also pursuing an aggressive strategy to promote innovation that reins in tuition costs. We've got lower costs so that young people are not burdened by enormous debt when they make the right decision to get higher education. And next week, Michelle and I will bring together college presidents and non-profits to lead a campaign to help more low-income students attend and succeed in college. (Applause.)

But while higher education may be the surest path to the middle class, it's not the only one. So we should offer our people the best technical education in the world. That's why we've worked to connect local businesses with community colleges, so that workers young and old can earn the new skills that earn them more money.

And I've also embraced an idea that I know all of you at the Center for American Progress have championed—and, by the way, Republican governors in a couple of states have championed—and that's making high-quality preschool available to every child in America. (Applause.) We know that kids in these programs grow up likelier to get more education, earn higher wages, form more stable families of their own. It starts a virtuous cycle, not a vicious one. And we should invest in that. We should give all of our children that chance.

And as we empower our young people for future success, the third part of this middle-class economics is empowering our workers. It's time to ensure our collective bargaining laws function as they're supposed to—(applause)—so unions have a level playing field to organize for a better deal for workers and better wages for the middle class. It's time to pass the Paycheck Fairness Act so that women will have more tools to fight pay discrimination. (Applause.) It's time to pass the Employment Non-Discrimination Act so workers can't be fired for who they are or who they love. (Applause.)

And even though we're bringing manufacturing jobs back to America, we're creating more good-paying jobs in education and health care and business services; we know that we're going to have a greater and greater portion of our people in the service sector. And we know that there are airport workers, and fast-food workers, and nurse assistants, and retail salespeople who work their tails off and are still living at or barely above poverty. (Applause.) And that's why it's well past the time to raise a minimum wage that in real terms right now is below where it was when Harry Truman was in office. (Applause.)

This shouldn't be an ideological question. It was Adam Smith, the father of free-market economics, who once said, "They who feed, clothe, and lodge the whole body of the people should have such a share of the produce of their own labor as to be themselves tolerably well fed, clothed, and lodged." And for those of you who don't speak old-English—(laughter)—let me translate. It means if you work hard, you should make a decent living. (Applause.) If you work hard, you should be able to support a family.

Now, we all know the arguments that have been used against a higher minimum wage. Some say it actually hurts low-wage workers—businesses will be less likely to hire them. But there's no solid evidence that a higher minimum wage costs jobs, and research shows it raises incomes for low-wage workers and boosts short-term economic growth. (Applause.)

Others argue that if we raise the minimum wage, companies will just pass those costs on to consumers. But a growing chorus of businesses, small and large, argue differently. And already, there are extraordinary companies in America that provide decent wages, salaries, and benefits, and training for their workers, and deliver a great product to consumers.

SAS in North Carolina offers childcare and sick leave. REI, a company my Secretary of the Interior used to run, offers retirement plans and strives to cultivate a good work balance. There are companies out there that do right by their workers. They recognize that paying a decent wage actually helps their bottom line, reduces turnover. It means workers have more money to spend, to save, maybe eventually start a business of their own.

A broad majority of Americans agree we should raise the minimum wage. That's why, last month, voters in New Jersey decided to become the 20th state to raise theirs even higher. That's why, yesterday, the D.C. Council voted to do it, too. I agree with those voters. (Applause.) I agree with those voters, and I'm going to keep pushing until we get a higher minimum wage for hard-working Americans across the entire country. It will be good for our economy. It will be good for our families. (Applause.)

Number four, as I alluded to earlier, we still need targeted programs for the communities and workers that have been hit hardest by economic change and the Great Recession. These communities are no longer limited to the inner city. They're found in neighborhoods hammered by the housing crisis, manufacturing towns hit hard by years of plants packing up, landlocked rural areas where young folks oftentimes feel like they've got to leave just to find a job. There are communities that just aren't generating enough jobs anymore.

So we've put forward new plans to help these communities and their residents, because we've watched cities like Pittsburgh or my hometown of Chicago revamp themselves. And if we give more cities the tools to do it—not handouts, but a hand up—cities like Detroit can do it, too. So in a few weeks, we'll announce the first of these Promise Zones, urban and rural communities where we're going to support local efforts focused on a national goal—and that is a child's course in life should not be determined by the zip code he's born in, but by the strength of his work ethic and the scope of his dreams. (Applause.)

And we're also going to have to do more for the long-term unemployed. For people who have been out of work for more than six months, often through no fault of their own, life is a catch-22. Companies won't give their résumé an honest look because they've been laid off so long—but they've been laid off so long because companies won't give their résumé an honest look. (Laughter.) And that's why earlier this year, I challenged CEOs from some of America's best companies to give these Americans a fair shot. And next month, many of them will join us at the White House for an announcement about this.

Fifth, we've got to revamp retirement to protect Americans in their golden years, to make sure another housing collapse doesn't steal the savings in their homes. We've also got to strengthen our safety net for a new age, so it doesn't just protect people who hit a run of bad luck from falling into poverty, but also propels them back out of poverty.

Today, nearly half of full-time workers and 80 percent of part-time workers don't have a pension or retirement account at their job. About half of all households don't have any retirement savings. So we're going to have to do more to encourage private savings and shore up the promise of Social Security for future generations. And remember, these are promises we make to one another. We don't do it to replace the free market, but we do it to reduce risk in our society by giving people the ability to take a chance and catch them if they fall. One study shows that more than half of Americans will experience poverty at some point during their adult lives. Think about that. This is not an isolated situation. More than half of Americans at some point in their lives will experience poverty.

That's why we have nutrition assistance or the program known as SNAP, because it makes a difference for a mother who's working, but is just having a hard time putting food on the table for her kids. That's why we have unemployment insurance, because it makes a difference for a father who lost his job and is out there looking for a new one so that he can keep a roof over his kids' heads. By the way, Christmastime is no time for Congress to tell more than 1 million of these Americans that they have lost their unemployment insurance, which is what will happen if Congress does not act before they leave on their holiday vacation. (Applause.)

The point is these programs are not typically hammocks for people to just lie back and relax. These programs are almost always temporary means for hardworking people to stay afloat while they try to find a new job or go into school to retrain themselves for the jobs that are out there, or sometimes just to cope with a bout of bad luck. Progressives should be open to reforms that actually strengthen these programs and make them more responsive to a 21st-century economy. For example, we should be willing to look at fresh ideas to revamp unemployment and disability programs to encourage faster and higher rates of re-employment without cutting benefits. We shouldn't weaken fundamental protections built over generations, because given the constant churn in today's economy and the disabilities that many of our friends and neighbors live with, they're needed more than ever.

We should strengthen them and adapt them to new circumstances so they work even better.

But understand that these programs of social insurance benefit all of us, because we don't know when we might have a run of bad luck. (Applause.) We don't know when we might lose a job. Of course, for decades, there was one yawning gap in the safety net that did more than anything else to expose working families to the insecurities of today's economy—namely, our broken health care system.

That's why we fought for the Affordable Care Act—(applause)—because 14,000 Americans lost their health insurance every single day, and even more died each year because they didn't have health insurance at all. We did it because millions of families who thought they had coverage were driven into bankruptcy by out-of-pocket costs that they didn't realize would be there. Tens of millions of our fellow citizens couldn't get any coverage at all. And Dr. King once said, "Of all the forms of inequality, injustice in health care is the most shocking and inhumane."

Well, not anymore. (Applause.) Because in the three years since we passed this law, the share of Americans with insurance is up, the growth of health care costs are down to their slowest rate in 50 years. More people have insurance, and more have new benefits and protections—100 million Americans who have gained the right for free preventive care like mammograms and contraception; the more than 7 million Americans who have saved an average of $1,200 on their prescription medicine; every American who won't go broke when they get sick because their insurance can't limit their care anymore.

More people without insurance have gained insurance—more than 3 million young Americans who have been able to stay on their parents' plan, the more than half a million Americans and counting who are poised to get covered starting on January 1st, some for the very first time.

And it is these numbers—not the ones in any poll—that will ultimately determine the fate of this law. (Applause.) It's the measurable outcomes in reduced bankruptcies and reduced hours that have been lost because somebody couldn't make it to work, and healthier kids with better performance in schools, and young entrepreneurs who have the freedom to go out there and try a new idea—those are the things that will ultimately reduce a major source of inequality and help ensure more Americans get the start that they need to succeed in the future.

I have acknowledged more than once that we didn't roll out parts of this law as well as we should have. But the law is already working in major ways that benefit millions of Americans right now, even as we've begun to slow the rise in health care costs, which is good for family budgets, good for federal and state budgets, and good for the budgets of businesses small and large. So this law is going to work. And for the sake of our economic security, it needs to work. (Applause.)

And as people in states as different as California and Kentucky sign up every single day for health insurance, signing up in droves, they're proving they want that economic security. If the Senate Republican leader still thinks he is going to be able to repeal this someday, he might want to check with the more than 60,000 people in his home state who are already set to finally have coverage that frees them from the fear of financial ruin, and lets them afford to take their kids to see a doctor. (Applause.)

So let me end by addressing the elephant in the room here, which is the seeming inability to get anything done in Washington these days. I realize we are not going to resolve all of our political debates over the best ways to reduce inequality and increase upward mobility this year, or next year, or in the next five years. But it is important that we have a serious debate about these issues. For the longer that current trends are allowed to continue, the more it will feed the cynicism and fear that many Americans are feeling right now—that they'll never be able to repay the debt they took on to go to college, they'll never be able to save enough to retire, they'll never see their own children land a good job that supports a family.

And that's why, even as I will keep on offering my own ideas for expanding opportunity, I'll also keep challenging and welcoming those who oppose my ideas to offer their own. If Republicans have concrete plans that will actually reduce inequality, build the middle class, provide more ladders of opportunity to the poor, let's hear them. I want to know what they are. If you don't think we should raise the minimum wage, let's hear your idea to increase people's earnings. If you don't think every child should have access to preschool, tell us what you'd do differently to give them a better shot.

If you still don't like Obamacare—and I know you don't (laughter) even though it's built on market-based ideas of choice and competition in the private sector, then you should explain how, exactly, you'd cut costs, and cover more people, and make insurance more secure. You owe it to the American people to tell us what you are for, not just what you're against. (Applause.) That way we can have a vigorous and meaningful debate. That's what the American people deserve. That's what the times demand. It's not enough anymore to just say we should just get our government out of the way and let the unfettered market take care of it—for our experience tells us that's just not true. (Applause.)

Look, I've never believed that government can solve every problem or should— and neither do you. We know that ultimately our strength is grounded in our people—individuals out there, striving, working, making things happen. It depends on community, a rich and generous sense of community—that's at the core of what happens at THEARC here every day. You understand that turning back rising inequality and expanding opportunity requires parents taking responsibility for their kids, kids taking responsibility to work hard. It requires religious leaders who mobilize their congregations to rebuild neighborhoods block by block, requires civic organizations that can help train the unemployed, link them with businesses for the jobs of the future. It requires companies and CEOs to set an example by providing decent wages, and salaries, and benefits for their workers, and a shot for somebody who is down on his or her luck. We know that's our strength—our people, our communities, our businesses.

But government can't stand on the sidelines in our efforts. Because government is us. It can and should reflect our deepest values and commitments. And if we refocus our energies on building an economy that grows for everybody, and gives every child in this country a fair chance at success, then I remain confident that the future still looks brighter than the past, and that the best days for this country we love are still ahead. (Applause.)

Thank you, everybody. God bless you. God bless America.

President Barack Obama's State of the Union Address

By Barack Obama

In his 2014 State of the Union address, President Barack Obama speaks about a variety of issues facing Americans in 2014, including education, the economy, retirement, health care, and foreign policy. The State of the Union address is an annual speech given to a joint session of Congress that reports on the current state of the nation and outlines the future policy agenda for the White House. Obama begins with anecdotal examples of American life, illustrating the state of American industry and society. As he moves on to proposals for policy initiatives during the year, he speaks about federal support for alternative energy, including solar power, and asserts that the government must be more proactive in confronting climate change. Obama also addresses early childhood education and the need to further reform the higher education loan process to protect students. In defense of the American workforce, he supports the national effort to raise the minimum wage and promotes the ongoing federal effort to reform the healthcare system to ensure that all US citizens have health insurance. In terms of foreign policy, Obama states that diplomacy is the key to ending the terrorist conflicts of the twenty-first century and that the federal government will focus on diplomatic—rather than military—initiatives to promote peace abroad. Declaring his belief that the war in Afghanistan will be over by the end of the year, he states that the administration will work to disrupt terrorist networks forming in other parts of the world. Elected in 2008 and reelected in 2012, Obama is the forty-fourth president of the United States.

Mr. Speaker, Mr. Vice President, Members of Congress, my fellow Americans:

Today in America, a teacher spent extra time with a student who needed it, and did her part to lift America's graduation rate to its highest level in more than three decades.

An entrepreneur flipped on the lights in her tech startup, and did her part to add to the more than eight million new jobs our businesses have created over the past four years.

An autoworker fine-tuned some of the best, most fuel-efficient cars in the world, and did his part to help America wean itself off foreign oil.

A farmer prepared for the spring after the strongest five-year stretch of farm exports in our history. A rural doctor gave a young child the first prescription to treat asthma that his mother could afford. A man took the bus home from the graveyard shift, bone-tired but dreaming big dreams for his son. And in tight-knit communities across America, fathers and mothers will tuck in their kids, put an arm around

Delivered January 28, 2014, on the floor of the US House of Representatives, Washington, DC, by Barack Obama.

their spouse, remember fallen comrades, and give thanks for being home from a war that, after twelve long years, is finally coming to an end.

Tonight, this chamber speaks with one voice to the people we represent: it is you, our citizens, who make the state of our union strong.

Here are the results of your efforts: The lowest unemployment rate in over five years. A rebounding housing market. A manufacturing sector that's adding jobs for the first time since the 1990s. More oil produced at home than we buy from the rest of the world—the first time that's happened in nearly twenty years. Our deficits—cut by more than half. And for the first time in over a decade, business leaders around the world have declared that China is no longer the world's number one place to invest; America is.

That's why I believe this can be a breakthrough year for America. After five years of grit and determined effort, the United States is better-positioned for the 21st-century than any other nation on Earth.

The question for everyone in this chamber, running through every decision we make this year, is whether we are going to help or hinder this progress. For several years now, this town has been consumed by a rancorous argument over the proper size of the federal government. It's an important debate—one that dates back to our very founding. But when that debate prevents us from carrying out even the most basic functions of our democracy—when our differences shut down government or threaten the full faith and credit of the United States—then we are not doing right by the American people.

As President, I'm committed to making Washington work better, and rebuilding the trust of the people who sent us here. I believe most of you are, too. Last month, thanks to the work of Democrats and Republicans, this Congress finally produced a budget that undoes some of last year's severe cuts to priorities like education. Nobody got everything they wanted, and we can still do more to invest in this country's future while bringing down our deficit in a balanced way. But the budget compromise should leave us freer to focus on creating new jobs, not creating new crises.

In the coming months, let's see where else we can make progress together. Let's make this a year of action. That's what most Americans want—for all of us in this chamber to focus on their lives, their hopes, their aspirations. And what I believe unites the people of this nation, regardless of race or region or party, young or old, rich or poor, is the simple, profound belief in opportunity for all—the notion that if you work hard and take responsibility, you can get ahead.

Let's face it: that belief has suffered some serious blows. Over more than three decades, even before the Great Recession hit, massive shifts in technology and global competition had eliminated a lot of good, middle-class jobs, and weakened the economic foundations that families depend on.

Today, after four years of economic growth, corporate profits and stock prices have rarely been higher, and those at the top have never done better. But average wages have barely budged. Inequality has deepened. Upward mobility has stalled. The cold, hard fact is that even in the midst of recovery, too many Americans are working more than ever just to get by—let alone get ahead. And too many still aren't working at all.

Our job is to reverse these trends. It won't happen right away, and we won't agree on everything. But what I offer tonight is a set of concrete, practical proposals to speed up growth, strengthen the middle class, and build new ladders of opportunity into the middle class. Some require congressional action, and I'm eager to work with all of you. But America does not stand still—and neither will I. So wherever and whenever I can take steps without legislation to expand opportunity for more American families, that's what I'm going to do.

As usual, our First Lady sets a good example. Michelle's Let's Move partnership with schools, businesses, and local leaders has helped bring down childhood obesity rates for the first time in thirty years—an achievement that will improve lives and reduce health care costs for decades to come. The Joining Forces alliance that Michelle and Jill Biden launched has already encouraged employers to hire or train nearly 400,000 veterans and military spouses. Taking a page from that playbook, the White House just organized a College Opportunity Summit where already, 150 universities, businesses, and nonprofits have made concrete commitments to reduce inequality in access to higher education—and help every hardworking kid go to college and succeed when they get to campus. Across the country, we're partnering with mayors, governors, and state legislatures on issues from homelessness to marriage equality.

The point is, there are millions of Americans outside Washington who are tired of stale political arguments, and are moving this country forward. They believe, and I believe, that here in America, our success should depend not on accident of birth, but the strength of our work ethic and the scope of our dreams. That's what drew our forebears here. It's how the daughter of a factory worker is CEO of America's largest automaker; how the son of a barkeeper is Speaker of the House; how the son of a single mom can be president of the greatest nation on Earth.

Opportunity is who we are. And the defining project of our generation is to restore that promise.

We know where to start: the best measure of opportunity is access to a good job. With the economy picking up speed, companies say they intend to hire more people this year. And over half of big manufacturers say they're thinking of insourcing jobs from abroad.

So let's make that decision easier for more companies. Both Democrats and Republicans have argued that our tax code is riddled with wasteful, complicated loopholes that punish businesses investing here, and reward companies that keep profits abroad. Let's flip that equation. Let's work together to close those loopholes, end those incentives to ship jobs overseas, and lower tax rates for businesses that create jobs here at home.

Moreover, we can take the money we save with this transition to tax reform to create jobs rebuilding our roads, upgrading our ports, unclogging our commutes— because in today's global economy, first-class jobs gravitate to first-class infrastructure. We'll need Congress to protect more than three million jobs by finishing transportation and waterways bills this summer. But I will act on my own to slash bureaucracy and streamline the permitting process for key projects, so we can get more construction workers on the job as fast as possible.

We also have the chance, right now, to beat other countries in the race for the next wave of high-tech manufacturing jobs. My administration has launched two hubs for high-tech manufacturing in Raleigh and Youngstown, where we've connected businesses to research universities that can help America lead the world in advanced technologies. Tonight, I'm announcing we'll launch six more this year. Bipartisan bills in both houses could double the number of these hubs and the jobs they create. So get those bills to my desk and put more Americans back to work.

Let's do more to help the entrepreneurs and small business owners who create most new jobs in America. Over the past five years, my administration has made more loans to small business owners than any other. And when 98 percent of our exporters are small businesses, new trade partnerships with Europe and the Asia-Pacific will help them create more jobs. We need to work together on tools like bipartisan trade promotion authority to protect our workers, protect our environment, and open new markets to new goods stamped "Made in the USA." China and Europe aren't standing on the sidelines. Neither should we.

We know that the nation that goes all-in on innovation today will own the global economy tomorrow. This is an edge America cannot surrender. Federally funded research helped lead to the ideas and inventions behind Google and smartphones. That's why Congress should undo the damage done by last year's cuts to basic research so we can unleash the next great American discovery—whether it's vaccines that stay ahead of drug-resistant bacteria, or paper-thin material that's stronger than steel. And let's pass a patent reform bill that allows our businesses to stay focused on innovation, not costly, needless litigation.

Now, one of the biggest factors in bringing more jobs back is our commitment to American energy. The all-of-the-above energy strategy I announced a few years ago is working, and today, America is closer to energy independence than we've been in decades.

One of the reasons why is natural gas—if extracted safely, it's the bridge fuel that can power our economy with less of the carbon pollution that causes climate change. Businesses plan to invest almost $100 billion in new factories that use natural gas. I'll cut red tape to help states get those factories built, and this Congress can help by putting people to work building fueling stations that shift more cars and trucks from foreign oil to American natural gas. My administration will keep working with the industry to sustain production and job growth while strengthening protection of our air, our water, and our communities. And while we're at it, I'll use my authority to protect more of our pristine federal lands for future generations.

It's not just oil and natural gas production that's booming; we're becoming a global leader in solar, too. Every four minutes, another American home or business goes solar; every panel pounded into place by a worker whose job can't be outsourced. Let's continue that progress with a smarter tax policy that stops giving $4 billion a year to fossil fuel industries that don't need it, so that we can invest more in fuels of the future that do.

And even as we've increased energy production, we've partnered with businesses, builders, and local communities to reduce the energy we consume. When we rescued our automakers, for example, we worked with them to set higher fuel efficiency standards for our cars. In the coming months, I'll build on that success by setting new standards for our trucks, so we can keep driving down oil imports and what we pay at the pump.

Taken together, our energy policy is creating jobs and leading to a cleaner, safer planet. Over the past eight years, the United States has reduced our total carbon pollution more than any other nation on Earth. But we have to act with more urgency—because a changing climate is already harming western communities struggling with drought, and coastal cities dealing with floods. That's why I directed my administration to work with states, utilities, and others to set new standards on the amount of carbon pollution our power plants are allowed to dump into the air. The shift to a cleaner energy economy won't happen overnight, and it will require tough choices along the way. But the debate is settled. Climate change is a fact. And when our children's children look us in the eye and ask if we did all we could to leave them a safer, more stable world, with new sources of energy, I want us to be able to say yes, we did.

Finally, if we are serious about economic growth, it is time to heed the call of business leaders, labor leaders, faith leaders, and law enforcement—and fix our broken immigration system. Republicans and Democrats in the Senate have acted. I know that members of both parties in the House want to do the same. Independent economists say immigration reform will grow our economy and shrink our deficits by almost $1 trillion in the next two decades. And for good reason: when people come here to fulfill their dreams—to study, invent, and contribute to our culture—they make our country a more attractive place for businesses to locate and create jobs for everyone. So let's get immigration reform done this year.

The ideas I've outlined so far can speed up growth and create more jobs. But in this rapidly-changing economy, we have to make sure that every American has the skills to fill those jobs.

The good news is, we know how to do it. Two years ago, as the auto industry came roaring back, Andra Rush opened up a manufacturing firm in Detroit. She knew that Ford needed parts for the best-selling truck in America, and she knew how to make them. She just needed the workforce. So she dialed up what we call an American Job Center—places where folks can walk in to get the help or training they need to find a new job, or better job. She was flooded with new workers. And today, Detroit Manufacturing Systems has more than 700 employees.

What Andra and her employees experienced is how it should be for every employer—and every job seeker. So tonight, I've asked Vice President Biden to lead an across-the-board reform of America's training programs to make sure they have one mission: train Americans with the skills employers need, and match them to good jobs that need to be filled right now. That means more on-the-job training, and more apprenticeships that set a young worker on an upward trajectory for life. It means connecting companies to community colleges that can help design training to fill their specific needs. And if Congress wants to help, you can concentrate funding on proven programs that connect more ready-to-work Americans with ready-to-be-filled jobs.

I'm also convinced we can help Americans return to the workforce faster by reforming unemployment insurance so that it's more effective in today's economy. But first, this Congress needs to restore the unemployment insurance you just let expire for 1.6 million people.

Let me tell you why.

Misty DeMars is a mother of two young boys. She'd been steadily employed since she was a teenager. She put herself through college. She'd never collected unemployment benefits. In May, she and her husband used their life savings to buy their first home. A week later, budget cuts claimed the job she loved. Last month, when their unemployment insurance was cut off, she sat down and wrote me a letter—the kind I get every day. "We are the face of the unemployment crisis," she wrote. "I am not dependent on the government. . . .Our country depends on people like us who build careers, contribute to society . . . care about our neighbors . . . I am confident that in time I will find a job . . . I will pay my taxes, and we will raise our children in their own home in the community we love. Please give us this chance."

Congress, give these hardworking, responsible Americans that chance. They need our help, but more important, this country needs them in the game. That's why I've been asking CEOs to give more long-term unemployed workers a fair shot at that new job and new chance to support their families; this week, many will come to the White House to make that commitment real. Tonight, I ask every business leader in America to join us and to do the same—because we are stronger when America fields a full team.

Of course, it's not enough to train today's workforce. We also have to prepare tomorrow's workforce, by guaranteeing every child access to a world-class education.

Estiven Rodriguez couldn't speak a word of English when he moved to New York City at age nine. But last month, thanks to the support of great teachers and an innovative tutoring program, he led a march of his classmates—through a crowd of cheering parents and neighbors—from their high school to the post office, where they mailed off their college applications. And this son of a factory worker just found out he's going to college this fall.

Five years ago, we set out to change the odds for all our kids. We worked with lenders to reform student loans, and today, more young people are earning college degrees than ever before. Race to the Top, with the help of governors from both parties, has helped states raise expectations and performance. Teachers and principals in schools from Tennessee to Washington, D.C. are making big strides in preparing students with skills for the new economy—problem solving, critical thinking, science, technology, engineering, and math. Some of this change is hard. It requires everything from more challenging curriculums and more demanding parents to better support for teachers and new ways to measure how well our kids think, not how well they can fill in a bubble on a test. But it's worth it—and it's working.

The problem is we're still not reaching enough kids, and we're not reaching them in time. That has to change.

Research shows that one of the best investments we can make in a child's life is high-quality early education. Last year, I asked this Congress to help states make high-quality pre-K available to every four year-old. As a parent as well as a president, I repeat that request tonight. But in the meantime, thirty states have raised pre-K funding on their own. They know we can't wait. So just as we worked with states to reform our schools, this year, we'll invest in new partnerships with states and communities across the country in a race to the top for our youngest children. And as Congress decides what it's going to do, I'm going to pull together a coalition of elected officials, business leaders, and philanthropists willing to help more kids access the high-quality pre-K they need.

Last year, I also pledged to connect 99 percent of our students to high-speed broadband over the next four years. Tonight, I can announce that with the support of the FCC and companies like Apple, Microsoft, Sprint, and Verizon, we've got a down payment to start connecting more than 15,000 schools and twenty million students over the next two years, without adding a dime to the deficit.

We're working to redesign high schools and partner them with colleges and employers that offer the real-world education and hands-on training that can lead directly to a job and career. We're shaking up our system of higher education to give parents more information, and colleges more incentives to offer better value, so that no middle-class kid is priced out of a college education. We're offering millions the opportunity to cap their monthly student loan payments to 10 percent of their income, and I want to work with Congress to see how we can help even more Americans who feel trapped by student loan debt. And I'm reaching out to some of America's leading foundations and corporations on a new initiative to help more young men of color facing tough odds stay on track and reach their full potential.

The bottom line is, Michelle and I want every child to have the same chance this country gave us. But we know our opportunity agenda won't be complete—and too many young people entering the workforce today will see the American Dream as an empty promise—unless we do more to make sure our economy honors the dignity of work, and hard work pays off for every single American.

Today, women make up about half our workforce. But they still make 77 cents for every dollar a man earns. That is wrong, and in 2014, it's an embarrassment. A woman deserves equal pay for equal work. She deserves to have a baby without sacrificing her job. A mother deserves a day off to care for a sick child or sick parent without running into hardship—and you know what, a father does, too. It's time to do away with workplace policies that belong in a "Mad Men" episode. This year, let's all come together—Congress, the White House, and businesses from Wall Street to Main Street—to give every woman the opportunity she deserves. Because I firmly believe when women succeed, America succeeds.

Now, women hold a majority of lower-wage jobs—but they're not the only ones stifled by stagnant wages. Americans understand that some people will earn more than others, and we don't resent those who, by virtue of their efforts, achieve incredible success. But Americans overwhelmingly agree that no one who works full time should ever have to raise a family in poverty.

In the year since I asked this Congress to raise the minimum wage, five states have passed laws to raise theirs. Many businesses have done it on their own. Nick Chute is here tonight with his boss, John Soranno. John's an owner of Punch Pizza in Minneapolis, and Nick helps make the dough. Only now he makes more of it: John just gave his employees a raise, to ten bucks an hour—a decision that eased their financial stress and boosted their morale.

Tonight, I ask more of America's business leaders to follow John's lead and do what you can to raise your employees' wages. To every mayor, governor, and state legislator in America, I say, you don't have to wait for Congress to act; Americans will support you if you take this on. And as a chief executive, I intend to lead by example. Profitable corporations like Costco see higher wages as the smart way to boost productivity and reduce turnover. We should too. In the coming weeks, I will issue an executive order requiring federal contractors to pay their federally-funded employees a fair wage of at least $10.10 an hour—because if you cook our troops' meals or wash their dishes, you shouldn't have to live in poverty.

Of course, to reach millions more, Congress needs to get on board. Today, the federal minimum wage is worth about 20 percent less than it was when Ronald Reagan first stood here. Tom Harkin and George Miller have a bill to fix that by lifting the minimum wage to $10.10. This will help families. It will give businesses customers with more money to spend. It doesn't involve any new bureaucratic program. So join the rest of the country. Say yes. Give America a raise.

There are other steps we can take to help families make ends meet, and few are more effective at reducing inequality and helping families pull themselves up through hard work than the Earned Income Tax Credit. Right now, it helps about half of all parents at some point. But I agree with Republicans like Senator Rubio that it doesn't do enough for single workers who don't have kids. So let's work together to strengthen the credit, reward work, and help more Americans get ahead.

Let's do more to help Americans save for retirement. Today, most workers don't have a pension. A Social Security check often isn't enough on its own. And while the stock market has doubled over the last five years, that doesn't help folks who don't have 401(k)s. That's why, tomorrow, I will direct the Treasury to create a new way for working Americans to start their own retirement savings: MyRA. It's a new savings bond that encourages folks to build a nest egg. MyRA guarantees a decent return with no risk of losing what you put in. And if this Congress wants to help, work with me to fix an upside-down tax code that gives big tax breaks to help the wealthy save, but does little to nothing for middle-class Americans. Offer every American access to an automatic IRA on the job, so they can save at work just like everyone in this chamber can. And since the most important investment many families make is their home, send me legislation that protects taxpayers from footing the bill for a housing crisis ever again, and keeps the dream of homeownership alive for future generations of Americans.

One last point on financial security. For decades, few things exposed hard-working families to economic hardship more than a broken health care system. And in case you haven't heard, we're in the process of fixing that.

A preexisting condition used to mean that someone like Amanda Shelley, a physician assistant and single mom from Arizona, couldn't get health insurance. But on January 1st, she got covered. On January 3rd, she felt a sharp pain. On January 6th, she had emergency surgery. Just one week earlier, Amanda said, that surgery would've meant bankruptcy.

That's what health insurance reform is all about—the peace of mind that if misfortune strikes, you don't have to lose everything.

Already, because of the Affordable Care Act, more than three million Americans under age 26 have gained coverage under their parents' plans.

More than nine million Americans have signed up for private health insurance or Medicaid coverage.

And here's another number: zero. Because of this law, no American can ever again be dropped or denied coverage for a preexisting condition like asthma, back pain, or cancer. No woman can ever be charged more just because she's a woman. And we did all this while adding years to Medicare's finances, keeping Medicare premiums flat, and lowering prescription costs for millions of seniors.

Now, I don't expect to convince my Republican friends on the merits of this law. But I know that the American people aren't interested in refighting old battles. So again, if you have specific plans to cut costs, cover more people, and increase choice—tell America what you'd do differently. Let's see if the numbers add up. But let's not have another forty-something votes to repeal a law that's already helping millions of Americans like Amanda. The first forty were plenty. We got it. We all owe it to the American people to say what we're for, not just what we're against.

And if you want to know the real impact this law is having, just talk to Governor Steve Beshear of Kentucky, who's here tonight. Kentucky's not the most liberal part of the country, but he's like a man possessed when it comes to covering his commonwealth's families. "They are our friends and neighbors," he said. "They are people we shop and go to church with . . . farmers out on the tractors . . . grocery clerks . . . they are people who go to work every morning praying they don't get sick. No one deserves to live that way."

Steve's right. That's why, tonight, I ask every American who knows someone without health insurance to help them get covered by March 31st. Moms, get on your kids to sign up. Kids, call your mom and walk her through the application. It will give her some peace of mind—plus, she'll appreciate hearing from you.

After all, that's the spirit that has always moved this nation forward. It's the spirit of citizenship—the recognition that through hard work and responsibility, we can pursue our individual dreams, but still come together as one American family to make sure the next generation can pursue its dreams as well.

Citizenship means standing up for everyone's right to vote. Last year, part of the Voting Rights Act was weakened. But conservative Republicans and liberal Democrats are working together to strengthen it; and the bipartisan commission I appointed last year has offered reforms so that no one has to wait more than a half hour to vote. Let's support these efforts. It should be the power of our vote, not the size of our bank account, that drives our democracy.

Citizenship means standing up for the lives that gun violence steals from us each day. I have seen the courage of parents, students, pastors, and police officers all over this country who say, "We are not afraid," and I intend to keep trying, with or without Congress, to help stop more tragedies from visiting innocent Americans in our movie theaters, shopping malls, or schools like Sandy Hook.

Citizenship demands a sense of common cause; participation in the hard work of self-government; an obligation to serve to our communities. And I know this chamber agrees that few Americans give more to their country than our diplomats and the men and women of the United States Armed Forces.

Tonight, because of the extraordinary troops and civilians who risk and lay down their lives to keep us free, the United States is more secure. When I took office, nearly 180,000 Americans were serving in Iraq and Afghanistan. Today, all our troops are out of Iraq. More than 60,000 of our troops have already come home from Afghanistan. With Afghan forces now in the lead for their own security, our troops have moved to a support role. Together with our allies, we will complete our mission there by the end of this year, and America's longest war will finally be over.

After 2014, we will support a unified Afghanistan as it takes responsibility for its own future. If the Afghan government signs a security agreement that we have negotiated, a small force of Americans could remain in Afghanistan with NATO allies to carry out two narrow missions: training and assisting Afghan forces, and counterterrorism operations to pursue any remnants of al Qaeda. For while our relationship with Afghanistan will change, one thing will not: our resolve that terrorists do not launch attacks against our country.

The fact is, that danger remains. While we have put al Qaeda's core leadership on a path to defeat, the threat has evolved, as al Qaeda affiliates and other extremists take root in different parts of the world. In Yemen, Somalia, Iraq, and Mali, we have to keep working with partners to disrupt and disable these networks. In Syria, we'll support the opposition that rejects the agenda of terrorist networks. Here at home, we'll keep strengthening our defenses, and combat new threats like cyberattacks. And as we reform our defense budget, we have to keep faith with our men and women in uniform, and invest in the capabilities they need to succeed in future missions.

We have to remain vigilant. But I strongly believe our leadership and our security cannot depend on our military alone. As commander-in-chief, I have used force when needed to protect the American people, and I will never hesitate to do so as long as I hold this office. But I will not send our troops into harm's way unless it's truly necessary; nor will I allow our sons and daughters to be mired in open-ended conflicts. We must fight the battles that need to be fought, not those that terrorists prefer from us—large-scale deployments that drain our strength and may ultimately feed extremism.

So, even as we aggressively pursue terrorist networks—through more targeted efforts and by building the capacity of our foreign partners—America must move off a permanent war footing. That's why I've imposed prudent limits on the use of drones—for we will not be safer if people abroad believe we strike within their countries without regard for the consequence. That's why, working with this Congress, I will reform our surveillance programs—because the vital work of our intelligence community depends on public confidence, here and abroad, that the privacy of ordinary people is not being violated. And with the Afghan war ending, this needs to be the year Congress lifts the remaining restrictions on detainee transfers and we close the prison at Guantanamo Bay—because we counter terrorism not just through intelligence and military action, but by remaining true to our constitutional ideals, and setting an example for the rest of the world.

You see, in a world of complex threats, our security and leadership depends on all elements of our power—including strong and principled diplomacy. American diplomacy has rallied more than fifty countries to prevent nuclear materials from falling into the wrong hands, and allowed us to reduce our own reliance on Cold War stockpiles. American diplomacy, backed by the threat of force, is why Syria's chemical weapons are being eliminated, and we will continue to work with the international community to usher in the future the Syrian people deserve—a future free of dictatorship, terror and fear. As we speak, American diplomacy is supporting Israelis and Palestinians as they engage in difficult but necessary talks to end the conflict there; to achieve dignity and an independent state for Palestinians, and lasting peace and security for the State of Israel—a Jewish state that knows America will always be at their side.

And it is American diplomacy, backed by pressure, that has halted the progress of Iran's nuclear program—and rolled parts of that program back—for the very first time in a decade. As we gather here tonight, Iran has begun to eliminate its stockpile of higher levels of enriched uranium. It is not installing advanced centrifuges. Unprecedented inspections help the world verify, every day, that Iran is not building a bomb. And with our allies and partners, we're engaged in negotiations to see if we can peacefully achieve a goal we all share: preventing Iran from obtaining a nuclear weapon.

These negotiations will be difficult. They may not succeed. We are clear-eyed about Iran's support for terrorist organizations like Hezbollah, which threaten our allies; and the mistrust between our nations cannot be wished away. But these negotiations do not rely on trust; any long-term deal we agree to must be based on verifiable action that convinces us and the international community that Iran is not building a nuclear bomb. If John F. Kennedy and Ronald Reagan could negotiate with the Soviet Union, then surely a strong and confident America can negotiate with less powerful adversaries today.

The sanctions that we put in place helped make this opportunity possible. But let me be clear: if this Congress sends me a new sanctions bill now that threatens to derail these talks, I will veto it. For the sake of our national security, we must give diplomacy a chance to succeed. If Iran's leaders do not seize this opportunity, then I will be the first to call for more sanctions, and stand ready to exercise all options to make sure Iran does not build a nuclear weapon. But if Iran's leaders do seize the chance, then Iran could take an important step to rejoin the community of nations, and we will have resolved one of the leading security challenges of our time without the risks of war.

Finally, let's remember that our leadership is defined not just by our defense against threats, but by the enormous opportunities to do good and promote understanding around the globe—to forge greater cooperation, to expand new markets, to free people from fear and want. And no one is better positioned to take advantage of those opportunities than America.

Our alliance with Europe remains the strongest the world has ever known. From Tunisia to Burma, we're supporting those who are willing to do the hard work of building democracy. In Ukraine, we stand for the principle that all people have the right to express themselves freely and peacefully, and have a say in their country's future. Across Africa, we're bringing together businesses and governments to double access to electricity and help end extreme poverty. In the Americas, we are building new ties of commerce, but we're also expanding cultural and educational exchanges among young people. And we will continue to focus on the Asia-Pacific, where we support our allies, shape a future of greater security and prosperity, and extend a hand to those devastated by disaster—as we did in the Philippines, when our Marines and civilians rushed to aid those battered by a typhoon, and were greeted with words like, "We will never forget your kindness" and "God bless America!"

We do these things because they help promote our long-term security. And we do them because we believe in the inherent dignity and equality of every human being, regardless of race or religion, creed or sexual orientation. And next week, the world will see one expression of that commitment—when Team USA marches the red, white, and blue into the Olympic Stadium—and brings home the gold.

My fellow Americans, no other country in the world does what we do. On every issue, the world turns to us, not simply because of the size of our economy or our military might—but because of the ideals we stand for, and the burdens we bear to advance them.

No one knows this better than those who serve in uniform. As this time of war draws to a close, a new generation of heroes returns to civilian life. We'll keep slashing that backlog so our veterans receive the benefits they've earned, and our wounded warriors receive the health care—including the mental health care—that they need. We'll keep working to help all our veterans translate their skills and leadership into jobs here at home. And we all continue to join forces to honor and support our remarkable military families.

Let me tell you about one of those families I've come to know.

I first met Cory Remsburg, a proud Army Ranger, at Omaha Beach on the 65th anniversary of D-Day. Along with some of his fellow Rangers, he walked me through the program—a strong, impressive young man, with an easy manner, sharp as a tack. We joked around, and took pictures, and I told him to stay in touch.

A few months later, on his tenth deployment, Cory was nearly killed by a massive roadside bomb in Afghanistan. His comrades found him in a canal, face down, underwater, shrapnel in his brain.

For months, he lay in a coma. The next time I met him, in the hospital, he couldn't speak; he could barely move. Over the years, he's endured dozens of surgeries and procedures, and hours of grueling rehab every day.

Even now, Cory is still blind in one eye. He still struggles on his left side. But slowly, steadily, with the support of caregivers like his dad Craig, and the community around him, Cory has grown stronger. Day by day, he's learned to speak again and stand again and walk again—and he's working toward the day when he can serve his country again.

"My recovery has not been easy," he says. "Nothing in life that's worth anything is easy."

Cory is here tonight. And like the Army he loves, like the America he serves, Sergeant First Class Cory Remsburg never gives up, and he does not quit.

My fellow Americans, men and women like Cory remind us that America has never come easy. Our freedom, our democracy, has never been easy. Sometimes we stumble; we make mistakes; we get frustrated or discouraged. But for more than two hundred years, we have put those things aside and placed our collective shoulder to the wheel of progress—to create and build and expand the possibilities of individual achievement; to free other nations from tyranny and fear; to promote justice, and fairness, and equality under the law, so that the words set to paper by our founders are made real for every citizen. The America we want for our kids—a rising America where honest work is plentiful and communities are strong; where prosperity is widely shared and opportunity for all lets us go as far as our dreams and toil will take us—none of it is easy. But if we work together; if we summon what is best in us, with our feet planted firmly in today but our eyes cast towards tomorrow—I know it's within our reach.

Believe it.

God bless you, and God bless the United States of America.

Land of Hope and Dreams: Rock and Roll, Economics, and Rebuilding the Middle Class

By Alan B. Krueger

In this speech, chair of the Council of Economic Advisers Alan B. Krueger speaks about economics and restoring the middle-class economy to a group assembled at the Rock and Roll Hall of Fame in June 2013. Krueger's speech was one of a series of public lectures hosted by the Rock and Roll Hall of Fame covering social and cultural issues connected to the music industry. Krueger explains that both the music industry and the modern economy can be characterized as "superstar economies," in which a small number of lucky and talented individuals are able to dominate the economy, and explains how the globalization of economic systems has made it increasingly possible for privileged groups or individuals to take an increasing percentage of available revenues from every industry. Krueger then explains how the gulf between the top and bottom earners continues to increase, and speaks about "fairness" and the fact that American companies are now less likely to share profits with all employees than they were in the 1970s and 1980s. Ultimately, Krueger argues that the focus of economic revitalization needs to be the middle income brackets, inspiring a "middle out" pattern of growth that will better reach each facet of the economy than starting renewal at either the top or bottom of the income spectrum. Alan Krueger has been a member of the White House Council of Economic Advisers since 2011. Before joining the White House, Krueger was a professor of economics at Princeton University and a research associate for the National Bureau of Economic Research.

Thank you very much for your kind introduction. I have always felt that this is a magnificent museum, one of the few in the world that brings people of all backgrounds together, young and old, rich and poor—there is something here for everyone to marvel at. Particularly at a time when economic forces have been chipping away at the middle class for decades, I think it is essential to have institutions like the Rock and Roll Hall of Fame that can bring people together, and remind us that we are one nation, united by our hopes and dreams.

I gave this talk the title, "Land of Hope and Dreams: Rock and Roll, Economics and Rebuilding the Middle Class" because many of the forces that are buffeting the U.S. economy can be understood in the context of the music industry. I have also learned from 25 years of teaching that the best way to explain economics is through the example of the rock 'n roll industry.

Delivered June 12, 2013, at the Rock and Roll Hall of Fame, Cleveland, Ohio, by Alan B. Krueger.

The music industry is a microcosm of what is happening in the U.S. economy at large. We are increasingly becoming a "winner-take-all economy," a phenomenon that the music industry has long experienced. Over recent decades, technological change, globalization and an erosion of the institutions and practices that support shared prosperity in the U.S. have put the middle class under increasing stress. The lucky and the talented—and it is often hard to tell the difference—have been doing better and better, while the vast majority has struggled to keep up.

These same forces are affecting the music industry. Indeed, the music industry is an extreme example of a "super star economy," in which a small number of artists take home the lion's share of income.

The music industry has undergone a profound shift over the last 30 years. The price of the average concert ticket increased by nearly 400 percent from 1981 to 2012, much faster than the 150 percent rise in overall consumer price inflation.

Concert Ticket Prices Have Risen Much Faster Than Overall Consumer Price Inflation

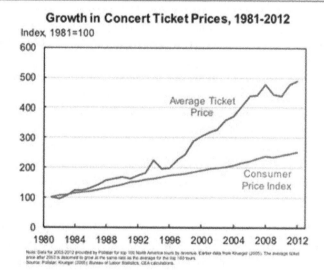

And prices for the best seats for the best performers have increased even faster.

At the same time, the share of concert revenue taken home by the top 1 percent of performers has more than doubled, rising from 26 percent in 1982 to 56 percent in 2003.

The top 5 percent take home almost 90 percent of all concert revenues.

This is an extreme version of what has happened to the U.S. income distribution as a whole. The top 1 percent of families doubled their share of income from 1979 to 2011.

The Top Artists are Getting a Larger Share of Total Ticket Revenue...

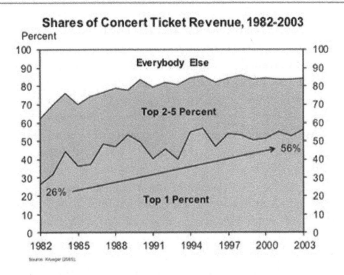

...As the Top Earners are Getting a Larger Share of National Income

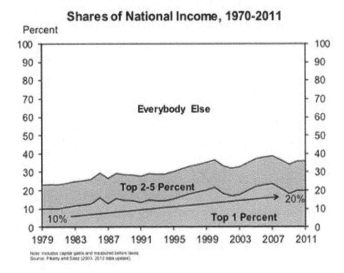

In 1979, the top 1 percent took home 10 percent of national income, and in 2011 they took home 20 percent. By this measure, incomes in the entire U.S. economy today are almost as skewed as they were in the rock and roll industry when Bruce Springsteen cut "Born in the U.S.A."

In my talk, I will focus on why these dramatic changes are taking place and explore their consequences. I will also describe President Obama's vision for providing more opportunities for middle-class families and those struggling to get into the middle class.

I should be clear about my overall theme: while the U.S. economy is recovering from the worst financial and economic crisis since the Great Depression, we must also take steps to strengthen the middle class and provide more opportunities for those born to less fortunate circumstances. If we don't, we will fail to live up to our promise as a nation and be susceptible to the kinds of forces that created economic instability in the past. *To rebuild the economy from the middle out, the private sector will have to step up and reinvigorate the norms and institutions that have supported inclusive growth in the past.* The government has an important role to play as well, but with severe budget constraints and limited political will, the government can only set the conditions for the private sector to grow, and provide more jobs and opportunities for middle-class families. It is, to a considerable extent, up to private-sector businesses, organizations and communities to ensure that economic growth leads to widely shared prosperity and a decent living for the vast majority of our people.

Let me start with the economics of the music industry, and then turn to the economy at large.

Rockonomics

I want to highlight four factors that are important in generating a superstar economy. These are technology, scale, luck and an erosion of social norms that compress prices and incomes. All of these factors are affecting the music industry.

The idea of a "super star economy" is very old. It goes back to Alfred Marshall, the father of modern microeconomics. In the late 1800s, Marshall was trying to explain why some exceptional businessmen amassed great fortunes while the incomes of ordinary artisans and others fell. He concluded that changes in communications technology allowed "a man exceptionally favored by genius and good luck" to command "undertakings vaster, and extending over a wider area, than ever before."

Ironically, his example of a profession where the best performers were unable to achieve such super star status was music. Marshall wrote, "so long as the number of persons who can be reached by a human voice is strictly limited, it is not very likely that any singer will make an advance on the £10,000 said to have been earned in a season by Mrs. Billington at the beginning of the last century, nearly as great [an increase] as that which the business leaders of the present generation have made on those of the last."

Elizabeth Billington reputedly was a great soprano with a strong voice, but she did not have access to a microphone or amplifier in 1798, let alone to MTV, CDs, iTunes, and Pandora. She could only reach a small audience. This limited her ability to dominate the market.

Modern economists have elaborated on Alfred Marshall's insights. The economist Sherwin Rosen developed a theoretical model in which superstar effects are driven by "imperfect substitution" and "scale" in production. Simply put, imperfect substitution means that you would rather listen to one song by your favorite singer than a song and a half by someone else. Or, in another context, it means that if you need to have heart surgery, you would rather have the best surgeon in Cleveland perform it rather than the second and third best together.

Scale means that one performer can reach a large audience.

Technological changes through the centuries have long made the music industry a superstar industry. Advances over time including amplification, radio, records, 8-tracks, music videos, CDs, iPods, etc., have made it possible for the best performers to reach an ever wider audience with high fidelity.

And the increasing globalization of the world economy has vastly increased the reach and notoriety of the most popular performers. They literally can be heard on a worldwide stage.

But advances in technology have also had an unexpected effect. Recorded music has become cheap to replicate and distribute, and it is difficult to police unauthorized reproductions. This has cut into the revenue stream of the best performers, and caused them to raise their prices for live performances.

My research suggests that this is the primary reason why concert prices have risen so much since the late 1990s. In this spirit, David Bowie once predicted that "music itself is going to become like running water or electricity," and, that as a result, artists should "be prepared for doing a lot of touring because that's really the only unique situation that's going to be left." While concerts used to be a loss leader to sell albums, today concerts are a profit center.

But there are limits to how much artists can charge their fans for concert tickets because of social pressures. Most people do not want to think of their favorite singer as greedy. There are a lot of great singers to choose from. Would you rather listen to a singer who is committed to social causes you identify with, or one who is only in it for the money? Part of what you are buying when you buy a recording or concert ticket is the image of the performers. The image and the music are intrinsically linked.

Some of our greatest artists have also been great champions of important social and economic causes, including George Harrison, Joan Baez and Bono.

If artists charge too much for their tickets, they risk losing their appeal. In this sense, the market for rock 'n roll music is different from the market for commodities, or stocks and bonds. Considerations of fair treatment exert pressure on how much musicians can charge, even superstars.

Along these lines, one of my favorite performers, Tom Petty, once said, "I don't see how carving out the best seats and charging a lot more for them has anything to do with rock & roll."

And artists like Garth Brooks and, more recently, Kid Rock have made a point of charging a low price for all of the seats in the house when they perform.

In fact, the best seats for the hottest concerts have historically been underpriced. This is a major reason why there is a market for scalped tickets.

But many artists have been reluctant to raise prices to what the market will bear for fear of garnering a reputation of gouging their fans.

They also protest when tickets sell for a higher price on the secondary market, and often try to prevent the secondary market entirely. And it is considered scandalous when performers sell tickets on the secondary market themselves.

This behavior can only be explained in light of fairness considerations. Singers want to be viewed as treating their fans fairly, rather than charging them what supply and demand dictate. Indeed, you can think of market demand as depending on the perception of fairness.

In many respects, concerts could be thought of as a giant block party instead of a traditional market. While it is socially appropriate to charge neighbors some fee for coming to a block party to pay for the provisions, it is inappropriate to charge them enough to make a hefty profit. There is a compact that fans come and bring their enthusiasm and support for the band, and the band charges a reasonable price and puts on a good show.

Now, as inequality has increased in society in general, norms of fairness have been under pressure and have evolved.

Prices have risen for the best seats at the hottest shows—and made it possible for the best artists to make over $100 million for one tour—but this has come with a backlash from many fans who feel that rock 'n roll is straying from its roots. And this is a risk to the entire industry.

Let me next turn to the role of luck. I said "best artists," but I also could have added luckiest artists. Luck plays a major role in the rock 'n roll industry. Success is hard to judge ahead of time, and definitely not guaranteed, even for the best performers. Tastes are fickle, and herd behavior often takes over.

Even the experts, with much at stake, have difficulty picking winners. Columbia Records turned down Elvis Presley in 1955 and the Beatles in 1963. They turned down Bob Dylan in 1963, and almost rejected "Like a Rolling Stone" in 1965, which was later named the greatest rock 'n roll song ever by *Rolling Stone* magazine.

Or consider Sixto Rodriguez, the subject of the documentary movie *Searching for Sugar Man*. Rodriguez recorded two-and-a-half albums from 1970 to 1975, which were commercial flops. But he was a huge success in South Africa, and his music became the battle hymn of the anti-Apartheid movement. And—amazingly—he was unaware of his fame and influence.

Both good and bad luck play a huge role in the rock 'n roll industry. And the impact of luck is amplified in a superstar economy.

This was clearly demonstrated in a fascinating experiment conducted by the sociologists Matt Salganik and Duncan Watts. With the musicians' permission, the researchers posted 48 songs in an online music library. Subjects were invited to log on to the library and sample the songs, with the opportunity to download the songs for free.

Role of Luck in Popular Music:
Design of Music Market Experiment

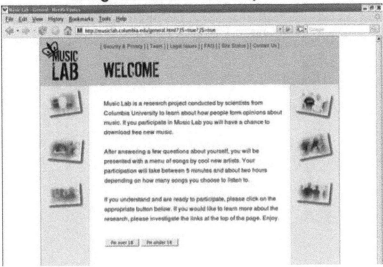

Participants could see the list of songs, ranked by the number of times each one had been downloaded up to that point. They could also see the exact download counts, so they were aware of the popularity of each song based on the collective opinions of other participants.

Role of Luck in Popular Music:
Subjects Can See Download Counts and Rank

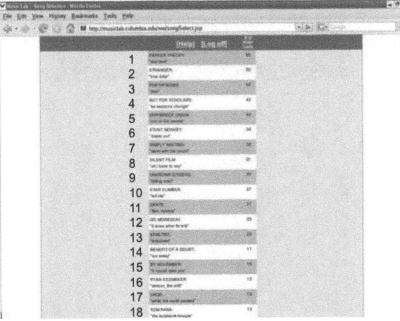

From there, the subjects could click on a song to play it, and then were given the option to download the song for free.

Role of Luck in Popular Music: Can Listen To and Download Songs

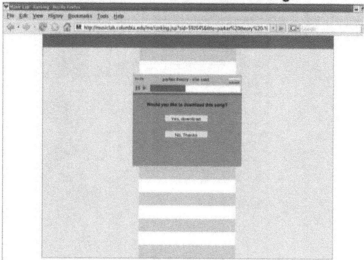

For the first 750 participants, the researchers faithfully tallied and displayed the number of downloads. However, the subsequent 6,000 participants were randomly—and unknowingly—assigned to one of two alternative universes. In one universe, they continued to see the true download counts.

Role of Luck in Popular Music: "Alternative Universe" With Flipped Rankings

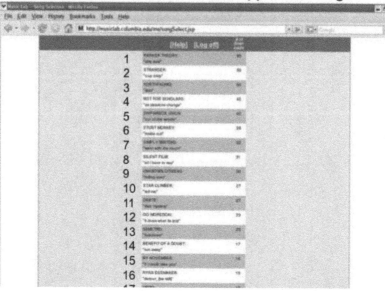

For the other participants, the researchers deviously created an alternative universe where the download counts had been flipped, so that the 48th song was listed as the most popular song, the 47th song was listed as the number two song, and so on. After this one-time inversion in the ranking, the researchers let the download tallies grow on their own. They wanted to see if the cream would rise to the top, or if the boost in ranking that the worst song received would lead it to become popular.

Here's what happened in the world where the download counts were presented accurately.

The *Belief* that a Song is Popular has a Profound Effect on its Popularity, Even if it Wasn't Truly Popular to Begin With

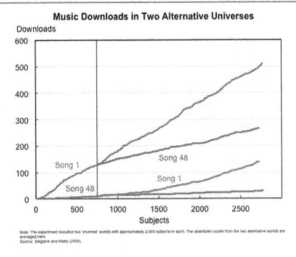

Music Downloads in Two Alternative Universes

By the end of the experiment, the top song ("She Said" by Parker Theory) had been downloaded over 500 times, while the least popular song ("Florence" by Post Break Tragedy) had been downloaded just 29 times—so the natural outcome of the experiment was that the most popular song was nearly 20 times more popular than the least popular song.

Now let's see what happened when the download counts were flipped, so that the new participants *thought* the least popular song was actually the most popular. As you can see, the download count for the least popular song grew much more quickly when it was artificially placed at the top of the list. And the download count for the most popular song grew much more slowly when it was artificially placed at the bottom of the list.

In the alternative world that began with the true rankings reversed, the least popular song did surprisingly well, and, in fact, held onto its artificially bestowed top ranking. The most popular song rose in the rankings, so fundamental quality did have some effect. But, overall—across all 48 songs—the final ranking from the experiment that began with the reversed popularity ordering bore absolutely no relationship to the final ranking from the experiment that began with the true ordering. This demonstrates that the belief that a song is popular has a profound effect on its popularity, even if it wasn't truly popular to start with.

A more general lesson is that, in addition to talent, arbitrary factors can lead to success or failure, like whether another band happens to release a more popular song than your band at the same time. The difference between a *Sugar Man*, a Dylan and a Post Break Tragedy depends a lot more on luck than is commonly acknowledged.

Decent Wages

Let me next turn to the economy more generally. The same forces of technology, scale, luck and the erosion of social pressures for fairness that are making rock 'n roll more of a superstar industry also are causing the U.S. economy to become more of a winner-take-all affair.

The effects of technological change and globalization on inequality have been well documented in the past.

It is abundantly clear that computer and information technology has revolution- ized the way work is done in the U.S. In 1984, less than a quarter of workers directly used a computer on their job. Today, nearly two thirds of workers directly touch a keyboard at work, and millions of others have had their jobs altered by embedded computers and information technology. Computer and information technology has reduced the demand for jobs that can be routinized, and increased the demand for highly educated workers who can use the technology to increase their productivity.

The U.S. economy has also become much more integrated with the world econ- omy in recent decades. While exports and imports made up only 11 percent of GDP in 1970, they made up 31 percent last year. You see signs of globalization ev- erywhere: for example, American bands tour much more internationally today than they used to. A more globally connected economy increases the reach of successful entrepreneurs and artists, but also brings many more low-wage workers into compe- tition with our workforce.

These developments have contributed to some of the momentous changes we have seen in the U.S. economy. This chart shows the share of total income going to the top 1 percent of families starting in 1920.

In the U.S., the Share of Income Earned by the Top 1 Percent Has Doubled Since 1979

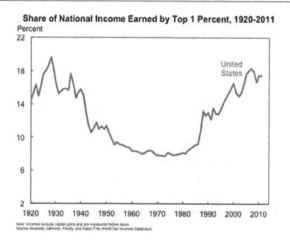

Share of National Income Earned by Top 1 Percent, 1920-2011

During the Roaring Twenties inequality was very high, with the top 1 percent taking in nearly 20 percent of total income. This remained the case until World War II. Price and wage controls and the patriotic spirit that "we're all in it together" during World War II caused inequality to fall. Interestingly, the compression in income gaps brought about by World War II persisted through the 1950s, 1960s and 1970s. Beginning in the 1980s, however, inequality rose significantly in the U.S., with the share of income accruing to the top 1 percent rising to heights last seen in the Roaring Twenties.

After World War II, a social compact ensured that workers received a fair share of the gains of economic growth. This was enforced by labor unions, progressive taxation, a minimum wage that increased in value, anti-discrimination legislation and expanding educational opportunities.

This social compact was good for business and good for the economy. But the social compact began to fray in the 1980s. You can see from the following chart that wages of production and nonsupervisory workers moved pretty much in lockstep with productivity until the late 1970s.

Since the 1980s, however, labor compensation has failed to keep pace with productivity growth, and this has put stress on middle-class workers.

Beginning in the 1980s, Compensation for Production and Non-Supervisory Workers Failed to Keep Pace With Productivity

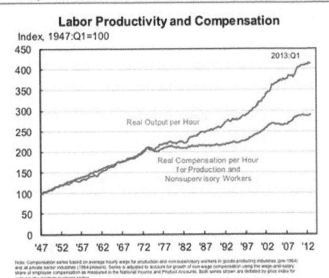

The next two charts show what has happened to income growth in other parts of the distribution. The charts show average annual income growth for families broken down to whether they are in the poorest fifth, second poorest fifth, and so on.

First look at the postwar period through 1979.

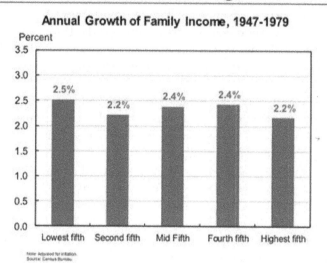

All segments grew together. But since 1979, the top has done better than the middle—which has barely grown over three decades—and those in the bottom have done even worse, with real income declining.

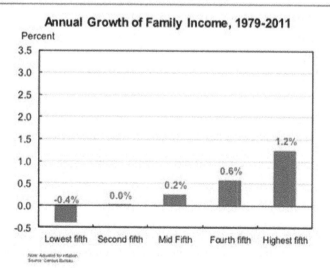

Since 1979, the Top has Done Better than the Middle

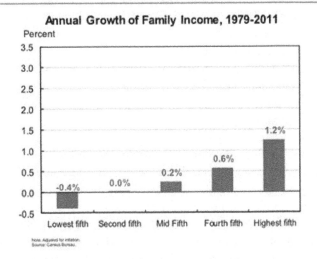

Annual Growth of Family Income, 1979-2011

An astonishing 84 percent of total income growth from 1979 to 2011 went to the top 1 percent of families, and more than 100 percent of it from 2000 to 2007 went to the top 1 percent.

These trends are driven by a pulling apart of wages, with much faster wage growth for the highest income earners over the last three decades, and wages barely keeping pace with inflation or falling behind for everyone else.

Now the forces that brought about these changes were not unique to the U.S., but they have had a more dramatic effect in the U.S. Consider the following chart again with other countries added.

Top Income Shares Vary Across Countries

Share of National Income Earned by Top 1 Percent, 1920-2011

Inequality has followed a broadly similar trend in the U.K., France and Sweden, for example. But notice that the level of inequality varies considerably across these countries, and the rise in the share going to the top 1 percent varies considerably as well. In Sweden, for example, the share of income brought home by the top 1 percent rose just 3 percentage points, from 4 percent in 1980 to 7 percent in 2011, while in the U.S. it doubled from 10 percent to 20 percent.

The widely differing responses to globalization and technological change suggest that other factors mediate these forces.

This brings me to discuss the role of luck, education and institutions that ensure that prosperity is broadly shared.

Globalization and technological change have increased the payoff to completing more education. Countries that have expanded access to education have weathered the polarizing effects of technological change and globalization to a better extent.

To demonstrate the economic benefit of education, I'll describe a study that a colleague and I conducted not very far from here, in Twinsburg, Ohio. For four summers in a row in the 1990s, we went to the Twins Days Festival in Twinsburg. We interviewed identical twins about their education and their incomes. We were particularly interested in knowing whether a twin who had more education than his sibling also had higher income.

The following graph shows the difference in wage rates and years of education between pairs of twins. You can see that, on average, twins with higher education tend to earn more than their other half with less education.

Twins With Higher Education Tend to Earn More Than Their Other Half With Less Education

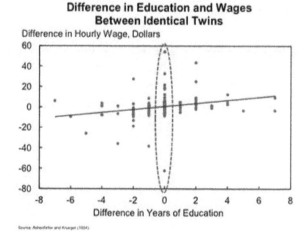

Difference in Education and Wages Between Identical Twins

On average, we find that completing four more years of education is associated with 60 percent higher wages. This and other studies demonstrate that education has a high payoff, on average.

But as we saw in the rock 'n roll industry, luck also matters. Consider identical twins with the same level of education. They were raised by the same family, under the same roof, and typically were dressed alike and went to the same school. They are as alike as two peas in a pod.

Yet in most cases they have very different economic outcomes as adults. Earnings differed by 25 percent or more for pairs of identical twins in half of our sample. And earnings differed by more than 50 percent in a quarter of identical twins with identical school levels.

These discrepancies for such similar workers suggest that luck is an important factor in the labor market, as well as in the music industry.

As in the music industry, the effect of luck is amplified in a winner-take-all economy. Consider the pay of CEOs.

The pay of top executives relative to their workers has soared since the 1980s. In 1965 the average CEO earned about 18 times as much as the average worker; now the average CEO earns over 200 times as much.

A Typical CEO Made 18 Times the Average Worker in 1965, but Today CEOs Make Over 200 Times the Average Worker

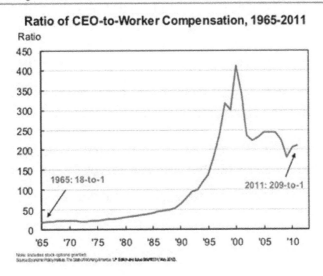

Ratio of CEO-to-Worker Compensation, 1965-2011

As in Alfred Marshall's time, successful executives can now command undertakings on a much vaster scale. This undoubtedly has played a role.

But luck and an erosion of norms of fairness have also boosted CEO pay in many cases. For example, Marianne Bertrand and Sendhil Mullainathan show that the compensation paid to CEOs of oil companies jumps when the price of oil rises. Since the price of oil is set on a world market, with gyrations caused by geopolitical forces well beyond the control of CEOs, movements in the price of oil have nothing to do with their job performance. Yet they benefit when the price of oil rises.

Next, let me consider the role that fairness plays in the economy. We already saw that social pressures for fairness affect the concert industry.

Workers, like music fans, expect to be treated fairly, and if they perceive they are paid unfairly their morale and productivity suffer.

To examine the role of fairness at the workplace, in a recent experiment Ernst Fehr and coauthors randomly varied the pay of members of pairs of workers who were hired to sell membership cards to discotheques in Germany. Obviously, it is not fair if, by luck of the draw, your pay is lower than that of your co-worker who was hired to do the exact same job. They found that increasing the disparity in pay between pairs of workers *decreased* the productivity of the two workers combined. Their findings suggest that a more equal distribution of wages would be good for business because it would raise morale and productivity.

This conclusion is reinforced by fascinating new research by Alex Edmans of Wharton. Edmans finds that when a company makes the list of the "100 Best Companies to Work for in America" its stock market value subsequently rises by 2 to 4 percent per year. Because employee morale suggests that treating workers fairly is in shareholders' interests. Unfortunately, too many executives have strayed from this ethic, to the detriment of their shareholders and the economy.

The notion that profitable companies should share some of their success with their workforce used to be ingrained in U.S. companies. Earlier studies have found that companies and industries that are profitable tend to pay *all* of their workers relatively well, the managers as well as the janitors. In economics we call this "rent sharing." While this is still the case, the practice has been eroded. The following chart shows the relationship between the average pay of managers and janitors across industries in the 2000s.

In Industries Where Managers are Well-Paid, Janitors are also Paid Better, Showing that to Some Extent Profits are Shared

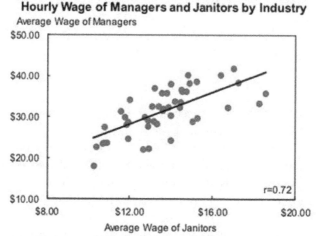

Hourly Wage of Managers and Janitors by Industry

Note: Data covers 2003-2012. Wages in 2012 dollars.
Source: Current Population Survey. OEA calculations.

The correlation is 0.7, indicating that pay is higher for janitors in industries where managers are relatively well paid. If the same analysis is done using data for the 1980s, however, the correlation is higher (0.8), indicating that there used to be a stronger tendency for janitors' pay to move together with that of managers in their industry. This suggests that companies are less likely to share their profits with all workers.

It is not hard to find reasons why the institutions and practices that long enforced norms of fairness in the labor market have been eroded. At a time when market forces were pushing an increasing share of before-tax income toward the wealthiest Americans, the previous administration cut taxes disproportionately for the well-off.

Even earlier, in the 1980s when inequality was starting to take off, the nominal value of the minimum wage was left unchanged from 1981 to 1989, causing it to decline in the value by 27 percent after accounting for inflation. The minimum wage serves as an important anchor for other wages, and the whole wage scale was brought down by the decline in the minimum wage.

A lower minimum wage and regressive tax changes sent a clear signal that maintaining fairness was not a priority.

And policies and tactics that undermined the ability of workers to join unions and exercise their right to collectively bargain weakened a critical institution that has long fought for fairness in the labor market, and served to strengthen the middle class, both for union members and nonmembers.

Consequences

While we rightly celebrate the achievements of those who have been able to scale new heights of success in our economy, the shift toward becoming more of a winner-take-all economy has also had a number of adverse consequences for the U.S. economy that merit great concern.

I'll highlight three.

First, the three-decades-long stagnation in real income for the bottom half of families threatens our long cherished goal of equality of opportunity. In a winner-take-all society, children born to disadvantaged circumstances have much longer odds of climbing the economic ladder of success. Indeed, research has found that countries that have a high degree of inequality also tend to have less economic mobility across generations.

This is shown in the next chart, which displays a plot of the degree of income mobility across generations in a country on the Y-axis (the intergenerational income elasticity) against a measure of the extent of inequality in that country in the mid-1980s (the Gini coefficient for after-tax income) on the X-axis.

A little over a year ago, I called this relationship "the Great Gatsby curve" because F. Scott Fitzgerald's novel highlighted the inequality of the Roaring Twenties and class distinctions—I had no idea they would remake the movie as a result!

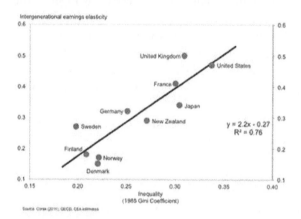

Each point in the graph represents a country. Higher values along the X-axis reflect greater inequality in family resources roughly around the time that the children were growing up. Higher values on the Y-axis indicate a *lower* degree of economic mobility across generations. The points cluster around an upward sloping line, indicating that countries that had more inequality across households also had more persistence in income from one generation to the next. Note that the U.S. is on the upper right of the line, indicating that we have both high inequality and low mobility.

The rise in inequality since the 1980s is likely to move us further out on the Great Gatsby Curve.

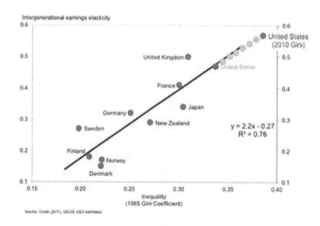

Quantitatively, the persistence in the advantages and disadvantages of income passed from parents to children is predicted to rise by about one quarter for the next generation as a result of the rise in inequality that the U.S. has experienced over the last 25 years.

We are already seeing a growing gap in the enrichment activities provided to children born to higher- and lower-income families.

This next chart shows that since the 1970s expenditures on education-related activities—including music and art lessons, books and tutoring—have been growing for children in families in the top 20 percent of income earner but have been stagnant for children in the bottom 20 percent.

The Gap in Spending on Child Enrichment Has Widened

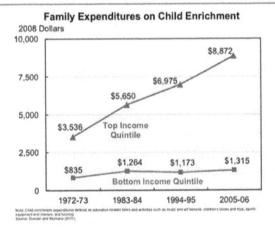

And the following chart shows that there is a growing gap between the top and bottom in participation in extracurricular activities at school.

The Gap in Participation in Extracurricular Activities Has Widened

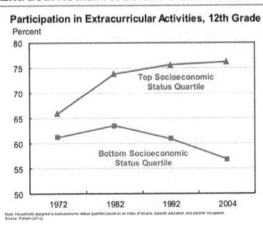

And there is also a widening gap in participation in music, dance, and art outside school.

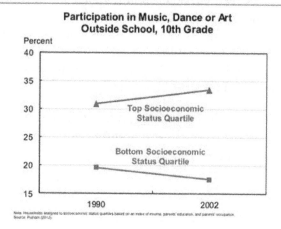

The Gap in Participation in Music, Dance and Art Outside of School Has Widened

Children of wealthy parents already have much more access to opportunities to succeed than do children of poor parents, and this is likely to be increasingly the case in the future unless we ensure that all children have access to quality education, health care, a safe environment and other opportunities that are necessary to have a fair shot at economic success.

There is a significant cost to the economy and society if children from low-income families do not have anything close to the opportunities to develop and apply their talents as their more fortunate counterparts from better-off families, who can attend better schools, receive college prep tutoring, and draw on a network of family connections in the job market.

Diverse observers from Raghuram Rajan of the University of Chicago to Robert Reich of Berkeley have suggested a **second** way in which rising inequality and slow income growth for the vast middle class have harmed the U.S. economy—namely, by encouraging families to borrow to try to maintain consumption, a practice which cannot go on forever, and by reducing aggregate consumption. As a result of the rise in inequality, the amount of income going to the top 1 percent of American families has increased by about $1 trillion on an annual basis. Because the middle class has a higher propensity to spend their income than the top 1 percent, this curbs consumption. An increasingly top-heavy distribution of income is a drag on aggregate demand and economic growth, and a contributing factor to credit bubbles.

President Obama made this point very clearly in a speech in Osawatomie, Kansas: "When middle-class families can no longer afford to buy the goods and services that businesses are selling, it drags down the entire economy, from top to bottom."

Third, an active line of research examines the connection between inequality and longer-term economic growth. In a seminal study, Torsten Persson and Guido

Tabellini found that in a society where income inequality is greater, political decisions are likely to result in policies that lead to less growth.

A recent IMF paper also finds that more equality in the income distribution is associated with more stable economic growth.

Historically, a growing middle class has led to new markets, supported economic growth and built stronger communities.

Growing the Economy from the Middle Out

In this year's State of the Union Address, President Obama said, "We can either settle for a country where a shrinking number of people do really well, while a growing number of Americans barely get by, or we can restore an economy where everyone gets a fair shot, and everyone does their fair share, and everyone plays by the same set of rules."

He went on to outline a robust set of proposals to grow the economy from the middle out, by creating more middle-class jobs and opportunities for those who are struggling to make it to the middle class.

I'll conclude by explaining why the president's agenda makes so much sense for our economy. This slide summarizes key elements of the president's proposals to rebuild the middle class.

Obama Administration Policies for Growing and Strengthening the Middle Class

- **Ladders of Opportunity: E.g., Pre-school for all**
- **Promise Zones: Revitalizing hard-hit communities**
- **Affordable Care Act: Affordable, high quality health care**
- **Raise the minimum wage**
- **Restore fairness to the tax code with ATRA and by closing loopholes**
- **Support a renaissance in U.S. manufacturing**
- **Invest in 21st Century Infrastructure**
- **Balanced Deficit Reduction**

First, we need to provide ladders of opportunity so we can fully utilize and develop the talents of everyone in our country. One example of such a policy is preschool education. Much research has found that high-quality preschool pays for itself many times over down the road. All children should have access to a safe learning environment.

Second, *the only force stronger than globalization is the strength of community*. There are synergies within local areas. There is the reason why tech companies agglomerate in Silicon Valley or movie producers in Hollywood. And it is why Motown produced so much great music. There can be positive spillovers within communities.

Research by the economist Enrico Moretti, for example, shows that high school graduates benefit when the number of college graduates rise in an area.

Education Has Spillover Effects: High School Grads Benefit from Living in a City with More College Grads

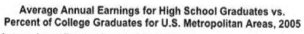

Average Annual Earnings for High School Graduates vs. Percent of College Graduates for U.S. Metropolitan Areas, 2005

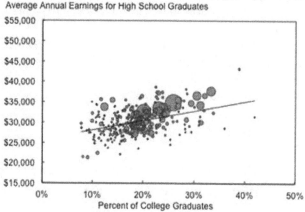

The Obama administration is committed to revitalizing distressed communities. The president's budget proposed to designate 20 of the communities hardest hit by the recession as "Promise Zones." These "Promise Zones" will benefit from co-ordinated federal support to reduce crime, build more affordable housing, revamp schools, and attract private investment.

Third, the landmark Affordable Care Act expands access to health insurance coverage by providing subsidies for low- and moderate-income families, creates more competition and transparency in the insurance market, and gives providers and insurers new incentives to keep costs down.

Fourth, to restore fairness to our economy, President Obama has proposed rais-ing the minimum wage to $9 an hour and indexing it so it rises with inflation. This would bring the real value of the minimum wage back to where it was in 1981.

Government actions and the use of the bully pulpit can also strengthen norms of fairness when it comes to private-sector pay.

As part of the Wall Street Reform Act, for example, the president signed legisla-tion that requires a nonbinding shareholder vote on the pay of top executives at pub-lic companies, called "Say-on-Pay." About 3 percent of companies had shareholders vote against executive pay packages in Say-on-Pay votes in 2012. Although this may seem small, there were some very consequential and newsworthy negative votes, including at Citigroup and Hewlett-Packard. About one in four of the companies that lost Say-on-Pay votes in 2011 subsequently replaced their CEO. Moreover, the fact that pay packages must now be aired in front of shareholders should cause at least some compensation committees to moderate their proposals.

President Obama has also proposed limiting the pay of federal contractors to the same salary received by the president himself, which was $400,000 this year (before he voluntarily returned 5 percent of his salary to the Treasury out of sympathy for federal workers who were forced to take pay cuts due to furloughs under the budget sequester). The current rules governing pay for federal contractors permits top managers at these firms to be reimbursed in line with the pay of top CEOs. The contractor reimbursement level has skyrocketed by more than 300 percent since the mid-1990s, and the top rate is slated to rise from $763,000 to $950,000 this year if action is not taken. This proposal not only reduces waste and inefficiency in government, but also represents another step towards strengthening norms of fairness in pay setting.

In addition, the American Taxpayer Relief Act, which passed at the beginning of this year and allows tax rates on the top 2 percent of income earners to return to where they were in the Clinton years, restores more fairness to our tax code, while maintaining tax breaks for middle-class families.

The manufacturing and construction industries were hit particularly hard by the Great Recession, and manufacturing languished before the recession. These industries provide relatively many middle-class jobs, especially for workers with less than a college degree. To revitalize manufacturing, the president has proposed to create Institutes of Manufacturing Innovation, and one has already been launched in Youngstown, Ohio. He has also proposed investing more in our infrastructure. It makes tremendous economic sense to repair and rebuild our roads and highways, ports and airports, when unemployment is high in the construction sector and interest rates are low. This would put more people back to work today and improve our competitiveness tomorrow.

Finally, all of the president's proposals were made in the context of a sustainable federal budget. The budget is a means to an end, not an end in itself. President Obama has insisted on a balanced approach to deficit reduction that closes loopholes for the well-off and well-connected and addresses our long-run entitlement problems, while protecting the middle class and making key investments in infrastructure and research and development, which will raise our living standards in the future.

We should not expect problems that have built up over decades to be solved overnight, but the president's proposal would put us on a path to rebuild the middle class.

Conclusion

One of my predecessors as chairman of the Council of Economic Advisers, Arthur Okun, wrote an influential book called, *Equality and Efficiency: The Big Tradeoff.* Okun argued that policies that increase equality often reduce efficiency.

But given the dramatic rise in inequality in the U.S. over the past three decades, we have reached the point where inequality is hurting the economy. Today, a reduction in inequality would be good for efficiency, economic growth and stability.

Growing the economy from the middle out is not only an economic necessity; it is also a national imperative. Our system of government as well as our economy work better when we have a rising, thriving middle class, with broad common interests.

The expanding middle class in the postwar period was a defining experience for our country. Just like music, this shared growth and prosperity helped bring the nation together.

President Obama captured the changes sweeping our economy well when he said, "The world is faster and the playing field is larger and the challenges are more complex. But what hasn't changed—what can never change—are the values that got us this far. We still have a stake in each other's success. We still believe that this should be a place where you can make it if you try. And we still believe, in the words of . . . [Theodore Roosevelt that] 'The fundamental rule of our national life, the rule which underlies all others—is that, on the whole, and in the long run, we shall go up or down together.'" And I agree with the president that America is still on the way up.

Unfair Shares

By Andrew G. Haldane

In this speech, Andrew G. Haldane, currently chief economist and executive director of monetary analysis and statistics for the Bank of England, speaks to an audience gathered in Bristol, England, on May 21, 2014, about inequality in the modern economy. Haldane's speech was part of the Bristol Festival of Ideas, an annual lecture series held in Bristol. Haldane begins by speaking about how inequality became one of the most-discussed topics in modern economics, citing statistics regarding the distribution of wealth in the United States and the United Kingdom that indicate the top 1 percent of the population controls as much as a third of the wealth. Haldane addresses the fact that a central bank can do little to address inequality in the economy directly, and cites his belief that, in the future, central banks may be in a better position to preempt financial crises through regulatory action. Drawing from research about short-term and long-term corporate strategies, Haldane argues that the United States and the United Kingdom have created a situation in which business is failing to invest in human capital and therefore, will have reduced productivity and growth over the long term. Haldane suggests corporate governance reform, such as tying corporate incentives to long-term company value, as a way to make the corporate structure reflect the interests of a wider proportion of the company's stakeholders. Haldane has been with the Bank of England since 1989, and has also worked for the International Monetary Fund. Haldane was one of the chief architects of the Bank of England's new regulatory framework developed in 2012.

Inequality has become the issue *du jour*—especially, it seems, when it is expressed in French. Yet until recently, inequality was a deeply unfashionable topic among academics and policymakers. Until the crisis, it is difficult to identify a period in the past 50 years when inequality was close to the top of the public policy or academic agenda (Stiglitz, 2012).

The past few years have changed all that. Key milestones include:
- The emerging facts. As ever, dispute rages about the precise statistics. But the long-term patterns are clear enough—and remarkable. Almost half of the growth in US national income between 1975 and 2007 accrued to the top 1% (OECD, 2014). In the UK and US, the top 1%'s share of the income pie has more than doubled since 1980 to around 15% and their share of the wealth pie has been estimated at up to a third—more than the whole bottom half of the population put together (ONS, 2014; Wolff, 2012). The five

Delivered May 21, 2014, at the Bristol Festival of Ideas, Bristol, England, by Andrew G. Haldane.

richest households in the UK have greater wealth than the bottom fifth of the population (Ocfam, 2014). Even among the 1% there has been a striking polarizaition. In 1990, a similarly skilled banker, lawyer and accountant were paid roughly the same. By 2006, the banker was earning between three and four times as much (Philippon and Reshef, 2009).

- The global financial crisis. On standard metrics, the crisis probably reduced wealth inequalities because the collapse of asset values hit hardest existing asset-owners. But the global financial crisis also shrunk the global income and wealth pie, in some countries materially so. This added momentum to the squeeze on real incomes at the very bottom end of the income scale experienced in a number of Western countries (Economic Policy Institute, 2012; Joyce et al., 2010). Financial crises are known to disadvantage disproportionately the poor because they are least able to absorb income shocks (Honohan, 2005). This crisis appears to have been no different. Meanwhile, the crisis-induced narrowing of wealth inequalities has been at least partially reversed as asset prices have reflated rapidly over recent years.

- The Occupy movement. They took up the baton for the 99% in 2011. At least at first, Occupy were treated with all of the seriousness of a local student protest. But rather remarkably Occupy became a global outfit, albeit a rather loosely-fitting one. Occupy touched a moral nerve among the many. The 1%ers in Davos had inequality as their main theme this year. In the words I used when addressing Occupy in 2012, there is now a broader acceptance that "they were right" in their diagnosis (Haldane, 2012). Criticism of Occupy today tends to focus not on their diagnosis, but on their lack of prescription for curing the ills of inequality.

- Bill de Blasio. He was elected mayor of New York in November 2013 on a signature theme of tackling widening inequality in the city. His campaign slogan was "a tale of two cities.".And this was no ordinary victory. Bill de Blasio won with a remarkable 73% of the popular vote.

- And finally, Thomas Piketty. Enough has already been said and written about a book bought by many, read by few and understood by even fewer (Piketty, 2014). I am guilty on all three charges. I suspect never, in the field of human endeavor, has so simple a line chart done so much to fuel the debate among so many, not just in the salons of Paris but in the Starbucks of London and New York.

Suffice to say, the inequality issue seems unlikely to be a French fashion. It is a global public policy trend and a rising one. Inequality is emerging after a half-century in the wilderness. The surprise may be that it has taken so long. It is well-known, from survey and experimental evidence, that a sense of "fairness" is a deeply-held and richly-valued psychological trait in humans (Bowles, 2012). And if Piketty is right, inequality trends are self-perpetuating as wealth begets wealth.

Economic and Financial Stability

That naturally begs the question of whether anything should be done. On the face of it, this is not the business of a central banker. There is considerable truth in that. The tools at the disposal of a central bank—interest rates, the money supply, regulation—have an impact on inequality which is, at best, indirect, inadvertent and transient. Central banks can do nothing, durably, to reshape long-term structural trends in the economy, much less in broader society.

Yet inequality has appeared on central banks' radar during the course of the crisis, sometimes flashing red. That is because, at least over the shorter term, central bank policies can and probably have reshaped patterns of inequality. Some have gone further, arguing that central bank policies of extraordinary monetary accommodation have, by boosting asset prices and wealth, exacerbated inequalities (Saiki and Frost, 2014). In effect, central banks stand accused of having provided an extra spin to the Piketty cycle. It is worth viewing this claim in context.

In response to the Great Recession, monetary policy globally went into overdrive. Interest rates fell to the floor and central bank money supply rose to the ceiling—so-called quantitative easing or QE. Interest rates have never been so low, nor central bank money supply so high (relative to money spending), in the Bank of England's 320-year history. Extraordinary times heralded truly extraordinary measures.

This action was taken with the best of intentions: to cushion the economy from the sharpest downturn in economic activity since the Great Depression. Monetary policy aimed to do so by lowering borrowing costs for debtors whose income and employment prospects were squeezed and by boosting risk-taking, and hence asset prices, otherwise held back by fearful investors.

It is impossible to know for sure how the economy would have performed in the absence of this monetary action. But it seems near-certain the economy would have been materially smaller, and asset prices materially lower, had this action not been taken. On the Bank's own estimates, the UK economy today would have been at least 6 percentage points smaller today without the combined effects of lower interest rates and large doses of QE. Or, in money terms, we as a nation would have been perhaps £80-100 billion poorer. The income pie would have been materially smaller.

It is harder still to gauge the impact of monetary policy measures on asset prices. But the facts are striking. Equity prices are almost 90% higher than in 2009 when QE commenced in the UK. Corporate bond prices are over 40% higher and government bond prices 15% higher. In the US, the numbers are 120%, 30%, and 12%, respectively. In other words the wealth, as well as the income, pie would most probably have been materially smaller absent extraordinary monetary stimulus.

During this reflationary process, shares of the income and wealth pie have not remained constant. All public policy is re-distributional and monetary policy is no exception. *Relative* winners have included debtors, whose borrowing costs have collapsed. *Relative* losers are likely to have included savers reliant on bank deposits for income, due to falling bank deposit rates. Studies have tended to confirm that distributional pattern (McKinsey Global Institute, 2013).

But these relativities need to be seen against the backcloth of a rising, not retreating, income and wealth tide. The majority of people—savers and borrowers, old and young—appear to have been made better off *absolutely* as a result of extraordinary monetary measures. For what it is worth, the Bank's own research points firmly in that direction (Bank of England, 2012).

Of course, some of the losses may be more visible than the gains and some of the relative losers more audible than the gainers. For example, low yields have reduced annuity rates for some pensioners, lowering income streams. But those same low yields have boosted asset prices, raising the value of pension pots. The net effect appears on average to have been positive. And extraordinary monetary measures will not, of course, last forever. When they unwind, so too will any distributional effects. In others words, central banks' influence on income and wealth shares is likely to be temporary.

Yet even if, over the medium term, central banks cannot influence inequality, the reverse may not be true. There is rising evidence that inequality can have an important bearing on the objectives central banks hold dear—the stability of the financial system and growth in the economy. Were inequality to jeopardize these public goods, it could make the everyday job of central banks somewhat harder. This means that, even if they cannot influence it, central banks have a strong vested interest in inequality issues too.

In his book *Fault Lines*, Raghu Rajan—now Governor of the Reserve Bank of India—dug up the deep roots of America's subprime crisis (Rajan, 2010). Many conventional crisis explanations have focused on the combined effects of venal bankers, Byzantine risk models and somnambulating regulators. Rajan suggested these missed the deeper cause—rising US inequality. Facing this fault-line, US policymakers had chosen a policy of cheap and plentiful credit, expanded home-ownership and rising asset prices—a "let them eat credit" policy. Bank balance sheets grew to distribute this rapidly expanding credit cake, with banks taking their own healthy slice en route.

Interestingly, this would not be the first time rising inequality has preceded crisis. The self-same pattern preceded the financial crash of 1929 and the resulting Great Depression (Kumhoff and Ranciere, 2010). Between 1920 and 1928, the income share of the top 5% rose from little more than a quarter to more than a third. Household debt relative to GDP doubled. Inequalities widened and balance sheets fattened. And the upshot was the same: a huge economic contraction when the credit bubble popped.

If this is a fair reading of history, then inequality may have a direct bearing on the fragility of the financial system. And while of historical interest when describing the past, its greater significance may be in highlighting risks for the future. As in the 1920s and the 2000s, rising inequality could build pressure for a credit balm to sooth the symptoms. Yet temporary pain relief, through a credit boom, would risk sowing the seeds of tomorrow's crisis.

The good news is that central banks may, in future, be better placed to head off these pressures by taking preemptive regulatory policy action. This is the essence of so-called macro-prudential policy. In the UK, it is the responsibility of the Bank of England's Financial Policy Committee (FPC). The FPC aims to curb excess credit at source. A large and growing number of other countries are putting macro-pruden-tial frameworks in place, and taking macro-prudential actions, to serve similar ends (Haldane, 2014).

There is a second way in which inequality could affect central bank policy objec-tives. Based on a detailed cross-country study, IMF research has found that lower income inequality delivers faster and more durable growth (Ostry et al., 2014). Moreover redistributive policies, provided they are not excessive, have benign direct growth effects—and positive indirect effects—by lowering inequality. Or, put dif-ferently, the IMF's research suggests that increasing inequality shrinks the pie.

Unfair Shares

This link between growth and inequality is, at present, no more than an empirical regularity. The IMF's research does not tell us the channels through which in-equality may have dented growth. And without an appreciation of those channels, it is difficult to know where public policy could make inroads into the problem. Nonetheless, it is useful to piece together evidence on possible channels of causa-tion.

Growth is rooted in investment, specifically the accumulation of human capital by individuals (education, skills, experience) and physical capital by firms (research and development). Both boost productivity, the elixir of economic life. And both require inter-temporal sacrifice—patience, a willingness to defer gratification. This is a topic I have researched in recent years (Haldane, 2010; Davies et al., 2014).

Individuals' patience, and hence human capital accumulation, is a complex pro-cess. But it is affected importantly by their financial environment. An important new book by psychologists Mullainathan and Shafir (MS) illustrates the impact of financial circumstances on decision-making (Mullainathan and Shafir, 2013). Solving everyday problems of scarcity—of time, money, friendship—absorbs huge amounts of the mind's energy. It taxes cognitive bandwidth. And this can have dra-matic effects on behavior.

In one experiment, two groups—one wealthy, one poor—are IQ-tested, asked to contemplate suffering a significant monetary loss and then retested. The remark-able finding is that merely contemplating monetary loss is sufficient to reduce sig-nificantly the measured IQs of the poor, lowering scores from "average" to "seriously deficient." This is a dramatic, environmentally induced, loss of cognitive power, the direct result of minds being impoverished by financial insecurity concerns. Being poor taxes the mind every bit as much as the wallet.

It does not end there. Financial scarcity is also shown by MS to damage deci-sion-making over time. The mind-absorbing effects of making ends meet can lead to an excessive focus on the present at the expense of the future—that is, financial in-security generates impatience or myopia. This, too, can have damaging implications for life choices. As MS demonstrate, it may lead people to under-invest in education and skills and to over-borrow at high interest rates and short maturities.

MS call this a scarcity or myopia trap. It is a trap because it is self-fulfilling. Scarcity generates myopia and myopia is the enemy of human capital accumulation. For individuals, this means that scarcity traps may, over time, create poverty (lack of income) or unemployment (lack of skills) traps. And at the level of the aggregate economy, it means that scarcity traps, by taxing human capital accumulation, may generate lower growth and productivity.

Physical capital accumulation, such as research and development, also relies on patient decision-making. It requires a willingness to defer gratification, either on the part of managers of firms (for example, through lower salaries and bonuses) and/or shareholders in those firms (for example, through lower dividends and share buybacks). Unfortunately, the evidence suggests neither have found it easy to do so. Public companies suffer from "short-termism" (Kay, 2012).

One example is found in the high and smoothed payout ratios to both executives and shareholders of public companies even when underlying company profitability is low, perhaps even negative. Another is that longer-term cashflows from company projects appear to be "excessively" discounted (Davies et al., 2014). This can lead to projects which boost the long-run value of the company being wrongly rejected. Consistent with that hypothesis, privately owned companies seem to invest more than otherwise identical public companies (Davies et al., 2014).

There is some debate about where the blame for this corporate myopia problem may lie. Some place it at the door of shareholders, driven to demand short-term returns by short holding periods. Others blame management for seeking short-term financial gain given their short tenure. This distinction may anyway be artificial. In a world where executive compensation is largely in stock, the two are one and the same, their incentives largely indistinguishable.

So how does all of this link to inequality? If impatient (money-scarce) individuals are failing to invest sufficiently in skills, and impatient (short-termist) companies are failing to invest sufficiently in capital, this is a recipe for weak (human and physical) capital accumulation. This will show up in weak long-term investment and skills deficits. The most likely casualties from this are productivity and growth.

If there are legs to this story, then one important element is corporate governance. This defines decision-making within firms—how much to invest, how much to distribute, and to whom. Company law in a number of countries, such as the UK, gives primacy to the interests of shareholders when defining the objectives of a company and its decision-making. The objectives and rights of a broader set of stakeholders, including workers, suppliers and wider society, tend to be secondary (Mayer, 2013).

This governance structure has stood the test of time. But it is not without distributional consequences. If power resides in the hands of one set of stakeholders, and they are short-termist, then we might expect high distribution of profits to this cohort, at the expense of ploughing back these profits (as increased investment) or distributing them to workers (as increased real wages). To some extent, this matches the stylized facts on rising inequality—rising executive and shareholder compensation and faltering real wage growth. The shareholder model may, ironically, have contributed to unfair shares.

If so, this suggests that one avenue worth considering further is corporate governance reform. A set of corporate incentives which had as its fulcrum long-term company value and which more fully reflected the interests of a wider set of stakeholders might help rebalance the scales—for example, towards investing rather than distributing. Such an alternative model is certainly not without precedent. It is found in a number of countries around the world (Mayer, 2013).

Inequality and corporate governance are deep, structural issues. Central banks do not have many, perhaps any, of the solutions to these problems. But the stakes— a more stable, faster growing, fairer society—could not be higher. There is a collective public policy interest in getting them right.

Bibliography

Alvaredo, F., Atkinson, A. B., Saez, E. and Piketty, T., 'The world top incomes database'

Bank of England (2012), "The Distributional Effects of Asset Purchases", July. Available at: http://www.bankofengland.co.uk/publications/Documents/news/2012/nr073.pdf

Bowles, S. (2012), "The New Economics of Inequality and Redistribution", Cambridge University Press.

Cribb, J., Hood, A., Joyce, R. and Phillips, D. (2013), "Living standards, poverty and inequality in the UK: 2013", IFS Report R81.

Davies, R., Haldane, A., Nielsen, M. and Pezzini, S. (2014), "Measuring the costs of short-termism", Journal of Financial Stability, 12 (2014) 16–25.

Economic Policy Institute (2012), "The State of Working America, 12th Edition", Cornell University Press, November.

Haldane, A. G. (2010), "Patience and Finance", speech delivered at the Oxford China Business Forum, Beijing. Available at: http://www.bankofengland.co.uk/archive/Documents/historicpubs/speeches/2010/speech445.pdf

Haldane, A. G. and Davies, R. (2011), "The short long", speech to 29th Société Universitaire Européene de Recherches Financières Colloquium: New Paradigms in Money and Finance?, May. Available at: http://www.bankofengland.co.uk/publications/Documents/speeches/2011/speech495.pdf

Haldane, A. G. (2012), "A leaf being turned", speech to Occupy Economics, "Socially useful banking", October. Available at: http://www.bankofengland.co.uk/publications/Documents/speeches/2012/speech616.pdf

Haldane, A. G. (2014), "Ambidexterity", speech delivered at the American Economic Association Annual Meeting, Philadelphia on 3 January 2014. Available at: http://www.bankofengland.co.uk/publications/Documents/speeches/2014/speech713.pdf

Honohan, P. (2005), "Banking sector crises and inequality", World Bank Policy Research Working Paper 3659, July.

Kay, J. (2012), "The Kay Review of UK Equity Markets and Long-Term Decision Making", Department for Investment, Business and Skills, July.

Kumhoff, M. and Ranciere, R. (2010), 'Inequality, Leverage and Crises', IMF Working Paper WP/10/268, November.

Joyce, R., Muriel, A., Phillips, D. and Sibieta, L. (2010), "Poverty and inequality in the UK: 2010", IFS Commentary C116.

Mayer, C. (2013), "Firm Commitment: why the corporation is failing us and how to restore trust in it", Oxford University Press.

McKinsey Global Institute (2013), "QE and ultra-low interest rates: distributional effects and risks", Discussion paper, November.

Mullainathan, S. and Shafir, E. (2013), "Scarcity: Why Having Too Little Means So Much", Times Books.

OECD (2014). "Focus on Top Incomes and Taxation in OECD Countries: Was the crisis a game changer?", May.

ONS (2013), "Wealth in Great Britain Wave 3, 2010–2012", May.

Ostry, J. D., Berg, A. and Tsangarides, C. G. (2014), "Redistribution, Inequality, and Growth", IMF Staff Discusssion Note SDN/14/02, February.

Oxfam (2014), "A Tale of Two Britains: Inequality in the UK", March.

Philippon, T. and Reshef, A. (2009), "Wages and Human Capital in the U.S. Financial Industry: 1909–2006", NBER Working Paper 14644, National Bureau of Economic Research, Inc.

Piketty, T. (2014), "Capital in the Twenty-First Century", Harvard University Press.

Rajan, R. G. (2010), "Fault Lines: how hidden fractures still threaten the world economy", Princeton University Press.

Saiki, A. and Frost J. (2014), "How Does Unconventional Monetary Policy Affect Inequality? Evidence from Japan", DNB Working Paper No. 423, May.

Stiglitz, J. E., (2012), "The Price of Inequality", W.W. Norton and Company.

Wolff, E. N. (2012), "The Asset Price Meltdown and the Wealth of the Middle Class", New York University.

Fiscal Policy and Income Inequality

By David Lipton

In this speech, David Lipton, first deputy managing director of the International Monetary Fund (IMF), presents the findings of an IMF study on fiscal policy and income inequality at the Peterson Institute for International Economics on March 13, 2014. Lipton begins by speaking about the reason for the IMF study, the fact that income inequality has been increasing in most economies around the world. Lipton explains that the share of wealth among the top income earners has increased drastically in the United States in recent decades. He discusses various features of global economies that contribute to income inequality, including poorly designed social spending programs. Lipton then gives four suggestions for how to design efficient systems to encourage the redistribution of wealth, including making income tax systems more progressive, opting for a system that does not encourage tax evasion at the upper end and yet provides tax relief primarily to those at the lower end of the income bracket. Lipton also recommends progressive spending on education and health at the lower income brackets. In closing, Lipton explains that broad fiscal policies can be a tool to help governments combat rising levels of inequality, and that the design of redistributive policies should be carefully implemented to encourage growth. Lipton has been first deputy managing director of the IMF since 2011. Before joining the IMF, Lipton was an economic advisor to the White House and a managing director at Citi Corporation.

Thank you for providing me the opportunity to present the key findings of a new IMF study on fiscal policy and income inequality.

Income inequality has been rising in many parts of the world in recent decades. This, and the social tensions associated with fiscal consolidation that many have faced in part stemming from the global financial crisis, have put the distributional impact of governments' tax and spending policies at the heart of the public debate in many countries. Of course, the question of just how much redistribution the state should do is, at its core, a political one that economic analysis cannot answer. But I think that we can all agree that whatever degree of redistribution governments choose, it should be done with fiscal instruments that achieve their distributional objectives at a minimum cost to economic efficiency.

The design of these growth-friendly, efficient redistributive fiscal policies is the focus of my presentation today.

Some may be surprised that the Fund is engaging in this debate on the design of redistributive policies. The truth of the matter is that we have been at this for a long time. Assessing the effect of tax and expenditure policies on efficiency, and any

Delivered March 13, 2014, at the Peterson Institute for International Economics, Washington, DC, by David Lipton.

potential tradeoffs with distributional goals, has long been an important component of the IMF's policy advice. Furthermore, the design of Fund-supported programs is inevitably influenced by the authorities' distributional objectives. Whenever we discuss social safety net programs, or the level of health and education expenditures, and how to generate the revenues or finance to sustain them, subjects we routinely address, we are discussing redistribution policy.

Our record for protecting the poor in the design of Fund-supported programs has a longstanding history, going back to the Camdessus era in the 1980s.

So, this paper should thus be seen as the Fund's advice to its membership, based on our extensive experience. Of course, one reason why we are discussing this issue today is that the interest in redistribution as reflected in public surveys and our discussions with our members is higher than in the past. Our members want to explore with us how they can pursue distributive policies in an efficient manner.

The key message that I want to convey today is that when it comes to fiscal redistribution, design matters. This is consistent with a recent IMF staff study by Ostry et al., which finds that, on average, inequality is associated with lower growth. Thus fiscal redistribution can help support growth because it reduces inequality. What we see is a diversity of experience across countries with redistributive policies. Some redistributive fiscal policies can help improve efficiency and support growth, such as those that enhance the human capital of low-income households. Let me be clear, redistributive policies can generate a tradeoff between equality and efficiency, and if misconceived, this tradeoff can be very costly. I will cite examples of this problem later on. But as I said, design matters, and smart design can help to minimize the adverse effects of redistributive policies on incentives to work, save, and invest.

My presentation today will cover three broad topics, including trends in inequality, the experience of countries in using redistributive policy, and options for achieving more efficient redistribution.

Inequality has been increasing in most economies

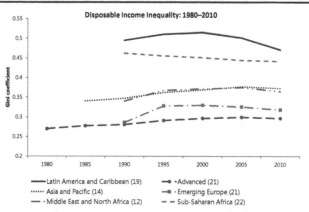

Let us first move to the discussion of trends in inequality. This figure presents the trends in the average Gini coefficient for disposable income. Gini coefficient ranges from 0 to 1, with larger values representing higher inequality. Disposable income is market income after income and wealth taxes and cash transfers. Over the last three decades, the Gini coefficient has increased in most countries, indicating an increase in inequality. In Latin America and sub-Saharan Africa, however, there has been a declining level of inequality more recently. What is most striking in the figure, however, are the persistent differences across regions, with Latin America having the highest inequality and the advanced economies having the lowest.

More recently, the focus has been on the rising income share of top income earners

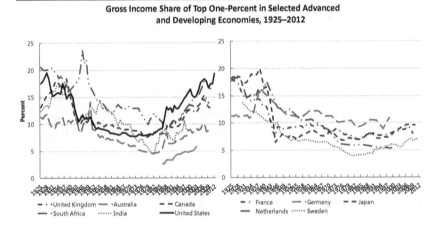

Gross Income Share of Top One-Percent in Selected Advanced and Developing Economies, 1925–2012

More recently, there has been great attention to the rising share of top income earners. The trends across countries appear mixed. In some economies, such as the United States and South Africa, the share of the top 1 percent has increased dramatically in recent decades, but not so in continental Europe and Japan, where it has been largely unchanged. There are differing views of the causes of the rising share of the top 1 percent. Some emphasize the impact of globalization and new technologies, while others highlight policy choices, such as reductions in tax rates, and others the rent-seeking behavior of executives.

If we compare the distribution of income with that of wealth, we can see that wealth is much more unequally distributed, as indicated by the higher Gini coefficients. In a similar vein, a recent Oxfam study found that that the richest 85 people in the world own the same amount of wealth as the bottom half of the world's population. Both the high degree of inequality of wealth, and the increased share of the top 1 percent, have fueled the recent debate on income and wealth taxation.

Wealth is even more unequally distributed

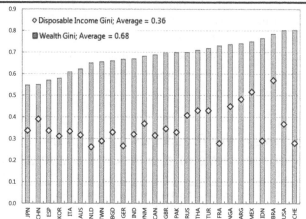

Redistributive fiscal policy reduces inequality by one-third in advanced economies, especially through spending

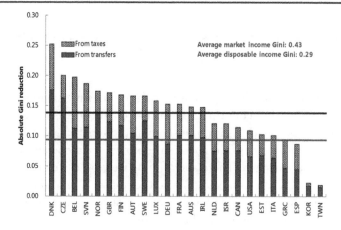

Let us now turn to country experience with different instruments for fiscal redistribution. We will start with the advanced economies, where countries are already doing a substantial amount of redistribution. The average market income Gini, i.e., in the absence of any fiscal redistribution, is 0.43. Redistributive transfers and taxes reduce inequality by about a third, with about two-thirds of this coming from transfers.

In-kind spending further reduces inequality in advanced economies

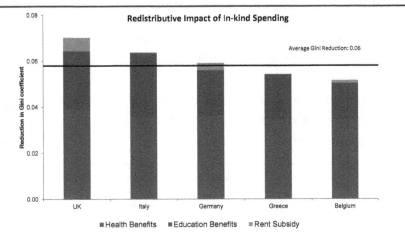

The previous slide does not include the impact of in-kind benefits, such as public spending on health, education, and housing. In the countries selected here, it is estimated that in-kind transfers further reduce the market Gini, on average, by more than 10 percent. Thus, we can conclude that based on both direct and in-kind benefits, fiscal policy has played a major role in reducing inequality in advanced economies, although its extent varies across countries.

The level and composition of fiscal policy reduces its redistributive impact in developing economies

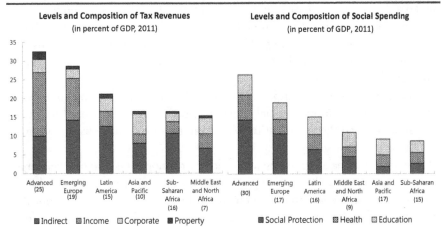

So what about developing economies? Developing economies here include both emerging and low-income countries. It appears that fiscal policy has played a much more modest role there. Let's first look at the tax side. The levels of tax revenues are significantly lower in developing economies, with the exception of emerging Europe. In terms of composition, indirect taxes, like the VAT, account for a much larger share, which tend to be less progressive than direct taxes such as the income tax. On the expenditure side, again, levels of redistributive expenditures are much lower, particularly when it comes to social protection.

Furthermore, a large share of the benefits from spending often goes to higher-income groups

Social Protection Coverage and Benefit Share of Poorest 40 Percent

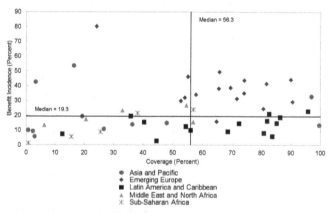

Social protection includes pensions and social assistance transfers.

A lot of the social spending in developing economies is not well designed and targeted and actually increases inequality. With the exception of emerging Europe, the poorest 40 percent of the population receive less than 20 percent of the benefits of social protection spending. The coverage of social benefits, in terms of the percentage of poor households that receive benefits, is also low, except in emerging Europe and Latin America.

In this context, it is also important to note that many developing countries use energy subsidies as a form of social assistance. But as we underscored in the work we presented at the Peterson Institute last year, these subsidies disproportionately benefit upper-income groups.

Education and health spending in developing economies is also not well targeted and exacerbates inequality. In many developing economies, for example, the poorest 40 percent receive less than 40 percent of the total benefits, which contributes to inequality of opportunity and low intergenerational mobility. One reason for this is that the poor often lack access to these services, reflecting the fact that many of them live in poor rural areas while services are concentrated in urban areas.

In-kind social spending is also regressive in many developing economies

In-kind Social Spending Benefit Share of Poorest 40 Percent

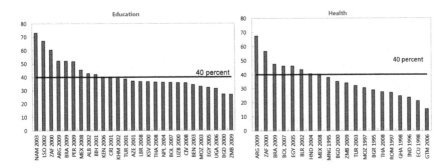

This discussion of the redistributive effect of fiscal policy in advanced and developing economies has important implications for the design of fiscal consolidation packages. As shown in our paper, a number of economies have adopted progressive adjustment measures during their recent fiscal consolidations. As a result, the burden of these adjustment measures on the bottom 20 percent of the population was lower than that of upper income groups. For example, in Greece, Latvia, Portugal, Romania, and Spain, cuts in public-sector pay had a smaller effect on civil servants toward the bottom of the pay-scale. In Spain and the United Kingdom, increases in income taxation were borne more heavily by upper-income groups.

Designing efficient redistributive fiscal policy

- ❏ **Redistributive fiscal policy should be consistent with macroeconomic objectives**
- ❏ **The impact of tax and spending policies should be evaluated jointly**
- ❏ **Tax and expenditure policies need to be carefully designed to balance distributional and efficiency objectives**
- ❏ **Design should take into account administrative capacity**

Let us now turn to options for designing fiscal redistribution in an efficient manner. We see four key considerations in designing efficient redistributive fiscal policy:

First, redistributive fiscal policy should be consistent with macroeconomic policy objectives. The level of spending on redistribution, for example, should be consistent with macroeconomic stability. In addition, the benefits of additional spending on redistribution should be compared with the benefits of raising spending in other priority areas, such as infrastructure.

Second, taxes and expenditures should be evaluated jointly. For example, an increase in VAT revenues, used to finance higher spending in secondary education, could—on net—be progressive.

Third, the design of redistribution policies should account for both redistributive and efficiency objectives. Some redistributive policies may in fact enhance efficiency, such as those that strengthen human capital. But with others there may be the need to manage a tradeoff.

And fourth, design should take into account administrative capacity.

Based on these principles, we examine a range of options for achieving redistribution efficiently. The paper provides an extensive discussion of instruments. In the interest of time, I will focus on a few of the most important options discussed in the paper. These measures could be implemented as part of long-term fiscal reforms aimed at achieving redistributive objectives more efficiently. They could also be integrated into the design of fiscal consolidation strategies that aim to help governments achieve redistributive goals at a lower fiscal cost.

Reform options to achieve more efficient redistribution of taxation

Direct taxes	Advanced	Developing
Implement progressive personal income tax (PIT) rate structures	✓	✓
Expand coverage of PIT		✓
Utilize better the opportunities for recurrent property taxes	✓	✓

Indirect taxes		
Minimize VAT exemptions and special VAT rates	✓	✓

The primary contribution of taxation to reducing income inequality is through its financing of redistributive spending measures in a way that it does not harm growth. Nevertheless, taxes can also have a direct effect on redistribution. This is particularly the case for income taxes.

To start, countries could consider making their income tax systems more progressive. For example, in economies where a flat rate is used, there may be scope for more tax progression at the top. Since the mid 1990s, 27 countries—especially in Central and Eastern Europe and Central Asia—have introduced flat tax systems, usually with a low marginal rate. The top personal income tax rate must, however, be set with care. If it is too high, taxpayers will find ways to avoid or evade the tax and a higher rate may no longer raise extra revenue. In many developing economies, both fairness and equity could be enhanced by bringing more informal operators into the personal income tax.

There is also scope to more fully utilize property taxes, both as a source of revenue and as an efficient redistributive instrument. This applies also to developing economies, where only Colombia, Namibia, Russia, South Africa, and Uruguay collect more than 1 percent of GDP through recurrent property taxes.

Indirect taxes, including the VAT, are generally less effective in achieving redistributive goals than direct taxes. On the VAT, the recommendation is thus to minimize exemptions and special rates, in order to efficiently raise revenues to help finance pro-poor spending. For instance, elimination of reduced VAT rates in the United Kingdom, and using the proceeds to increase social benefits, would significantly reduce inequality. Earlier work at the IMF has shown that in Ethiopia, the net impact of a uniform VAT, with the proceeds used for general spending on education and health, would have a strong progressive impact. However, where capacity constraints prevent spending programs from reaching the poor, there can be a case for some differentiation in VAT rates, for example for basic foods that are a large part of the spending of the poor.

Reform options to achieve more efficient redistribution of social spending

Education	Advanced	Developing
Improve access to education of low-income families	✓	✓

Health		
Expand coverage of publicly financed basic health package		✓
Maintain access of low-income groups to essential health services	✓	

On the expenditure side, I would like to start first with education. Improving the access of low-income families to education is an efficient tool for boosting equality of opportunity, and over the long run, it can also reduce income inequality. In advanced economies, this entails increasing the access to tertiary education for low-income families, including through scholarships and loans. For developing economies, a strengthening of access to quality secondary education is also required, for example, by eliminating tuition fees.

Along the same lines, improving the access of the poor to health care services in developing economies can provide a head start to greater opportunity and do so in an efficient manner. Some countries, including China, Ghana, India, and Mexico, have taken important steps toward universal coverage in recent years. In advanced economies, maintaining the access of the poor to health services during periods of expenditure constraint is also consistent with efficient redistribution.

Reform options to achieve more efficient redistribution of social spending

Social transfers	Advanced	Developing
Intensify the use of active labor market programs and in-work benefits	✓	
Expand conditional cash transfer (CCT) programs as administrative capacity improves		✓
Increase effective pension retirement age	✓	✓
Expand noncontributory means-tested social pensions		✓

To make social transfers more efficient in advanced economies, there could be greater use of active labor market programs and in-work benefits for social benefit recipients. This would, for example, require beneficiaries to participate in active labor market programs, such as job training, as a condition for receiving benefits, as done in Belgium, the Slovak Republic, and Slovenia.

The second reform measure that I will focus on is to expand conditional cash transfer programs in developing economies. These programs make benefits conditional on the attendance of children at health clinics and at school. Means-testing helps keep the fiscal cost low. This policy can help boost both equality of opportunity and income inequality. For instance, the direct impact of such transfers in Brazil and Mexico accounts for one-fifth of the reduction in inequality between 1995 and 2004 in these two countries. A strengthening of administrative capacity, however, is required for implementing these programs in many developing economies.

Pensions have played an important role in reducing income inequality. To improve the sustainability of pension systems and maintain their role in protecting the elderly poor, many economies could consider increasing effective retirement ages. This would need to be accompanied by measures to ensure that lower-income workers are fully protected, as needed, with disability pensions and social assistance if they are unable to work. In developing economies, to ensure wider coverage of pensions at a reasonable fiscal cost, a viable option is to expand noncontributory, means-tested social pensions. Social pensions in some form exist in both emerging and low-income developing countries, including in Chile, Ethiopia, India, and South Africa.

Many countries have been grappling with the twin challenge of putting their pension systems on sound financial footing while safeguarding or expanding their important role in alleviating old-age poverty. I would like to take this opportunity to bring your attention to a new IMF book, *Equitable and Sustainable Pensions: Challenges and Experience,* which we are also launching today. The book examines the complex equity issues involved in designing pension systems, including generational and gender equity. It also presents 12 country cases studies to help draw lessons for designing sustainable and equitable pension systems.

Let me end where I started. Many advanced and developing economies are facing the challenge of rising inequality. Fiscal policy has played a major role in reducing inequality in the past and is the primary tool available for governments to affect income distribution. Whether these policies help or hurt growth is all a matter of design. And the details matter. Thus, debates on the impact of the government's redistributive policies must go far beyond a mere discussion of tax and spending ratios. In the end, it is design that matters. And on this, the good news is that quite a lot is now known about how governments can best address the challenges of squaring their equity and efficiency concerns, a task on which the Fund stands ready to help.

Thank you.

Economic Inclusion and Financial Integrity—An Address to the Conference on Inclusive Capitalism

By Christine Lagarde

In this speech, Christine Lagarde, managing director of the International Monetary Fund (IMF), speaks to a group gathered in London, England, on May 27, 2014, to attend the Inclusive Capitalism Conference. The conference was held by the Inclusive Capitalism Initiative (ISI), a nonprofit organization formed by American and British business leaders and legislators in 2011 to investigate equality and inclusion in the capitalist system. Lagarde begins by defining "inclusive capitalism," the idea of creating a capitalist system that supports the greatest number of people at all levels of the financial system. Lagarde argues that making capitalism more inclusive must involve restoring public trust, which has eroded as global income disparity has grown. She then cites IMF research indicating that the countries with the highest levels of income inequality also had lower economic growth, and suggests potential strategies to address this, including instituting more progressive income tax systems and expanding access to education. Lagarde speaks about financial integrity, contending that the 2008–09 financial crisis was largely the result of a lack of integrity and a culture of excess in the financial sector. Lagarde explains that financial reform is the key to preventing this type of mismanagement, and notes the success of the Basel Committee on Banking Supervision, which has produced new regulations designed to make banks safer and more service-oriented. Christine Lagarde has been managing director of the IMF since 2011. Prior to this assignment, she was minister of finance for France from 2007 to 2011. She has also worked in the French Ministry of Agriculture and the Ministry of Commerce and Industry.

Good morning. What a great privilege to be here among such illustrious guests to discuss such an important topic.

Let me thank Lady Lynn de Rothschild and the Inclusive Capitalism Initiative for convening today's event. I would also like to recognize the great civic leaders here today—His Royal Highness, the Prince of Wales; President Clinton, and Fiona Woolf, Lord Mayor of the City of London.

We are all here to discuss "inclusive capitalism"—which must be Lynn's idea! But what does it mean? As I struggled with the answer to that, I turned to etymology and to history.

Capitalism originates from the Latin *caput*, "cattle heads," and refers to possessions. Capital is used in the 12th century and designates the use of funds. The term

Delivered May 27, 2014, at the Inclusive Capitalism Conference, London, England, by Christine Lagarde.

capitalism is only used for the first time in 1854 by an Englishman, the novelist William Thackeray—and he simply meant private ownership of money.

The consecration of capitalism comes during the 19th century. With the industrial revolution came Karl Marx who focused on the appropriation of the means of production—and who predicted that capitalism, in its excesses, carried the seeds of its own destruction, the accumulation of capital in the hands of a few, mostly focused on the accumulation of profits, leading to major conflicts, and cyclical crises.

So is *inclusive capitalism* an oxymoron? Or is it the response to Marx's dire prediction that will lead to capitalism's survival and regeneration—to make it truly the engine for shared prosperity?

If so, what would the attributes of inclusive capitalism be? Trust, opportunity, rewards for all within a market economy—allowing everyone's talents to flourish. Certainly, that is the vision.

Most recently, however, capitalism has been characterized by "excess"—in risk-taking, leverage, opacity, complexity, and compensation. It led to massive destruction of value. It has also been associated with high unemployment, rising social tensions, and growing political disillusion—all of this happening in the wake of the Great Recession.

One of the main casualties has been trust—in leaders, in institutions, in the free-market system itself. The most recent poll conducted by the Edelman Trust Barometer, for example, showed that less than a fifth of those surveyed believed that governments or business leaders would tell the truth on an important issue.

This is a wake-up call. Trust is the lifeblood of the modern business economy. Yet, in a world that is more networked than ever, trust is harder to earn and easier to lose. Or as the Belgians say, "la confiance part à cheval et revient à pied" ("confidence leaves on a horse and comes back on foot").

So the big question is: how can we restore and sustain trust?

First and foremost, by making sure that growth is more inclusive and that the rules of the game lead to a level playing field—favoring the many, not just the few; prizing broad participation over narrow patronage.

By making capitalism more inclusive, we make capitalism more effective, and possibly more sustainable. But if inclusive capitalism is not an oxymoron, it is not intuitive either, and it is more of a constant quest than a definitive destination.

I will talk about two dimensions of this quest—more inclusion in economic growth, and more integrity in the financial system.

Inclusion in Economic Growth

Let me begin with economic inclusion. One of the leading economic stories of our time is rising income inequality, and the dark shadow it casts across the global economy.

The facts are familiar. Since 1980, the richest 1 percent increased their share of income in 24 out of 26 countries for which we have data.

In the US, the share of income taken home by the top 1 percent more than doubled since the 1980s, returning to where it was on the eve of the Great Depression.

In the UK, France, and Germany, the share of private capital in national income is now back to levels last seen almost a century ago.

The 85 richest people in the world, who could fit into a single London double-decker, control as much wealth as the poorest half of the global population—that is 3.5 billion people.

With facts like these, it is no wonder that rising inequality has risen to the top of the agenda—not only among groups normally focused on social justice, but also increasingly among politicians, central bankers, and business leaders.

Many would argue, however, that we should ultimately care about equality of opportunity, not equality of outcome. The problem is that opportunities are not equal. Money will always buy better-quality education and health care, for example. But due to current levels of inequality, too many people in too many countries have only the most basic access to these services, if at all. The evidence also shows that social mobility is more stunted in less equal societies.

Fundamentally, excessive inequality makes capitalism less inclusive. It hinders people from participating fully and developing their potential.

Disparity also brings division. The principles of solidarity and reciprocity that bind societies together are more likely to erode in excessively unequal societies. History also teaches us that democracy begins to fray at the edges once political battles separate the haves against the have-nots.

A greater concentration of wealth could—if unchecked—even undermine the principles of meritocracy and democracy. It could undermine the principle of equal rights proclaimed in the 1948 Universal Declaration of Human Rights.

Pope Francis recently put this in stark terms when he called increasing inequality "the root of social evil."

It is therefore not surprising that IMF research—which looked at 173 countries over the last 50 years—found that more unequal countries tend to have lower and less durable economic growth.

So much for the diagnosis—what can be done about it? We have done some recent work on this as well. We focused on the fiscal policy dimension—which is part of the IMF's core business. We found that, in general, fiscal policies have a good record of reducing social disparities—for example, transfers and income taxes have been able to reduce inequality by about a third, on average, among the advanced economies.

But it is a complex issue and policy choices need to be made carefully. Fiscal discipline is often the first victim on the political battlefield, and we obviously want to choose measures that do the most good and the least harm.

Some potentially beneficial options can include making income tax systems more progressive without being excessive; making greater use of property taxes; expanding access to education and health; and relying more on active labor market programs and in-work social benefits.

But we must recognize that reducing inequality is not easy. Redistributive policies always produce winners and losers. Yet if we want capitalism to do its job—enabling as many people as possible to participate and benefit from the economy—then it needs to be more inclusive. That means addressing extreme income disparity.

Integrity in the Financial System

Let me now turn to the second dimension of inclusive capitalism that I have chosen to address—integrity in the financial system.

In this age of diminished trust, it is the financial sector that takes last place in opinion surveys. This might not be surprising in light of some of the behavior that triggered the global financial crisis. But it is nevertheless disturbing. As many have pointed out, the very word *credit* derives from the Latin word for "trust."

We are all familiar with the factors behind the crisis—a financial sector that near-ly collapsed because of excess. A sector that, like Icarus, in its hubris flew too close to the sun, and then fell back to earth—taking the global economy down with it.

We can trace the problems to the evolution of the financial sector before the crisis. Financial actors were allowed to take excessive risks, leading to a situation whereby the profits on the upside went to the industry—and the losses on the downside were picked up by the public.

Some of the greatest problems, still outstanding today, lay with the so-called too-big-to-fail firms. In the decade prior to the crisis, the balance sheets of the world's largest banks increased by two- to fourfold. With rising size came rising risk—in the form of lower capital, less stable funding, greater complexity, and more trading.

This kind of capitalism was more extractive than inclusive. The size and com-plexity of the megabanks meant that, in some ways, they could hold policymakers to ransom. The implicit subsidy they derived from being too-big-too-fail came from their ability to borrow more cheaply than smaller banks—magnifying risk and un-dercutting competition.

Completing the Financial Reform Agenda

Thankfully, the crisis has prompted a major course correction—with the under-standing that the true role of the financial sector is to serve, not to rule, the econ-omy. Its real job is to benefit people, especially by financing investment and thus helping with the creation of jobs and growth.

As Winston Churchill once remarked, "I would rather see finance less proud and industry more content."

The good news is that the international community has made progress on the reform agenda. This is especially true for banking regulation under the auspices of the Basel Committee, where we are moving forward with stronger capital and li-quidity requirements. This should make the system safer, sounder, and more service oriented.

The bad news is that progress is still too slow, and the finish line is still too far off. Some of this arises from the sheer complexity of the task at hand. Yet, we must acknowledge that it also stems from fierce industry pushback, and from the fatigue that is bound to set in at this point in a long race.

A big gap is that the too-big-to-fail problem has not yet been solved. A recent study by IMF staff shows that these banks are still major sources of systemic risk. Their implicit subsidy is still going strongly—amounting to about $70 billion in the US, and up to $300 billion in the Euro Area.

So clearly, ending too-big-to-fail must be a priority. That means tougher regulation and tighter supervision.

Here, I believe that the new capital surcharges for systemic banks can work. We estimated that increasing the capital ratio on these banks by 2½ percent, beyond the Basel III standard, can reduce the systemic risk of a trillion dollar bank by a quarter. This is a big deal.

Yet the problem will not go away without steps to reduce the potential for contagion. First on the agenda should be an agreement on cross-border resolution of megabanks—providing a framework to unwind them in an orderly way in case of failure. This is a gaping hole in the financial architecture right now, and it calls for countries to put the global good of financial stability ahead of their parochial concerns.

And we should not give up just because it is hard. Let me quote John Fitzgerald Kennedy here, who famously said that "we choose to go to the moon not because it is easy, but because it is hard."

We also need more vigor across the rest of the reform agenda—better rules for nonbanks, better monitoring of shadow banks, and better safety and transparency over derivatives, an area that is still today excessively obscure and complex. To reduce the scope for contagion, I would like to see much more progress on cross-border issues, for example, in the mutual recognition of rules for derivatives markets.

Again, this is complex, and we need to be mindful of the risks of fragmenting the global financial system and hampering the flow of credit to finance investment. But complexity is not an excuse for complacency and delay.

Changing Behavior and Culture

As well as regulation, we need stronger supervision. Rules are only as good as their implementation. This calls for greater resources, and independence, for the supervisors who perform such a vital public duty, day in and day out.

Yet regulation and supervision by themselves are still not enough. Rules can certainly affect behavior—think of compensation practices, for example. But people who want to skirt the rules will always find creative ways of doing so.

So we also need to turn our attention to the culture of financial institutions, and to the individual behavior that lies beneath. Incentives must be aligned with expected behavior and be made transparent.

Here, the work of the FSB on Principles for Sound Compensation Practices, commissioned by the G20, is instrumental to realign incentives with actual performance. We must push on with implementation.

Why is this so important? Because the behavior of the financial sector has not changed fundamentally in a number of dimensions since the crisis. While some changes in behavior are taking place, these are not deep or broad enough. The industry still prizes short-term profit over long-term prudence, today's bonus over tomorrow's relationship.

Some prominent firms have even been mired in scandals that violate the most basic ethical norms—LIBOR and foreign exchange rigging, money laundering, illegal foreclosure.

To restore trust, we need a shift toward greater integrity and accountability. We need a stronger and systematic ethical dimension.

In grappling with this, it helps to go back to the ancient philosophers. They would have raised the most basic question—what is the social purpose of the financial sector? Or, as Aristotle would have asked: "what is its telos?"

He answered his own question: "Wealth is evidently not the good we are seeking; for it is merely useful and for the sake of something else." Or as Oscar Wilde put it, "the true perfection of man lies, not in what man has, but in what man is."

From this perspective, we can identify the true purpose of finance. Its goal is to put resources to productive use, to transform maturity, thereby contributing to the good of economic stability and full employment—and ultimately, to the wellbeing of people. In other words—to enrich society.

In Aristotle's framework, once we know the purpose, we can identify the virtues needed to fulfill it. It becomes a matter of every person doing the right thing.

When we think about finance, surely one of these core virtues is prudence—which is about stewardship, sustainability, and safeguarding the future. Prudence has long been a byword of banking, and yet has been sorely missing in action in recent times.

We know that regaining virtues like prudence will not happen overnight. Aristotle teaches us that virtue is molded from habit, from developing and nurturing good behavior over time. As with anything worth doing, practice makes perfect.

Getting back on the right path requires education and leadership that is sustained over many years. It requires alert watchdogs, including from civil society.

Most importantly of all, it requires investors and financial leaders taking values as seriously as valuation, culture as seriously as capital.

As Mark Carney pointed out in an admirable speech in Canada last year, the financial sector needs to be grounded in strong connections to clients and to communities—to the people served by the financial industry.

Ultimately, we need to ingrain a greater social consciousness—one that will seep into the financial world and forever change the way it does business.

The good news is that we are seeing some positive signs. The Inclusive Capitalism Initiative is one such example—pursuing practical ways to make capitalism an engine of economic opportunity for all.

We can draw some parallels here with our expanding environmental consciousness. Not so long ago, we had much higher levels of pollution, and littering was commonplace. Today, we are more educated about these issues, and more in the habit of respecting the planet.

By comparison, the equivalent kind of awareness in the financial sector—the idea that private misbehavior can have a broader social cost—is only in its early stages. It is akin to the initial period of environmental consciousness, which focused on the banning of lead from petroleum products.

Just as we have a long way to go to reduce our carbon footprint, we have an even longer way to go to reduce our "financial footprint."

Yet we must take those steps.

I realize that these are deeper questions than economists and policymakers are normally comfortable talking about. Yet I also believe the link is clear—ethical behavior is a major dimension of financial stability.

Conclusion

Let me conclude. The topic of inclusive capitalism is obviously a vast one. I could have talked about many different aspects: women's exclusion, disregard for the environment, corporate social responsibility.

Yet I wanted to focus my remarks today on the behavior that continues to deplete the treasury of trust and could again destabilize the global economy.

This is why the work of your Initiative is so important. It needs to infuse the consciousness of all economic leaders, across all sectors and countries.

At the end of the day, when the global economy is more inclusive, the gains are less elusive. The market is more effective, and a better future—for everyone—is more likely.

Thank you very much.

Remarks by the President on the Economy—Kansas City, MO

By Barack Obama

In this speech, delivered at the Uptown Theater in Kansas City, Missouri, in July 2014, President Barack Obama speaks about the US economy and federal strategies to promote economic improvement. He begins by explaining the process in which his correspondence office chooses ten letters—from around forty thousand—for the president to read each day to receive insight directly from his constituents. Obama describes, specifically, a letter he received from a man named Victor, who lives in Butler, a small city south of Kansas City. He relates Victor's difficulties due to unemployment, and how the Affordable Care Act and the income-based repayment plan for loans have helped Victor's situation. After the most recent economic crisis, Obama asserts, the measures initiated to restore the economy have begun to work, including increases in manufacturing, construction, and the auto industry. He also points out that the United States has again become the leading country for investment. In terms of the future, Obama outlines his idea for an "opportunity agenda," which he envisions as a series of initiatives to enhance opportunity for American workers. Among these initiatives, he mentions reinvestment in manufacturing and infrastructure, investment in research that helps to grow the technology industry, and a broader goal of raising the minimum wage around the country. Criticizing the Republican Party in Congress for failing to embrace equal-pay legislation, he also discusses tax support and breaks for the segments of the population most in need as well as a reduction in tax incentives for corporations and the wealthy. Obama is the forty-fourth president of the United States, elected to office in 2008 and reelected in 2012.

The President: Hello, Kansas City! (Applause.) Well, it is good to be back in Kansas City, back in the Midwest. (Applause.) And I have to say, I love these old theaters. I mean, they are unbelievable. This is just gorgeous.

It is good to see Governor Jay Nixon here today. (Applause.) Congressman Emanuel Cleaver is here. (Applause.) Congressman Lacy Clay is here. (Applause.) Mayor Sly James is here. (Applause.) And you're here! All of you are here. (Applause.)

Now, if you have a seat, feel free to sit down, because I don't want everybody starting to fall out. (Laughter.) If you don't have a seat, don't sit down. But bend your knees a little bit.

It's always good to spend a little time in Kansas City. Last night, I had a chance to get some barbecue at Arthur Bryant's. (Applause.) Now, they had run out of coleslaw,

Delivered July 30, 2014, at the Uptown Theater, Kansas City, Missouri, by Barack Obama.

which I asked—I said, did you save some coleslaw for me? They said, no, they hadn't saved any.

Audience Member: (Inaudible.)

The President: I'm sorry, what are you hollering about?

Audience Member: (Inaudible) to God—

The President: I believe in God. Thanks for the prayer. Amen. Thank you. (Applause.)

Audience: We love you! We love you!

The President: Thank you. I just want to be on record, though, because people have been asking me this question. I deal with a lot of tough issues—I am not going to decide who makes the best barbecue in Kansas City. (Laughter.) Bryant's barbecue was tasty. And Victor is right, I did plow through it pretty good. (Laughter.) But I have not had enough samples to make a definitive judgment, so I'm going to have to try some other barbecue the next time I come in. I have to say, by the way, Victor was not shy about eating either. (Laughter.) So I just want to be clear.

But I had a chance—I went there for the barbecue, but also I went there because I wanted to have a chance to talk to Victor and three other people from the area who took the time to sit down with me and talk, because they had written letters to me. Some of you may know—

Audience Member: I wrote you, too! (Laughter.)

The President: Well, you know what, if I had known, I would have had you over for dinner, too. (Laughter.)

But what happens is, every night I read 10 letters that we receive. We get 40,000 correspondence. And then our correspondence office chooses 10, sort of a sample for me to take a look at. And it gives me a chance to hear directly from the people I serve. And folks tell me their stories—they tell me their worries and their hopes and their hardships, their successes. Some say I'm doing a good job. (Applause.) But other people say, "You're an idiot."

Audience: No!

The President: No, no, I mean, this is how I know that I'm getting a good sample of letters. (Laughter.)

Last week, a young girl wrote to ask me why aren't there any women on our currency, and then she gave me like a long list of possible women to put on our dollar bills and quarters and stuff—which I thought was a pretty good idea.

Now, Victor wrote to me to tell me about his life in Butler, and he told me that he has been unemployed for a while after he and his wife had had their first child. But he refused to quit. He earned his degree, found a full-time job. He now helps folks with disabilities live independently. And he's just a good-hearted man. (Applause.) And you can tell, really, he's doing great stuff. And Victor described how he got through some tough times because of his Christian faith and his determination—which are things that government programs and policies can't replace. You got to have that sense of purpose and perseverance. That has to come from inside; you can't legislate that.

But he also said that he was able to afford health insurance because of the Affordable Care Act. (Applause.) And he also said that because of the income-based repayment plan that we had put in place, where you only have to pay 10 percent of your income maximum in repaying your loans each month, that was what allowed him and his family to keep a roof over their heads and support themselves.

And so I'm here because Victor is the sort of person I'm working for every single day, (applause) somebody who never quits, somebody who is doing everything right, somebody who believes in the American Dream. Somebody who just wants a chance to build a decent life for himself and his family. And that's the vast majority of Americans. That's who Im fighting for right here in Kansas City and all across this country. (Applause.) That's why I ran for President in the first place, to fight for folks like that. (Applause.)

Now, we all know it hasn't always been easy. The crisis that hit near the end of my campaign back in 2008, t would end up costing millions of Americans their jobs, their homes, their sense of security. But we have fought back. We have got back on our feet; we have dusted ourselves off. Today, our businesses have added nearly 10 million new jobs over the past 52 months. (Applause.) Construction is up. Manufacturing is back. Our energy, our technology, our auto industries, they're all booming.

The unemployment rate is at its lowest point since September of 2008. (Applause.) It's dropped faster than any time in 30 years. This morning, we found out that in the second quarter of this year our economy grew at a strong pace, and businesses are investing, workers are building new homes, consumers are spending, America is exporting goods around the world.

So the decisions that we made—to rescue our economy, to rescue the auto industry, to rebuild the economy on a new foundation, to invest in research and infrastructure, education—all those things are starting to pay off.

The world's number-one oil and gas producer—that's not Saudi Arabia; that's not Russia—it's the United States of America. (Applause.) We've tripled the amount of electricity we get from wind. (Applause.) We've increased by 10 times the amount of electricity we get from the sun. And all that is creating tens of thousands of jobs across the country.

Our high school graduation rate is at a record high. More young people are earning their college degrees than ever before. (Applause.) 401(k)s have recovered their value. Home prices are rising. And, yes, millions of families now have the peace of mind, just like Victor's family does, of getting quality, affordable health care when you need it. It makes a difference in people's lives. (Applause.)

And, look, Kansas City, none of this is an accident. It's thanks to the resilience and resolve of the American people. It's also thanks to some decisions that we made early on. And now America has recovered faster and come farther than just about any other advanced country on Earth. And for the first time in more than a decade, if you ask business leaders around the world what's the number-one place to invest, they don't say China anymore. They say the United States of America. (Applause.) And our lead is growing.

So sometimes you wouldn't know it if you were watching the news, but there are a lot of good reasons to be optimistic about America. We hold the best cards. Things are getting better. The decisions we make now can make things even better than that. In fact, the decisions we make now will determine whether the economic gains that we're generating are broad based, whether they just go to a few at the top or whether we got an economy in which the middle class is growing and folks who are trying to get into the middle class have more rungs on the ladder; whether ordinary folks are benefiting from growth.

And that's what's at stake right now—making sure our economy works for every American. See, I'm glad that GDP is growing, and I'm glad that corporate profits are high, and I'm glad that the stock market is booming. But what really I want to see is a guy working nine to five, and then working some overtime, I want that guy making more than the minimum wage. (Applause.)

And what I really want is somebody who has worked for 20, 30 years being able to retire with some dignity and some respect. (Applause.) What I really want is a family that they have the capacity to save so that when their child is ready to go to college, they know they can help and that it's affordable, and that that child is not going to be burdened down with debt. That's the measure of whether the economy is working; not just how well it's doing overall, but is it doing well for ordinary folks who are working hard every single day and aren't always getting a fair shot. That's what we're fighting for. That's why I ran for President. That's what I'm focused on every day. (Applause.)

And that's what sometimes Washington forgets. Your lives and what you're going through day to day—the struggles, but also the opportunities and the hopes and the good things, but sometimes the rough things that happen—that's more important than some of the phony scandals or the fleeting stories that you see. This is the challenge of our time—how do we make sure we've got an economy that is working for everybody?

Now, all of you are doing your part to help bring America back. You're doing your job. Imagine how much further along we'd be, how much stronger our economy would be, if Congress was doing its job, too. (Applause.) We'd be doing great. Every time I meet some of these folks who have written me letters, we sit down and talk, and they say, what's going on in Washington? Why—

What they tell me is, if Congress had the same priorities that ordinary families did, if they felt the same sense of urgency about things like the cost of college or the need for increases in the minimum wage, or how we're making child care more affordable and improving early childhood education—if that's what they were thinking about, we could help a lot more families. A lot more people would be getting ahead. The economy would be doing better. We could help a lot more families, and we should.

We should be relentlessly focused on what I call an opportunity agenda, one that creates more jobs by investing in what's always made our economy strong: making sure that we're on the cutting edge when it comes to clean energy; making sure that we're rebuilding our infrastructure—our roads, our bridges, our ports, our airports, our locks, our dams. (Applause.) Making sure that advanced manufacturing is happening right here in the United States so we can start bringing manufacturing jobs back to the Midwest and all across the country, jobs that pay a good wage. (Applause.) Investing in research and science that leads to new American industries. Training our workers—really making a job-training program and using our community colleges in ways that allow people to constantly retrain for the new opportunities that are out there and to prepare our kids for the global competition that they're going to face. Making sure that hard work pays off with higher wages and higher incomes.

If we do all these things, we're going to strengthen the middle class, we'll help more people get into the middle class. Businesses, by the way, will do better. If folks have more money in their pocket, then businesses have more customers. (Applause.) If businesses have more customers, they hire more workers. If you hire more workers, they spend more money. You spend more money, businesses have more customers—they hire even more workers. You start moving in the right direction. (Applause.) But it starts not from the top down, it starts from the middle out, the bottom up.

Now, so far this year, Republicans in Congress keep blocking or voting down just about every idea that would have some of the biggest impact on middle-class and working-class families. They've said no to raising the minimum wage. They've said no to fair pay, making sure that women have the ability to make sure that they're getting paid the same as men for doing the same job. They've said no to fixing our broken immigration system. Rather than investing in education, they actually voted to give another massive tax cut to the wealthiest Americans. And they've been pushing to gut the rules that we put in place after the financial crisis to make sure big banks and credit card companies wouldn't take advantage of consumers or cause another crisis. So they haven't been that helpful. (Laughter.) They have not been as constructive as I would have hoped. (Laughter.)

And these actions, they come with a cost. When you block policies that would help millions of Americans right now, not only are those families hurt, but the whole economy is hurt. So that's why this year, my administration, what we've said was we want to work with Congress, we want to work with Republicans and Democrats to get things going, but we can't wait. So if they're not going to do anything, we'll do what we can on our own. And we've taken more than 40 actions aimed at helping hardworking families like yours. (Applause.) That's when we act—when your Congress won't.

So when Congress failed to pass equal pay legislation, I made sure that women got more protection in their fight for fair pay in the workplace, because I think that when women succeed, everybody succeeds. (Applause.) I want my daughters paid the same as your sons for doing the same job. (Applause.)

Congress had the chance to pass a law that would help lower interest rates on student loans. They didn't pass it. I acted on my own to give millions of Americans a chance to cap their payments, the program that Victor has taken advantage of. I don't want our young people just saddled with debt before they've even gotten started in life. (Applause.)

When it comes to the minimum wage, last week marked five years since the last time the minimum wage went up. Now, you know the cost of living went up. The minimum wage didn't go up. So I went ahead on my own. When it came to federal contractors, I said, if you want to get a federal contract, you've got to pay your workers at least $10.10 an hour. (Applause.) And I've been trying to work with governors and mayors, and in some cases with business owners, just calling them up directly. How about giving your folks a raise? And some of them have done it.

And since I had first asked Congress to raise the minimum wage, businesses like the Gap—you've got 13 states and D.C.—they've gone ahead and raised their minimum wage. It makes a difference in people's lives. (Applause.) And, by the way, here's something interesting: The states that have increased their minimum wages this year, they've seen higher job growth than the states that didn't increase their minimum wage. (Applause.) So remember, you give them a little bit more money, businesses have more customers. They got more customers, they make more profit. They make more profit, what do they do? They hire more workers. America deserves a raise, and it's good for everybody.

So some of the things we're doing without Congress are making a difference, but we could do so much more if Congress would just come on and help out a little bit. (Applause.) Just come on. Come on and help out a little bit. Stop being mad all the time. (Applause.) Stop just hating all the time. Come on. (Applause.) Let's get some work done together. (Applause.)

They did pass this workforce training act, and it was bipartisan. There were Republicans and Democrats, and everybody was all pleased. They came, we had a bill signing, and they were all in their suits. I said, doesn't this feel good? (Laughter.) We're doing something. It's like, useful. Nobody is shouting at each other. (Laughter.) It was really nice. I said, let's do this again. Let's do it more often. (Applause.)

I know they're not that happy that I'm President, but that's okay. (Laughter.) Come on. I've only got a couple of years left. Come on, let's get some work done. Then you can be mad at the next president.

Look, we've got just today and tomorrow until Congress leaves town for a month. And we've still got some serious work to do. We've still got a chance to—we got to put people to work rebuilding roads and bridges. And the Highway Trust Fund is running out of money; we got to get that done. We've got to get some resources to fight wildfires out West. That's a serious situation. We need more resources to deal with the situation in the southern part of the border with some of those kids. We got to be able to deal with that in a proper way. (Applause.)

So there's a bunch of stuff that needs to get done. Unfortunately, I think the main vote—correct me if I'm wrong here, Congressman—the main vote that they've scheduled for today is whether or not they decide to sue me for doing my job.

Audience: Booo—

The President: No, no, no—first of all, here's something I always say—do not boo, vote. Booing doesn't help. Voting helps. (Applause.)

But think about this—they have announced that they're going to sue me for taking executive actions to help people. So they're mad because I'm doing my job.

And, by the way, I've told them—I said, I'd be happy to do it with you. So the only reason I'm doing it on my own is because you don't do anything. (Applause.) But if you want, let's work together.

I mean, everybody recognizes this is a political stunt, but it's worse than that, because every vote they're taking like that means a vote they're not taking to actually help you. When they have taken 50 votes to repeal the Affordable Care Act, that was time that could have been spent working constructively to help you on some things. (Applause.) And, by the way, you know who is paying for this suit they're going to file? You.

Audience Member: No!

The President: No, no—you're paying for it. And it's estimated that by the time the thing was done, I would have already left office. So it's not a productive thing to do.

But here's what I want people to remember. Every single day, as depressing sometimes as what goes on in Washington may be, I see the inherent goodness and generosity of the American people. I see it every day. I see it in all of you. I saw it in the four people that I had dinner with last night.

In addition to Victor, one guy who joined us was a guy named Mark Turner. He works with high school dropouts to help get them back on track. He used to be a successful corporate executive, decided he wanted to give something back. (Applause.) You got Valerie McCaw. Valerie is a single mom, engineer, owns a small business. She's doing great things. Even though sometimes it's a struggle making sure she keeps her business afloat, she's persevered and is helping her son get his college education. Then you got Becky Forrest. She's a fireplug. She's president of the Town Fork Creek Neighborhood Association. She's got so many things going on—after-school programs and mentoring programs, and basketball leagues, and all kinds of things at a community center—I couldn't keep track of all of them. (Laughter.)

And to listen to them talk, it made you optimistic. It reminded you there are good people out here. Everybody is out there trying to do their best, trying to look after their families, trying to raise their kids, trying to give something back—working with their church, working with their synagogues, working with their places of faith. Just trying to give something back and give some meaning to their lives. And they're responsible. And we all make mistakes and we all have regrets, but generally speaking, people are decent.

And so the question is, how can we do a better job at capturing that spirit in Washington, in our government? The American people are working harder than ever to support families, to strengthen communities. And so instead of suing me for doing my job, let's—I want Congress to do its job and make life a little better for the Americans who sent them there in the first place. (Applause.) Stop posturing.

And, by the way, there's one place to start. I talked about this last week, but I want to talk about this a little more. Right now, there's a loophole in the tax code that lets a small but growing group of corporations leave the country; they declare themselves no longer American companies just to get out of paying their fair share of taxes—even though most of their operations are here, they've always been American companies, they took advantage of all the benefits of being an American company, but now their accountant has convinced them maybe they can get out of paying some taxes.

They're renouncing their citizenship even though they're keeping most of their business here. I mean, it's just an accounting trick, but it hurts our country's finances, and it adds to the deficit and sticks you with the tab—because if they're not paying their share and stashing their money offshore, you don't have that option. It ain't right. Not only is it not right, it ain't right. (Laughter and applause.) It ain't right. I hope everybody is clear on the distinction. There are some things that are not right. And then there's some things that just ain't right. (Laughter and applause.) And this ain't right. (Laughter.)

I mean, you don't have accountants figuring all this stuff out for you, trying to game the system. These companies shouldn't either. And they shouldn't turn their back on the country that made their success possible. And, by the way, this can be fixed. For the last two years I've put forward plans to cut corporate taxes, close loopholes, make it more reliable, make it clearer. And to Republicans, I say, join with me. Let's work to close this unpatriotic tax loophole for good. Let's use the savings that we get from closing the loophole to invest in things like education that are good for everybody.

Don't double down on top-down economics. Let's really fight to make sure that everybody gets a chance and, by the way, that everybody plays by the same rules. (Applause.) We could do so much more if we got that kind of economic patriotism that says we rise or fall as one nation and as one people. And that's what Victor believes.

When Victor wrote me his letter, he said, "I believe, regardless of political party, we can all do something to help our citizens to have a chance at a job, have food in their stomachs, have access to great education and health care." That's what economic patriotism is. (Applause.) That's what we should all be working on.

Instead of tax breaks for folks who don't need them, let's give tax breaks to working families to help them pay for child care and college. Don't reward companies shipping jobs overseas; let's give tax breaks to companies investing right here in Missouri, right here in the Midwest. (Applause.) Let's give every citizen access to preschool and college and affordable health care. And let's make sure women get a fair wage. (Applause.) Let's make sure anybody who is working full-time isn't living in poverty. (Applause.)

These are not un-American ideas; these are patriotic ideas. This is how we built America. (Applause.)

So just remember this: The hardest thing to do is to bring about real change. It's hard. You've got a stubborn status quo. And folks in Washington, sometimes they're focused on everything but your concerns. And there are special interests and there are lobbyists, and they're paid to maintain the status quo that's working for somebody. And they're counting on you getting cynical, so you don't vote and you don't get involved, and people just say, you know what, none of this is going to make a difference. And the more you do that, then the more power the special interests have, and the more entrenched the status quo becomes.

You can't afford to be cynical. Cynicism is fashionable sometimes. You see it all over our culture, all over TV; everybody likes just putting stuff down and being cynical and being negative, and that shows somehow that you're sophisticated and you're cool. You know what—cynicism didn't put a man on the moon. Cynicism didn't win women the right to vote. Cynicism did not get a Civil Rights Act signed. Cynicism has never won a war. Cynicism has never cured a disease. Cynicism has never started a business. Cynicism has never fed a young mind. (Applause.)

I do not believe in a cynical America; I believe in an optimistic America that is making progress. (Applause.) And I believe, despite unyielding opposition, there are workers right now who have jobs who didn't have them before because of what we've done; and folks who got health care who didn't have it because of the work that we've done; and students who are going to college who couldn't afford it before; and troops who've come home after tour after tour of duty because of what we've done. (Applause.)

You don't have time to be cynical. Hope is a better choice. (Applause.) That's what I need you for.

Thank you very much, everybody. God bless you. (Applause.)

3

The Ocean

Ships are seen anchored in front of a refinery on Singapore's Bukom Island, July 6, 2014. About a quarter of the world's seaborne oil trade passes through the Malacca Strait, a choke point on the route between the Middle East and the energy-hungry economies of East Asia.

A Speech by the President of Iceland Ólafur Ragnar Grímsson at the Google Workshop Maritime Domain Awareness

By Ólafur Ragnar Grímsson

In this speech, President Ólafur Ragnar Grímsson of Iceland addresses a diverse group gathered at the Maritime Domain Awareness workshop hosted by the Internet company Google on April 23, 2014. The purpose of the workshop was to discuss applications of emerging technology to enhance the legal efforts of oceanic-wildlife protection through surveillance and monitoring. Grímsson describes the Icelandic model of oceanic management, explaining that this model provides a prime example of how to design a method of management and monitoring that does not interfere with the function of a profitable commercial fishing industry. Grímsson's speech focuses on three core proposals: that conservation efforts should be focused on the Arctic, where existing international agreements can be used to craft further international agreements; that protection efforts should be expanded to the global commons and that data on fishing activities should be made transparent so that public interest and input can be used to encourage adherence to national laws; and that sustainability can be improved by working toward more efficient utilization of oceanic resources. Grímsson believes that the global goal should be to utilize 99 percent of the nutrients and materials from every type of resource harvested from the ocean. President of Iceland since 1996, he has made climate change research and oceanic preservation a focus of his administration. His government founded the nonprofit think tank Arctic Circle in 2013 to coordinate cooperation between private companies and public agencies jointly interested in oceanic and Arctic preservation.

Distinguished participants
Dear friends

It is indeed a great honor to join you here today and tomorrow in a dialogue of the utmost importance, even urgency: a dialogue on the preservation of the ocean resources. I profoundly believe, based on the experience of my country, that this dialogue can now be furthered due to the extraordinary tools created by innovative information technologies.

It was at the World Ocean Summit, organized by *The Economist* two years ago in Singapore, that Jenifer and I started to explore how to bring the Icelandic monitoring model to the attention of others. Then we were privileged to host a delegation from Google in Iceland, organizing exploratory discussions with official institutions

Delivered April 23, 2014, at the Maritime Domain Awareness workshop, Mountain View, California, by Ólafur Ragnar Grímsson.

and also advanced IT companies. Last October, both Jenifer and Eric Schmidt participated in the first Assembly of the Arctic Circle, a new venue for international dialogue and cooperation on the Arctic, attended in Reykjavík by over 1,200 participants from 40 countries.

I wish to thank the Google Ocean Programme for bringing together now such a distinguished group of experts and visionaries; hopefully our dialogue will help to establish the necessary programs of actions and agreements.

We all know that time is short. Our present exploitation of the ocean resources allows us only a few decades to prevent its destruction.

The premise of our deliberations is the humble acknowledgement that we are still in the early stages of understanding the forces which dominate the seas and determine their future, the laws which govern the harmony between the different species and the balance which must prevail among the various bio-systems based in the salty waters. We certainly lack sufficient awareness of how the aggressive arrival of *homo economicus* is challenging the sustainability of the oceans.

International dialogue on the oceans, negotiations and discussion must take account of this awareness that our journey is still in its early stages. Our common knowledge is so limited that the oceans must always be given the benefit of the doubt and economic utilization must rest on sound scientific recommendations— otherwise we will risk destroying what to future generations will be the essence of their inheritance.

The gathering here today is a clear manifestation that, thanks to the advance of IT technologies, we can now work for a fundamental breakthrough and your Icelandic partners are proud to be in your coalition.

The Icelandic model of ocean management can be helpful, both as a reference point and as an inspiration that it is indeed possible to protect fish stocks in a program of sustainable utilization while at the same time building a highly successful and profitable fishing industry.

Because our struggle to extend our economic zone from 4 to 200 nautical miles was a direct continuation of our successful campaign for the establishment of the Republic, the people of Iceland have been deeply aware of our responsibility to preserve the resources of the ocean.

For decades, the Marine Research Institute has by law had a formal role in determining the annual catch of various species and the authority to close areas to fishing vessels when the protection of spawning fish so requires. At first, some politicians and local community leaders, and of course many fishermen, were not ready to accept its recommendations, believing that their own instinct was a better guide, but gradually our annual fisheries catches have become firmly based on scientific recommendations.

To strengthen this system, we developed in the 1980s a comprehensive regime of catch quotas for every vessel, making them transferable from the 1990s. Although this system is still hotly debated in my country, and certainly has its faults, especially regarding how commercially-based transfers by individual companies can affect the future of fishing communities, the result has been that Iceland is probably the

European country that has succeeded best in recent decades in maintaining its fish stocks at sustainable levels while making its fishing companies economically stronger and more profitable.

The scientifically-based quota system is also one of the reasons why Iceland has come out of the 2008 financial crisis earlier, and more effectively, than anyone expected, demonstrating a clear correlation between a sustainable fishing regime and recovery from a severe banking collapse!

Due to its significance for our economy, the fishing sector has furthermore served as the basis for technological innovations by a multitude of engineering and IT companies, opening routes for them to global markets.

Among those is the computerized system which the Icelandic Directorate of Fisheries has developed in cooperation with innovative IT companies like Track-Well. It allows the Directorate to have up-to-date information on the catch of each vessel, classified by species, port of landing, the fishing gear used, the fishing grounds and the buyers of the catch. This information is then immediately put on the Directorate's website and updated every six hours, so competing fishing companies can simultaneously check on each other and everybody else anywhere in the world can access their performance in a transparent way.

The nexus between IT and responsible fisheries is probably our best hope of reform, and therefore the dialogue initiated by Google is of great importance. I express my full support for its continuation and our readiness to offer assistance and advice. Let me conclude my opening remarks by offering three proposals to be considered in our continuous cooperation.

First. *Focus on the Arctic*. There are many reasons why: (a) The Arctic is fast acquiring global significance, especially since, following the Kiruna Ministerial Meeting, more than half of the G20 countries will be represented, in one way or another, at the Arctic table. (b) The aggressive melting of the sea-ice is creating a new ocean. For the first time in human history we are witnessing such a monumental transformation on planet Earth. (c) Climate change is already causing large movements of fish stocks; the recent mackerel dispute in the North Atlantic demonstrates how Arctic states and others now have to deal with migrating species in a new way. (d) The United Nations Law of the Sea is already a recognized and agreed framework within which to reach agreements.

In addition to these reasons there are already existing instruments ready to be used to promote responsible and monitored fisheries. One of these is the Arctic Circle, which we established last year and which succeeded so well that its First Assembly in Reykjavík became the most wide-ranging international forum on the Arctic.

We have already decided that ocean resources and fisheries, marine management and other related issues will be among the key sessions at the Second Assembly of the Arctic Circle in Reykjavík this fall. We have discussed the content of these sessions with the Director General of the FAO, Dr José Graziano da Silva, and the Assistant Director-General of FAO Fisheries and Aquaculture, Mr. Árni Mathiesen, both of whom have expressed an interest in attending the Assembly. Furthermore, marine research institutes and fishing companies from various countries will be represented there.

The Arctic Circle is also planning, in cooperation with the Government of Greenland, another smaller forum in Greenland to be held prior to the Assembly this fall, and next year, similar gatherings in Alaska and Singapore, the latter intended primarily to focus on the role of the Asian countries in the Arctic, some of which are leaders in the global fishing industry.

Thus, the Arctic Circle framework can offer the Google process many interesting ways to move forward on these issues, both by reporting on the conclusions reached at this meeting as well as gathering additional partners in these important endeavors.

I therefore take this opportunity, on behalf of the Arctic Circle, to offer Google a strategic relationship in the next few years in order to strengthen our common cause.

Second. *Country-by-country zones and the global commons.* These must be the core dimensions of our strategies. The record of global negotiations, the never-ending series of diplomatic gatherings, unfortunately is not a rapid road to success. Just look at the record from Kyoto to the present.

Therefore, I believe we should concentrate on country-by-country agreements, supported by both public and private partners who recognize that the existing IT technologies can enable them to protect their marine resources while at the same time building highly successful and profitable fishing industries.

This can be done by using tracking devices, similar to those which for years have been obligatory instruments on every Icelandic vessel, large and small. They send signals to satellites or other receivers, enabling the authorities to monitor where each vessel is at all times, creating a continuous record of vessel movements. This supports rescue efforts and enables companies to assemble data on the basis of which they can organize their fleet in a more profitable way.

All nations are linked to a strict international regime which obliges every airplane that takes off, whether large or small, to meet specific technical requirements. We should similarly advocate country-by-country agreements aimed at installing tracking instruments in every fishing vessel and thus transform the foundations on which a global system of responsible and safe fisheries can be firmly established.

Then we should extend this country-by-country cooperation to areas of the global commons, the oceans beyond the 200-mile zones; and use existing satellite technologies to monitor fishing vessels in the open oceans, list publicly their movements on open platforms and announce the location of vessels that have not accepted the tracking devices. Through the global social media and other IT instruments this information would then become public knowledge. Thus we can use the pressure created by transparency and public availability of data to transform fisheries, both within and outside the 200-mile zones.

Third. *Use 99%.* That should be our second slogan; our profound goal—together with the sustainability of the ocean resources. Let me explain.

It is not enough to protect the fish stocks. We should maximize the utilization of each fish brought out of the ocean. Unfortunately only 50% or even less of its volume and weight is now being utilized. We have created elaborate processes and industrial mechanisms to destroy half of the global fish stocks after they are caught.

This was also the case in Iceland until 30 years ago. We had thrown the fish heads and the backbones away after filleting the fish but then decided to create a drying process which enabled us to preserve them in perfect condition for up to two years with zero infrastructure, export them to African markets where they are used as key ingredients in great dishes. The drying process takes only about five days and the product lasts for a long time.

This gave us approximately 75–80% utilization. It left the fish skin, the inner organs and other parts previously thrown away. Now we have developed industrial processes which take the remaining 20% and create various health and cosmetic products like omega 3, calcium, enzymes, collagen and other items. Thus what is still thrown away by most fishing companies all over the world could bring great profits by being processed for the health, pharmaceutical and fashion markets.

At the seafood expo in Boston next year, a collection of Icelandic companies intends to present this case for commercially viable use of fish by-products. Thus the goal "Use 99%" is already a part of the Icelandic model.

My proposal is that we should try to explore ways to make that target global because it does not make sense to work hard to protect fish stocks and advocate sustainability of ocean resources if we then throw away half of what is caught due to ignorance and irresponsible business methods.

Here, also IT innovations can be helpful. By utilizing commercial stripe marking, the bar-code labeling we all know from our everyday shopping, putting it on every piece of fish product sold anywhere in the world, we can inform the customers whether the producers adhere to the "Use 99%" principle.

Icelandic companies have a well-established practice of using such bar-codes in both the European and US markets, indicating the vessel that caught the fish, the processing factory and even the individuals who handled the fish on its way from the ocean to the consumer. We now have the technological ability to allow buyers of fish, whether in Waitrose in London or Whole Foods in New York, to check on their Smartphones whether the companies adhere to sustainable fishing practices, respect the preservation of the stocks and follow the 99% method in their processing.

I hope that those three proposals will help to further our dialogue and cooperation. I can assure you that there are many interested and willing partners in Iceland, prepared to join a global campaign, aimed at preserving the resources of the oceans, inspired by the need to treasure the marine riches of Mother Earth.

Remarks of U.S. Consul General Jennifer McIntyre at the Maritime Trade and Security Conference

By Jennifer McIntyre

In this speech, Jennifer McIntyre, former US consul general in Chennai, India, addresses a group gathered for the Maritime Trade and Security Conference in Kochi, a port city in the West Indian state of Kerala. The Maritime Trade and Security Conference was a three-day conference held from June 10 to 13 in Chennai and Kochi, with a focus on the maritime politics of the Indo-Pacific Region. Individuals invited to attend included local and international policy makers, academic, environmental, and scientific specialists, and representatives of key industries and the military sector. McIntyre begins by speaking about the history of Kochi, a town located on the coast of the Arabian Sea with more than five thousand years history as a hub of trade between India and East Asia. McIntyre cites statistics showing that trade between India and Southeast Asia reached more than $76 billion in 2013. She assures the audience that helping to increase safety and connectivity in Asian waters is a priority for the United States, as US exports to the region accounted for $500 billion in 2013, supporting 2.8 million US jobs. To further these efforts, McIntyre says, the United States is working to build a Trans-Pacific Partnership that would advance the establishment of a Free Trade Area in the Asia-Pacific region. She then details the security measures that such an arrangement would require. Jennifer McIntyre was the US consul general in Chennai from August 2011 to July 2014, and began her career with the Senior Foreign Service in 2009. McIntyre has also served the US government in Pakistan, Eritrea, Turkey, and Cambodia.

KOCHI: Ladies and gentlemen, good morning! On behalf of the U.S. Consulate General Chennai, I welcome you all to South India for the second component of the Maritime Security Conference.

In Chennai, we discussed how a range of maritime issues affect Tamil Nadu and the surrounding region. Today, we'll have a Kerala perspective. Like Chennai, Kochi is a fitting place to discuss all things maritime.

Kochi is called the "Queen of the Arabian Sea." No visitor to Kochi can miss the Chinese fishing nets that adorn its beautiful shores.

Some local legends posit that they were introduced in Kochi by the Chinese explorer Zheng He from the court of Kublai Khan, although current research indicates they may have come by way of Portuguese settlers from Macau.

Delivered June 12, 2014, at the Maritime Trade and Security Conference, Kochi, Kerala, India, by Jennifer McIntyre.

Either way, they are reminders of the centuries-old trade and people-to-people links this part of India has with East Asia. In fact, as early as 5,000 years ago, Kerala established itself as a major center of the spice trade.

It had direct contacts across the Arabian Sea with all of the major Red Sea and Mediterranean ports, as well as ports in the Far East. The spice trade between Kerala and much of the world was one of the main drivers of the then global economy.

And today, the stretch of sea from the Indian Ocean through to the Pacific is one of the world's most vibrant trade and energy routes, linking world economies and driving development and prosperity.

This age-old goal of expanding trade now is joined by our 21st-century challenges of ensuring security and safe transit of our waterways, establishing international maritime rules of engagement, and protecting and conserving our maritime resources—all focus areas of discussion over the next few days.

In the area of promoting trade, India's "Look East" policy, established in 1991, placed a focus on developing significant partnerships in the region.

Today India is building closer and deeper economic ties with its eastern neighbors, expanding regional markets and increasing both investments and business ties. Published statistics cite India's trade with Southeast Asia as reaching 76 billion dollars in 2012–2013.

And enhanced economic engagements in Southeast Asia have resulted in the revitalizing and expansion of road, air, and sea links among India, Bangladesh, Burma, and the rapidly growing economies of ASEAN.

Nonetheless, by some measures, South Asia remains the least economically connected region in the world today. So there is a lot of potential for expanded opportunities.

Improved linkages and infrastructure investments between the economies of South Asia and Southeast Asia will be a critical component to integrating regional markets; accelerating economic development; and strengthening regional stability.

This growth in connectivity in the Asia-Pacific region is a priority for the United States, and with good reason: the United States realized over $500 billion in U.S. exports to the region last year which supported 2.8 million jobs in America. So the security and prosperity of the United States is also inextricably linked to the peaceful development of Asia and the Asian waterways.

Maritime connectivity is also essential to India's security and prosperity. It's important to note that by volume, 90% of the goods India trades are carried by sea. And, just as the U.S. exports to the Asia create U.S. jobs, Indian exports to the U.S. and the region generate economic activity and jobs here. We both gain from greater commercial interactions with and between the countries in the Asia-Pacific region.

Toward this end, within APEC, and as part of our ongoing rebalance toward Asia, the United States has been working to strengthen regional economic integration; to promote energy cooperation, private sector investments, and educational exchange; to reduce barriers to trade and investment; to improve connectivity; and to support sustainable growth.

The United States is also working with regional economies on a Trans-Pacific Partnership, or TPP, which will ultimately lead to APEC's goal of building a Free Trade Area of the Asia-Pacific. This realization of these shared objectives of economic integration, free trade and prosperity, require that the sea lanes throughout the Indo-Pacific remain open and secure. For that we need effective maritime security in the region.

The key to effective security is effective partnerships. Our countries' navies have a huge role to play in ensuring the security of the Asia-Pacific sea lanes. The United States is actively involved in a variety of partnerships specifically dealing with maritime security in the Indo-Pacific. For example, the U.S. most recently joined the Regional Cooperation Agreement on Combating Piracy and Armed Robbery against Ships in Asia, or ReCAAP.

In 2009, the United States helped establish the Contact Group on Piracy off the Coast of Somalia. As we all know, this piracy threatened trade flows to and from Asia. Working together to establish multinational naval patrols and to prosecute and incarcerate pirates has effectively checked this menace to trade and security.

As a founding member of this group, India has shown great leadership in confronting and combating piracy stemming from Somalian waters. Today, the Contact Group includes more than 80 nations, nongovernmental and international organizations, industry, and civil society groups, working together to fight piracy.

Thanks to the collective efforts of the international community, Somali pirate attacks declined 75 percent from 2011 to 2012, and there has not been a major incident of pirate attack in the Indian Ocean in nearly two years.

However, our collective gains against piracy are not irreversible, and the international community needs to maintain concerted efforts and cooperation to continue to suppress piracy.

Maritime security cooperation is a key component of U.S.– India defense and strategic cooperation. Our defense relationship today encompasses military-to-military dialogues, exercises, defense sales, professional military education exchanges, and practical cooperation.

My first trip to Kochi in October 2011 underscored to me the robust military cooperation between the U.S. and India as my trip was in conjunction with the visit of the U.S. Navy frigate USS *Ford* and professional exchanges between our naval professionals.

In just my three years as Consul General, the U.S. Consulate has had the opportunity to support four ship visits to South India to include two of the impressive bilateral Malabar exercises in the Bay of Bengal. These annual Malabar exercises are part of a continuing series of exchanges between the U.S. and Indian navies to advance maritime relationships and mutual security cooperation to include areas of humanitarian operations and search and rescue.

Finally, we cannot forget our commitment to protect our shared environment, and our shared seas. Our maritime resources are just too important to ignore. Accordingly, next week, Secretary of State John Kerry will host the "Our Ocean" Conference in Washington DC, which will bring together individuals, experts, practitioners, advocates, lawmakers, and the international ocean and foreign policy communities to share perspectives, lessons learned, and scientific insights, on effective actions and cooperation on issues such as sustainable fisheries, marine pollution, and ocean acidification.

Similarly, at this conference, a panel will discuss natural resources and environmental challenges in areas of energy, fisheries, and minerals and climate change.

Before I close, I would like to recognize the presence of Mr. Paul Antony, Chairman of the Cochin Port Trust; Vice Admiral Raman P. Suthan, former Commander in Chief of India's Eastern Naval Command; and Deputy Inspector General Chandran, Commander of the Indian Coast Guard, Kerala and Mahe. We thank you all for your support.

So, we have a lot to talk about and I wish you productive sessions throughout the day.

Thank you.

Secretary of State John Kerry and Leonardo DiCaprio on the Second Day of Our Ocean Conference

By John Kerry and Leonardo DiCaprio

In this speech, Secretary of State John Kerry and actor Leonardo DiCaprio speak to a crowd assembled at the Our Ocean Conference on June 17, 2014, in Washington, DC. The conference was a meeting of policy makers, industry leaders, academic researchers, and ocean activists to discuss issues regarding sustainable fishing, marine pollution, and ocean acidification. Secretary Kerry delivers an introduction for DiCaprio and compliments the actor on using his celebrity to support environmental activism, and for a recent $3 million donation to protect marine species. DiCaprio begins by voicing his support for White House plans to expand marine reserves and to develop stronger measures to combat illegal fishing. DiCaprio also describes his childhood dream of becoming a marine biologist as one of the reasons he supports oceanic conservation. DiCaprio explains that, as a frequent scuba diver, often revisiting the same locations, he has seen environmental devastation firsthand, from bleached coral reefs and spreading dead zones to pollution and acidification. DiCaprio praises recent efforts to increase government regulation and protection, but he says that activists must keep up a "constant drumbeat" to raise public awareness about ocean conservation. DiCaprio then announces that his foundation plans to invest $7 million over the next two years in ocean conservation projects. Former senator John Kerry has been secretary of state since 2013. Leonardo DiCaprio is an Academy Award–nominated actor who has been involved in numerous environmental charity efforts, including founding the Leonardo DiCaprio Foundation in 1998, which focuses on preserving wildlife in threatened locations, including Antarctica, the ocean, and rainforest habitats.

SECRETARY KERRY: Well, welcome back, everybody. Good morning to you all. And thank you, Mr. President, for that announcement. And I think many of you saw the sneak preview in the newspaper this morning, in *The Washington Post*, about a major announcement that John Podesta will share at lunchtime on behalf of the President. But obviously we intend to put meaning behind our words with actions, and you will see a very significant effort to follow up over the course of the next months.

One of the things I just want to say quickly—and I'll talk about it later—as we go through the morning, we need to think about how we all follow up on this. And we've thought of annualizing this effort so that we come back with a specific set of

Delivered June 17, 2014, at the Our Ocean Conference, Washington, DC, by John Kerry and Leonardo DiCaprio.

tasks that we can measure and people have to kind of report, in a sense, on the goals and missions that we set here so that we're really holding each other accountable to this effort going forward.

So I'm very appreciative for the President's announcement about the effort to deal with illegal fish that come to the marketplace. We can all do more, and if there's no market, we have an ability to really be able to begin to diminish the impact of illegal and undocumented, unwarranted fishing, and we want to do that, needless to say.

Now I know you're all very eager to hear from our special guest this morning, Leonardo DiCaprio. Here at the State Department, we are particularly grateful that Leo and his mother, Irmelin DiCaprio, are here, along with friends of the family and that they took the time to join our conference. I know he plans to hang around a little bit after he speaks so that he can hear some of the panels and particularly is interested in the deliverables.

I will refrain from a whole bunch of puns about the movie *Titanic* and the ocean. (Laughter.) Even—see, I just got away with that. (Laughter.) Even though "The Heart of the Ocean" is particularly apt for those of you who know what that is. But Leo's heard every one of them before, and I don't want to deter him from actually coming out here.

I will only say this. I got to know Leo particularly well during my campaign for president when he took time out of his life to put his celebrity to work on behalf of what he believed was the right choices for the country in terms of the environment particularly. And he packed halls and rallies all around the country, and I'm pleased to say he packed them not as a star of screen, but as a passionate advocate for the environment. He is a terrific example of how an artist, an actor, a person of celebrity can take that celebrity and make it meaningful in the context of things that matter to people's lives on a day-to-day base, more than being entertained. And he has used it to capture the public's attention on this particular issue about the oceans.

I was very, very struck during the course of our time together about his seriousness of purpose. He doesn't just lend his name to this kind of an effort casually. He does his homework. He knows the issues. He invests time to visit places where he can learn more about those issues. And he understands how to make the case effectively and persuasively. We have seen him do this through the Leonardo Di-Caprio Foundation, where he fights tiger poaching in Nepal, helps to preserve the rainforest in Sumatra, and proves that you can make a difference even to the lives of elephants and wild tigers and orangutans and that it matters to all of us that you do.

And just this year, he announced a $3 million donation to help protect the oceans' habitats for marine species, for marine animals, particularly including sharks. I might even say that he's been up close and personal. He was just telling me—I asked him about an incident where I heard a shark tried to eat him, and he said it was the first instance of a white shark jumping into a shark cage, where he promptly flattened himself and somehow avoided disaster. So that, my friends, is why he is here today.

It's a privilege for me to introduce an activist who has made it his mission to try to help convey to people just why it is so important that we act now on our common responsibility as stewards of this planet, whether on land or on sea, so join me in welcoming Leonardo DiCaprio. (Applause.)

MR. DICAPRIO: Good morning, everyone. And thank you, Secretary Kerry, for having me here today and thank you for your years of leadership working to protect our oceans.

It's fantastic to start off the day by hearing President Obama commit to expanding marine reserves in U.S. waters and taking serious steps to prevent illegally caught fish from entering the marketplace. Now before I wanted to be an actor, I dreamt about becoming a marine biologist. As a kid, I always had a fascination with the ocean and its wildlife. In fact, the first philanthropic dollar I ever contributed was to save the wild manatee in Florida. I had never seen a manatee before, but I somehow felt connected to the plight of these animals who had no voice and no ability to save themselves from the devastation caused by human activity.

Today I feel just as connected and inspired by ocean life that covers most of our planet. As an avid diver, I've been fortunate enough to experience some of the most pristine wild places on Earth, from my very first dive in the Great Barrier Reef to the Galapagos to Mozambique, Belize, and the islands of Thailand. And just last year, I got to visit Cocos Island, a national park off the shores of Costa Rica, where I had the opportunity to swim with 15 different species of shark—white tips, tiger sharks, and hammerheads—in one of the world's largest natural shark sanctuaries, and I came out unscathed.

These experiences haven't just been adventures. They've been educational for me. They've taught me just how fragile these ecosystems really are. Since my very first dive in the Great Barrier Reef in Australia 20 years ago to the dive I got to do in the very same location just two years ago, I've witnessed environmental devastation firsthand. What once had looked like an endless underwater utopia is now riddled with bleached coral reefs and massive dead zones. Recently on the Cocos Island dive, we stayed inside a marine-protected area where it was technically illegal to hunt sharks or other marine life within 10 miles of the sanctuary, but every night we hopelessly watched illegal fishing vessels invade the waters just one mile offshore.

I've learned that with each passing day, so many of our aquatic species are in jeopardy—not because of nature's unpredictability, but because of human activity. I've learned about the incredibly important role our oceans play on the survival of all life on Earth, and I've decided to join so many people and others that are working here today to protect this vital treasure.

Growing up, I remember hearing stories about the seemingly endless bounty that our oceans had to offer, how fishermen would cast a net a hundred years ago and catch 10-foot long tuna or 18-foot long sturgeon. It seemed like nothing would ever challenge the abundance the sea had to offer.

But today, we live in a very different reality. Because of modern industrialized fishing, ships are heading into ever-deeper waters in search of decent catch only to find ever-dwindling stocks. We have systematically devastated our global fisheries through destructive practices like bottom trawling, where huge nets drag across the bottom of the ocean for miles, literally scraping up everything in their path, permanently destroying abundant underwater forests teeming with every imaginable form of wildlife.

And while we've heard a lot about the impacts of climate change on dry land, the oceans will be the sink that absorbs the brunt of our pollution and the danger of higher temperatures. This is especially troubling since oceans are the source of most of our oxygen and life-giving nutrients on this planet. They dictate our climate, our weather patterns, and ultimately our own survival. Without healthy oceans we are in serious trouble, and the outlook for their health is not good.

I want to acknowledge the fact that significant commitments have been announced here over the last day to afford ocean protection. President Obama's announcement will help to preserve coral reefs and other vulnerable areas, and help to deter black market fishing and seafood fraud in our markets through traceability and transparency initiatives. I also commend President Tong of Kiribati who just announced yesterday the full closure of commercial fishing in the Phoenix Island Marine Protected Area by 2015. That means that an area of the ocean the size of California is now completely protected.

I applaud these pledges and others like them made here, and I look forward to working alongside those who have made these commitments to ensure their success. But this is just the beginning. We need to do much more to scale these commitments globally, continuously building more urgency and momentum to match the magnitude of this massive global challenge. This isn't simply an exercise in wildlife conservation. Several billion people a year depend on seafood as a source of protein, and yet we are failing to protect these vital waters. We are failing to set aside significant preserves that are off limits to fishing. We are failing to protect these critical ecosystems—the coral reefs, the forests of the sea, the tide pools, and the deep water canyons. We're plundering the ocean and its vital resources. And just because we can't see the devastation from dry land does not mean it's any less dangerous to life on Earth, and it has to stop.

Unfortunately today, there's no proper law enforcement capacity and little accountability for violating the law. It's the Wild West on the high seas. The ocean is an under-regulated marketplace right now. Even though the ocean covers 71 percent of our planet, less than 1 percent is fully protected as marine reserves where fishing is prohibited.

These last remaining underwater bio-gems are being destroyed because there isn't proper enforcement or sufficient cooperation among governments to protect them. People who depend on these oceans' resources for sustenance need to hear that governments are working to create strong systems of accountability for those who are destroying it. If we don't do something to save our oceans now, it won't be just the sharks and the dolphins that will suffer; it will be all of us including our children and our grandchildren.

You've all heard the bad news about the accelerated collapse of the West Antarctic Ice Sheet recently, which is incredibly scary. And you've probably heard about the growing concern in the scientific community about the methane emissions driving rapid climate change in ocean acidification. Methane is a greenhouse gas far more damaging than carbon dioxide. There seem to be new stories every week about methane's potential to send us beyond critical tipping points.

Yet these important stories are but a blip on the screen in mainstream media. What we need is a constant drumbeat about these tragedies unfolding before our very eyes and more attention towards the solutions that exist to avert them. Most importantly, what we need is action, sustained activism, and courageous political leadership. We cannot afford to be bystanders in this pre-apocalyptic scenario. We have to become the protagonists in the story of our own planet's salvation. We need to step up now.

Now the good news is we can do this together. As we've seen and heard in this conference, solutions exist all around us, but they will remain one-off projects or just ideas on paper until we commit to act on them on a global scale together. I'm standing here today as a concerned citizen of this planet who believes that this is the most important issue of our time. My foundation, as Secretary Kerry recently announced, gave a $3 million grant to the organization, Oceana, to support their efforts to support sharks, marine mammals, and key ocean habitat in the Eastern Pacific.

Today I am here to commit even more of my foundation's resources to this cause. I'm pledging an additional $7 million to meaningful ocean conservation projects over the next two years. (Applause.) But none of this can be implemented without proper worldwide leadership. This is our moment to move forward to protect our oceans, which are our lifeblood. Now working together, we can create and strengthen existing marine reserves that benefit coastal communities as well as the health of the world's oceans and their life-giving resources. Through my foundation, I'm committed to funding organizations, communities, and governments that are establishing meaningful marine reserves.

My partners and I, including Oceans 5, Pristine Seas, and Oceana, are prepared to provide significant resources to help design, establish, and implement reserves that are globally real and significant. Two years ago I learned an exciting opportunity in Antarctica, a magical place that is home to some of the world's largest populations of fish, penguins, seals, whales, and seabirds. I learned that many progressive governments were working to create large reserves in the Southern Ocean, and I wanted to help. My foundation became a proud supporter of the Antarctic Ocean Alliance, an international coalition of organizations working in partnership with Australia, New Zealand, and the European Union, and the United States.

Mr. Secretary, I remain excited and very optimistic about the prospects of a successful outcome. If there's anything we can do to help, please let us know. I was tremendously thankful for the response of over 1 million people around the world who expressed support for action in Antarctica. My foundation and our partners have also helped protect some of the 100 million sharks who are being killed each year due to overfishing, primarily for their fins.

Last spring, as a result of the efforts of several governments and an array of dedicated organizations, the Convention on Trade in Endangered Species approved proposals to protect several vulnerable shark species. It was a great example of success through collaboration, and together, it's time to create more of these examples on a global scale. We know we cannot do it alone. The only way to address problems of this scale is through smart collaboration among governments, communities, organizations, and scientists.

So I stand here today to challenge all of you to step up, to utilize your positions of authority, to ensure the health of the oceans that are so vital to people's lives all around the world. Together we can solve this problem, but it will not be easy. It will take courage, sacrifice, and true leadership. As it happens, we have here with us today many of you who have already shown leadership on this issue and are capable of doing much, much more. My ask is straightforward: Step up.

Mr. President, Secretary Kerry, all of you here today, we urge you, we're imploring you, we're cheering you on, we're watching you, and we need you to do the right thing. We'll be here to support you every step of the way, including right now with our actions in this conference, but you are the leaders we are looking towards to deliver the protection that our oceans deserve and require. We know you will make us proud. Right now we're launching an ambitious mission to protect the world's oceans, but we have a long, long road ahead of us. We must push ourselves to step up every chance we can get.

Thank you very much from me, from the wildlife in our ocean that has no voice, from the billions who depend on the abundance that the ocean must continue to provide, and from all of us and from the generations to come whom I hope will experience just as we have the beauty and abundance of our oceans. Thank you. (Applause.)

Global Solutions to Save the World's Oceans

By Maria Damanaki

In this speech, Maria Damanaki, commissioner for maritime affairs and fisheries for the European Commission, speaks about solutions to address global oceanic destruction to a group gathered on June 30, 2014, for the Re-energising the Oceans conference in Brussels, Belgium. Damanaki describes how emerging biotechnology and underwater industrial development have made the provisions of the United Nations Convention of the Law of the Sea (UNCLOS) insufficient to protect the ocean, especially in regard to preserving deep ocean territory. Damanaki says that the European Commission is therefore pushing for sweeping updates to UNCLOS provisions by August 2015. The primary changes proposed by the European Commission would include allowing for global protected marine areas, impact assessments, and new rules on the transfer of marine technology. Damanaki also describes how the EU has eliminated illegal, un-reported, and unregulated (IUU) fishing in European waters and has also initiated seafood trade sanctions with countries that have refused to adopt sustainable fishing policies, including complete trade bans with Belize and Cambodia. Damanaki believes that EU efforts to address pollution, fishing, and maritime trade could be examples for developing stronger UNCLOS provisions. Maria Damanaki is a Greek politician who has been a member of the Hellenic Parliament since 1977 and was the first female president of a political party in Greece. Damanaki became the Greek representative to the European Commission in 2009 and became commissioner of maritime affairs and fisheries in 2010.

Dear co-chairs of the GOC, ladies and gentlemen,

Good morning and welcome to "Re-Energising the Oceans."

Some of us have seen quite a lot of each other lately, in what we affectionately call now "the June of the oceans": a month that has been dense with high-level appointments on ocean governance.

And it's not just June: in the past few months discussions have gained pace, declarations have multiplied. Importantly, the media are starting to pick up the story of the oceans, and this is very positive. People should be aware of the issues at stake.

When the Global Ocean Commission was created, with the goal of finding workable solutions and feasible ideas on those issues, I was hopeful and relieved. Here in Europe, I was already trying to make a difference on ocean governance and painfully aware of the magnitude of problems.

Delivered June 30, 2014, at the Re-energising the Oceans conference, Brussels, Belgium, by Maria Damanaki.

Now, a year later, their Report comes with perfect timing. It will help to take the momentum further and energize the discussions that we have only just started.

When the United Nations Convention of the Law of the Sea was signed thirty-two years ago, it was a turning point in ocean governance.

And as Commissioner for Maritime Affairs and Fisheries, I am proud to say that the Convention has guided the EU ever since.

But three decades later, just like the Internet calls for rules against cybercrime, new bio-technologies or underwater systems call on us to regulate new activities especially in deep sea waters, in areas beyond national jurisdiction.

The current system is fragmented and uncoordinated. So far we have tried to palliate with ad-hoc arrangements between different bodies and countries, but in essence the system is ineffective. For instance it prevents us from having cumulative impact assessments or from having the marine protected areas recognized globally.

The kind of coordination we need can only be obtained through a systematic process; and this is why the European Union is so committed to an update of the rules through UNCLOS.

Clearly only a mix of elements would work, as the UN Working Group already agreed to in 2011: marine protected areas, environmental impact assessments, capacity building and rules on the transfer of marine technology, genetic resources and benefit sharing.

So let us agree to make progress; let us do away with any outstanding issues. The EU will work with all countries to ensure that we have a satisfactory result by August 2015.

Within the EU we have introduced transformational change with regard to fisheries. Since 1/1/2014 we have a new common fisheries policy, sustainable and science based, phasing out discarding and implementing the same principles for European vessels worldwide. Through this new policy we have banned all types of subsidies, at the European level, that lead to overcapacity and overfishing. Our European fund has no granting for fuel subsidies at all.

Allow me now to come to a global problem also mentioned in the GOC report: illegal fisheries.

Illegal fishing has to be eradicated from the high seas, and this is why the EU uses its diplomatic weight to push for rules like the UNCLOS or the United Nations Fish Stock Agreement to be enforced worldwide.

We also use our considerable market weight and I'm grateful to the Global Oceans Commission for highlighting this important aspect in its paper. In practice the EU requires that any fish import be accompanied by a catch certificate. In other words the fish has to be caught legally; otherwise it won't get into our market. And we go further.

We work with other world nations to promote compliance with international law. When a country clearly does not respect its international obligations, we give them a fair warning and time to set things straight. We have done so with 13 countries in the last two years. Ten of them then complied, but three didn't. So earlier this year the EU adopted our first ever trade ban with Cambodia, Belize and Guinea Conakry.

In just over four years the EU has become the frontrunner in the fight against IUU and we are making a difference. Many third countries are now taking their international duties much more seriously.

The EU is also stepping up its efforts to address the marine litter problem. It has agreed to set a reduction target for marine litter by 2020, to move towards Rio + 20 commitments. We in the European Commission are going to propose this target soon.

On offshore oil and gas the EU has put in place the highest risk-based standards for operation within its territory. We welcome, of course, binding efforts for reducing risk, as well as ensuring effective emerging response, regardless of where operations take place, in line with the polluter pays principle.

The other soft spot identified by the Global Oceans Commission is the performance of RFMOs. We cannot ignore their presence. I think the focus at least for right now should be on improving what we have.

How? you may ask.

We start from the basics—at least that is what the EU has done. Our new re-formed policy now tells us what to do: we are to improve the compliance committees of RFMOs, develop scientific knowledge and advice, manage stocks on a sustainable basis, apply effective and deterring penalties, carry out performance reviews and fix what needs to be fixed.

All this renews the thrust for our work in RFMOs, so I very much welcome the urgency you bring into this discussion. The GOC has made a recommendation for turning the high seas into a regeneration zone in case of no results. The vision is clear and highly ambitious. The European Union clearly supports the establishment of marine protected areas. Referring to the closing of all high seas fisheries we have a number of questions and concerns on the consequences for the fisheries in other areas and the complicated governance issues of such decisions. This issue needs further examination and discussion to be based on science, impartial decision-making procedures and control mechanisms.

Ladies and gentlemen,

What is needed at the international level is a change of perspective. We need to see the bigger picture. A holistic and comprehensive approach is the basic requirement for a healthy and resilient marine environment. As I said: no fences. Integration is the name of the game. It is gaining ground in all our Member States and beyond, as is our blue growth agenda. So far we have given special attention to promising maritime sectors such as marine biotech, aquaculture, ocean energy, deep sea mining and tourism. We think that with a focused research effort and steps to improve the environment for innovation, these sectors can prosper in a smart and sustainable way.

A key tool to ensure sufficient marine space for concurrent economic activities is maritime spatial planning. If all goes well our legislative proposal should enter into force after the summer and it is a historic achievement. For the first time in the world, countries have a legal obligation to cooperate in planning their seas across borders.

Spatial planning gives operators certainty on whether and what economic developments are possible, where and for how long. It will speed up licensing and permit procedures, and will provide good management of the cumulative impact of maritime activities. It a huge and real step for marine governance in Europe.

At the same time there is also an overall need to get a deeper and better understanding of how our oceans work, how they interact with the climate and how economic activities affect the marine environment.

Ocean observation, mapping and forecasting are essential in this vein. This is why the EU has directly and explicitly geared its financial support, and particularly its research funds, towards the sea.

Since last year, the EU, the United States and Canada have started a transatlantic research alliance which is to cover observing systems and ocean stressors, as well as research in the Arctic region, a fragile environment that is undergoing enormous change in terms of temperature and human activity.

We hope to see similar forms of cooperation with and between other countries in the future.

Needless to say, the private sector will have a big role to play in this sustainable growth model. Any firm operating in transport, oil and gas, fisheries, aquaculture or coastal tourism is entirely dependent on ocean resources, services and space. They will have to take up a corresponding responsibility for marine environmental protection, in Europe and in the world.

To conclude, ladies and gentlemen,

The EU perspective to the ocean challenge is one of caution and common sense. We don't want to open up the seas to unbridled growth or a lawless gold rush. But we think that controlled, smart and fair development is possible.

We need cooperation with the international community, to create one common front. And we need it now.

Thank you.

4

Embracing New Paradigms in Education

U.S. Secretary of Education Arne Duncan discusses the burden of student debt at the White House.

Remarks by the First Lady at Education Event with DC High School Sophomores

By Michelle Obama

In this speech, First Lady Michelle Obama speaks to students at Bell Multicultural High School in Washington, DC, about the state of American education and strategies for the future. Obama begins by speaking about President Barack Obama's "North Star" goal, which is for the United States to have the highest proportion of students graduating from college in the world by the year 2020. Obama states that, by 2020, nearly two-thirds of American jobs will require some form of postsecondary training or education and that college preparation therefore needs to be one of the central goals for the future evolution of the United States. In addition to improving the education system, Obama calls for students to take an active role in facilitating their own educational process and describes personal determination and effort as the keys to succeeding in the education system. She illustrates this by discussing her own experience; she was told it would be impossible for her to attend Princeton University, but she managed to secure a place at the university through hard work and funded her education through loans and grants. Michelle Obama became First Lady of the United States in 2008. Before her husband was elected to office, Obama worked for the University of Chicago Medical Center and was a member of the staff of Chicago mayor Richard M. Daley. As First Lady, Michelle Obama has focused on homelessness, education, LGBT rights, and childhood health.

Mrs. Obama: Well, good morning. How are you all doing? You good?

Students: Yes.

Mrs. Obama: Let me tell you, I'm thrilled to be back here at the Columbia Heights Education Campus. How many of you guys were here when the President and I were here the last time? (Applause.) Yes, show—applause is good. That will help me out. That's good.

So you guys have made some good progress, and now we're back because we are so proud of what you all have been doing here, and we thought that this was the best place to begin this conversation.

So let me start by thanking Menbere for that very kind introduction. She is a proud representative of what this school can do, and her story is one that we want you all to emulate.

I also want to recognize Mayor Gray, as well as Kaya Henderson, the Chancellor of the D.C. Public Schools. And of course, I want to recognize your principal, Principal Tukeva, and all of the faculty and staff here at Bell Multicultural High School. Thank you for hosting us.

Delivered November 12, 2013, at Bell Multicultural High School, Washington, DC, by Michelle Obama.

Of course, I want to thank Secretary Duncan for joining me today, as well as Jeff and Keshia and everyone from 106 and Park for helping to facilitate today's discussion. Let's give them all a big round of applause. (Applause.)

But most of all, I want to recognize all of the young people who are here with us, the sophomores here at CHEC. And I wanted to come here today because you guys and students like you across America are at the heart of one of my husband's most important goals as President.

See, when Barack came into office, one of the very first things he did was to set what he calls a North Star goal for the entire country—that by the year 2020, the year that all of you will be graduating from college, that this country will have the highest proportion of college graduates in the world.

Now, Barack set this goal because as a—a generation ago, we were number one in college graduates. But over the past couple of decades, this country has slipped all the way to 12th. We've slipped. And that's unacceptable, and we've all got a lot of work to do to turn that around and get back on top.

But Barack didn't just set that goal because it's good for our country. He did it because he knows how important higher education is to all of you as individuals. Because when the year 2020 rolls around, nearly two-thirds of all jobs in this country are going to require some form of training beyond high school. That means whether it's a vocational program, community college, a four-year university, you all are going to need some form of higher education in order to build the kind of lives that you want for yourselves, good careers, to be able to provide for your family.

And that's why the President and Secretary Duncan have been doing everything they can to make sure that kids like you get the best education possible and that you have everything you need to continue your education after high school. They've been fighting to strengthen your schools and to support your teachers. They've been working hard to make college more affordable for all young people in this country no matter where you come from or how much money your parents have. They've been working with parents, teachers, administrators, community leaders all across this country just to help you succeed.

But here's the thing—and I want you to listen to this—at the end of the day, no matter what the President does, no matter what your teachers and principals do or whatever is going on in your home or in your neighborhood, the person with the biggest impact on your education is you. It's that simple. It is you, the student. And more than anything else, meeting that 2020 goal is going to take young people like all of you across this country stepping up and taking control of your education.

And that's what we're going to talk about today. We're going to talk about the power that each of you has to commit to your education. We're going to talk about the power that you have to fulfill your potential and unlock opportunities that you can't even begin to imagine for yourselves right now. And when I talk about students needing to take responsibility for their education, I want you all to know that I'm speaking from my own personal life experience.

Like Menbere, growing up, I considered myself pretty lucky. Even though my parents didn't have a lot of money, they never went to college themselves, they had an unwavering belief in the power of education. So they always pushed me and my brother to do whatever it took to succeed in school. So when it came time for me to go to high school, they encouraged me to enroll in one of the best schools in Chicago. It was a school a lot like this one.

And listening to Menbere's story, it was so similar, because my school was way across the other side of the city from where I lived. So at 6:00 a.m. every morning, I had to get on a city bus and ride for an hour, sometimes more, just to get to school. And I was willing to do that because I was willing to do whatever it took for me to go to college.

I set my sights high. I decided I was going to Princeton. But I quickly realized that for me, a kid like me, getting into Princeton wasn't just going to happen on its own. See I went to a great school, but at my school we had so many kids, so few guidance counselors, they were dealing with hundreds of students so they didn't always have much time to help me personally get my applications together. Plus, I knew I couldn't afford to go on a bunch of college visits. I couldn't hire a personal tutor. I couldn't enroll in SAT prep classes. We didn't have the money.

And then—get this—some of my teachers straight up told me that I was setting my sights too high. They told me I was never going to get into a school like Princeton. I still hear that doubt ringing in my head. So it was clear to me that nobody was going to take my hand and lead me to where I needed to go.

Instead, it was going to be up to me to reach my goal. I would have to chart my own course. And I knew that the first thing I needed to do was have the strongest academic record possible.

So I worked hard to get the best grades I could in all of my classes. I got involved in leadership opportunities in school where I developed close relationships with some of my teachers and administrators. I knew I needed to present very solid and thoughtful college applications, so I stayed up late, got up early in the morning to work on my essays and personal statements. I knew my parents would not be able to pay for all of my tuition, so I made sure that I applied for financial aid on time. That FAFSA form was my best friend. I knew the deadlines, everything.

Most importantly, when I encountered doubters, when people told me I wasn't going to cut it, I didn't let that stop me—in fact, I did the opposite. I used that negativity to fuel me, to keep me going. And at the end, I got into Princeton, and that was one of the proudest days of my life.

But getting into Princeton was only the beginning. Graduating from Princeton was my ultimate goal. So I had to start all over again, developing and executing a plan that would lead me to my goal. And of course, I struggled a little bit. I had to work hard, again, to find a base of friends and build a community of support for myself in this Ivy League university.

I remember as a freshman I mistakenly enrolled into a class that was meant for juniors and seniors. And there were times when I felt like I could barely keep my head above water. But through it all, I kept that college diploma as my North Star. And four years later, I reached that goal, and then I went on to build a life I never could have imagined for myself.

I went to law school, became a lawyer. I've been a vice president for a hospital. I've been the head of a nonprofit organization. And I am here today because I want you to know that my story can be your story. The details might be a little different, but let me tell you, so many of the challenges and the triumphs will be just the same.

You might be dreaming of becoming a doctor or a teacher; maybe a mechanic or a software designer. Or you might not know what you want to do right now—and that's fine. But no matter what path you choose, no matter what dreams you have, you have got to do whatever it takes to continue your education after high school—again, whether that's going to community college, getting a technical certificate, or completing a training opportunity, or going off to a four-year college.

And once you've completed your education, you will have the foundation you need to build a successful life. That's how me, that's how Menbere, that's how so many other students have overcome adversities to reach our goals.

There's another young man, Roger Sanchez. He is another example of a CHEC alum who is working toward his North Star goal.

In fifth grade, Roger came to the United States from the Dominican Republic to live with his mother. When Roger arrived in America, he could barely speak a word of English. He often couldn't understand anything his teachers were saying, so he decided to put a piece of paper in his pocket so he could jot down all the new words he heard, and then he'd ask his friends and teachers to translate for him.

He went to the library and pored through books and videos and cassettes to help teach himself English. And after all those hours of studying and practicing, Roger arrived here at Bell ready to thrive. And every day, he put the same effort into his classes that he put into learning English. He joined the baseball, the football teams. He helped found your Global Kids Club so that students could discuss world issues. And last spring, he graduated with nearly a 4.0 GPA.

And today, Roger is a freshman at American University. He's majoring in international relations, and he also volunteers as a mentor. He's paying it forward. He's helping high school students just like all of you with their college applications and essays. And I had a chance to meet Roger, who's here today, and I'd like to—Roger, can you stand up if you're in the audience so we can give you a round of applause? We're so proud of you. There Roger is. (Applause.) Congratulations.

So every day, students like Menbere and Roger and all of you are proving that it is not your circumstances that define your future—it's your attitude. It's your commitment. You decide how high you set your goals. You decide how hard you're going to work for those goals. You decide how you're going to respond when something doesn't go your way.

And here's the thing: Studies show that those kinds of skills—skills like grit, determination, skills like optimism and resilience—those skills can be just as important as your test scores or your grade scores—or your grades. And so many of you already have those skills because of everything you've already overcome in your lives.

Maybe you've had problems at home and you've had to step up, take on extra responsibilities for your family. Maybe you come from a tough neighborhood, and you've been surrounded by things like violence and drugs. Maybe one of your parents has lost a job and you've had to struggle just to make it here today.

One of the most important things you all must understand about yourselves is that those experiences are not weaknesses. They're not something to be ashamed of. Experiences like those can make you stronger and more determined. They can teach you all kinds of skills that you could never learn in a classroom—the skills that will lead you to success anywhere in life. But first, you've got to apply those skills toward getting an education.

So what does that mean? That means, first and foremost, believing in yourselves no matter what obstacles you face. It means going to class every single day—that's what I did—not just showing up, but actually paying attention, taking some notes, asking questions.

It means doing your homework every single night—I did—studying hard for every test, even if it's not your favorite subject. It means reaching out to your teachers and counselors and coaches and asking for help whenever you need it. And when you stumble and fall—and I guarantee you, you will, because we all do—it means picking yourself up and trying again and again and again.

All of that is on you. You've got to own that part of it. You've got to step up as individuals. Because here's the key: If you step up, if you choose to own your future and commit to your education, and if you don't let anything stand in your way until you complete it, then you will not only lead our country to that North Star goal, but you will lead yourselves to whatever future you dream of.

That is my message for all of you today. And over these next few years, I'm going to continue sharing that message all across the country and all across the world to students just like you. We, with the help of Arne and the President and everyone in this administration, we're going to do everything we can to help connect you to all the resources that are available to help you on your journey—many resources that weren't around when I was your age.

For example, we're going to tell students about our College Navigator and College Scorecard that can help you find affordable programs that fit your interests, your goals. We also want to make sure that you know about websites like studentAid.gov, which helps you apply for grants and loans, and also provides you with a year-by-year checklist so you know what you need to be doing to get you to college, or whatever program you need to get to.

But I also believe that this conversation—it's got to be a two-way conversation. I know that you all have important things to say, you have important questions that you deserve answers to, and that that's why I want to make sure that I continue to hear your stories as well as talk to you. I want to hear about your dreams. I want to hear about the things you're worried about. I want folks like me and my husband and your teachers and parents, I want you to tell us what we can do to help you get to college and fulfill your dreams.

So that's what we're going to do next. I'm going to step away from the podium, and Secretary Duncan, Menbere, Jeff, and Keshia are going to come back out, and we're going to talk. We're going to ask you some questions; you're going to ask us some questions. We'll listen. I don't want you to be shy; I want you to be relaxed, okay? And we'll talk more about how do we get you to your goals, okay? And hopefully, this conversation here will help students around the country.

So are you all ready for that? You have questions?

Students: Yes.

Mrs. Obama: All right. Well, let's get it started. Let's bring out the other panelists. You all, thank you so much. We love you, and I'm so proud of you all. Keep going. (Applause.)

A Vision for Better Education:
Areas of Surprising Agreement

By Arne Duncan

Addressing the National Convention of the Parent Teacher Association (PTA), US sec-retary of education Arne Duncan talks about problems facing the American education system and suggests strategies to strengthen the system and help the next generation of students compete in the global marketplace. Duncan begins by describing how success is increasingly tied to how well people are able to use their knowledge and their critical thinking skills in conjunction with modern technology. He then discusses issues facing students, including the rising cost of tuition for college, the increasing importance of advanced college education for employment success, and the proliferation of violent events in American schools that prevents students from feeling safe in their learning environments. To address such issues, Duncan recommends increased transparency for parents and improved assessment measures for students and teachers, explaining his belief that education can be better served by spending time and resources promoting great teaching and reducing focus on test preparation. Additionally, Duncan cites the Pay as You Earn plan to cap college loan repayment and speaks about the development of educational programs that help students learn the supplementary skills necessary to succeed in their education, including determination, creativity, and problem solving. The ninth US secretary of education, Duncan came into office in 2009 under President Barack Obama. Prior to his service as secretary of education, he was chief executive officer of the Chicago Public Schools system.

I'm thrilled to be here and thank you so much for that kind introduction. Under Otha's extraordinary leadership, together with your state leaders and members, the PTA has been a vital force in raising expectations for every single child in this country.

You are helping people get the information they need about new, higher learning standards that many states have adopted—and about community eligibility for free meals.

You have helped raise funds for cash-strapped schools and put the spotlight on creative arts. And you have been a very thoughtful voice for discipline policies that treat every child fairly.

Parents are precious, precious assets in education and you help our nation's schools when you treat them that way. I join America's educators and families in a heartfelt thank-you.

So please give President Thornton and all of yourselves a round of applause.

Delivered June 20, 2014, at the National Convention of the Parent Teacher Association, Austin, Texas, by Arne Duncan.

As Otha said, I'm first and foremost a dad. We have a daughter going into the seventh grade, and a son going into fifth grade.

They're finishing school, actually, today.

When I was home Wednesday night, before I left for San Antonio, at dinner my wife and I talked with them about what were their best learning opportunities this school year—what was the most fun, and what they got the most out of.

It was really interesting—and not surprising—that it wasn't the traditional "sit in a row with 25 or 30 desks and hear the teacher lecture them."

So my son said, what he really enjoyed this year, was the chance to work a little bit ahead of grade level in math by using technology. He talked about how fascinating it was to learn how to operate a flight simulator as part of one of his classes.

My daughter, who's in sixth grade, going into seventh, she talked about the chance to be part of a Constitutional Convention—to have that debate, and to learn about the Civil War and again, rather than having to get a lecture, they had a Civil War Day where students, almost like at the college level, they got to pick which class they go to during the day. They had a bunch of different options.

One option was what it was like to be a child during the Civil War, what were children's roles during that time. They had a chance to see their clothing, go in a tent, touch the weapons, and experience those things. They had a mock trial for Mary Surratt, who was maybe, maybe not, an accomplice of John Wilkes Booth— they debated that, and they decided she was guilty.

But it's those kinds of opportunities that I think are so special. And why are those experiences so important? Because I think all of us—all of us as parents—want our children to be inspired, to be challenged, to be active participants in their own learning.

And here's why this matters so much:

Every child—every student—deserves an education that will prepare her for the future. And more and more, success in the real world won't be just about what you know, but what you can do with what you know.

It will be about your ability to make connections among ideas, to communicate them, and to be able to work in diverse groups to create, to analyze, and to find solutions to complex problems. It will be about a child's ability to understand technology not as an end in itself, but as a tool for a task.

Yes, knowledge matters, but not in a vacuum. It has to be connected with inquiry and problem solving.

Those skills will be precious currency for young people who might change jobs a dozen or more times across their careers. And the best jobs for our children, as columnist Tom Friedman has written about, will actually be the jobs they invent themselves.

Fluency with critical thinking, readiness for life-long learning—that's what will matter. That's what my wife and I want for our children.

And after thousands and thousands of conversations all over the country, I am more convinced than ever that's exactly what most parents and most teachers want for our nation's children as well.

Making that happen at scale—for the many, and not for the few—that will take real action.

If you remember only one thing from what I say today, please make it this: to prepare our children for the real future that they'll face, public education has to change. It has to evolve. And there is growing agreement in this country about what we need to do.

There's growing agreement on the results-driven improvements we can make right now to ensure a truly effective education for every student. There is growing agreement about how best to prepare every student for success in college, careers, and life.

Those changes have begun in many, many communities throughout this country. But there's also tough work ahead. It won't happen fast enough without the support of people like you, who are so committed to our nation's children.

So I'm going to lay out what that change looks like, and where I think we agree. And I'm also going to ask for your help.

This change isn't about pleasant platitudes or airy aspirations. These challenges have been decades in the making. But it's urgent for us to take action now. Because we all benefit if all students receive an education that truly challenges and motivates them. And we will all live with the consequences if they don't.

Let me ask you two questions.

If you could, please raise your hand if you're better off than your parents were.

Now, the second question—maybe the tougher question—please raise your hand if you think your kids will be better off than you are today.

Around this country, a lot of people wouldn't raise their hands on that last one right now, because they are worried that our children won't inherit a better America than the one we did.

We all want our kids to go further, to have more, than we have, to have a secure future. I know that's what my wife and I want. But many people question whether they can deliver on that future for their kids.

And as parents, that uncertainty and that worry, sometimes gnaws at us. It keeps us awake some nights.

Parents see children in places like Germany and Korea and China racing past ours educationally, and they suspect kids from those countries will be better positioned than ours in a globally competitive economy.

These worries are my worries, too. And they're backed up by facts:

Compared to 1970 and 1990, more young adults now live with their parents, and more are poor.

Fewer than one in three high school sophomores from middle-class families—and just one in seven from low-income families—go on to earn a bachelor's degree.

And in the last generation, the average tuition at a public four-year college more than tripled—while the typical family income has barely moved.

The statistics shouldn't surprise us. In many ways, the education system we have today was designed for a time when higher education was simply a privilege reserved for the elite. Those days have to end.

Other countries have retooled their education systems to meet that challenge; we are just beginning to.

Quality education can no longer be just for the wealthy few. Every student—no matter where they come from, what zip code they live in, or challenges they face—they desperately need and deserve the opportunity to truly learn and to be successful.

This fall, as we prepare for a new school year, we face a seminal moment in public education: for the first time in our nation's history, our Department projects that America's public schools will enroll a majority-minority student body. Our collective future depends on meeting the needs of all students, and particularly those minority students, better.

Let me be clear: our challenges are not isolated to poor or minority students. The absolute fact is that all students—regardless of race, income and geography—must learn at higher levels if we expect to catch up with our international competitors and to pass them by. No one—no one—is exempt from the call for educational improvement.

We owe it to each and every student to provide her the best possible skills and preparation for the new global economy. The schools she attends must look as different as her world will.

So let's talk about what school needs to look like—and what we need to do to make that happen.

First, school must be a supportive, joyful and safe place. For most of our young people, our schools are absolutely all of those things. But for a tragic number, schools have become a place of deadly violence.

A year and a half ago, I thought this country had to have reached a turning point with gun violence and schools. I thought that after the horrific massacre at Newtown, Connecticut, things could never be the same.

Sadly, I was wrong.

Since then, in just the past 18 months, there have been 70—70—school shootings on our school and college campuses, resulting in 36 deaths, including 22 students and two teachers. What ought to shock us, and jar us to act, has only become more routine.

This level of violence, of death, of heartbreak, and of devastation of families, simply doesn't happen in countries like Japan and England and Australia and Canada. And I refuse to believe, that's based on how they value their children more than we do.

I promise to work with anyone, anywhere, to keep our children safe and free from fear.

Collectively, that's the least that we can do.

Ensuring that schools are safe places for children to learn—that's our first job. But let's talk about what learning must look like to get every child ready for an innovation-driven world.

To prepare our young people for success in careers and life, we must prepare all of them for some form of college. That's never been the case before. Why is it today?

College does a lot more than prepare young people for work—but the economic facts alone are compelling. In the last generation, pay has climbed substantially for those with a bachelor's degree, and more for those with additional degrees—while it has actually fallen for those with only a high school diploma.

What does that all mean? According to M.I.T. economist David Autor, a male college graduate who entered the labor force in 1965 could expect to earn $213,000 more over a lifetime compared with someone with just a high school diploma.

By 2010, that pay differential reached $590,000. For women, the college advantage also more than doubled, to $370,000 from $129,000.

David Leonhardt, the Pulitzer prize-winning economics writer, reports that the pay gap between college graduates and everyone else has reached a record high: college grads today earn 98 percent more per hour.

He writes, and I quote: "For all the struggles that many young college graduates face, a four-year degree has probably never been more valuable."

In the years ahead, some form of postsecondary degree or credential will serve as the basic entry ticket in this economy. Today, our schools do a pretty decent job of persuading our kids to go to college—but a poor job of preparing them to succeed once they are there.

We can't accept that. Every student in America must be prepared to compete with—and actually to lead—the rest of the world.

As people invested in our kids and in our country, everyone here has a shared mission: to make sure that every student, everywhere, receives an effective education.

It's a mission that we can all agree on, and it's one that matters immensely.

That mission starts with access to high-quality early learning opportunities. We must help our babies enter kindergarten ready to be successful. It's the best investment we can make.

That mission continues with a great school—a school ready for the future. Schools ready for the future share seven key factors: First, inspiring, effective, well-supported teachers; second, high standards; third, engaged parents and families; fourth, motivated students; fifth, courageous, committed, accountable leaders; sixth, a safe, secure classroom environment; and finally, access to modern technology.

For the many, many schools that already have the ingredients for success, let's celebrate them and learn from them and empower them to achieve even more.

For schools that need help getting there, let's provide real and meaningful help now because I think we can all agree on so much of what we need to do.

Let's start with a huge area of agreement, and that's around teachers.

Great teachers and great leaders matter more than anything else in school. I think everyone here would agree that we must do even more to respect, reward, and retain them.

We have to stand up for great teachers. We have to celebrate them and create pathways and opportunities for them to shape and nurture the next generation of teacher talent.

While we know that, as a nation, we don't always act on those beliefs. If we did, we would provide teachers with better resources. We would pay them a lot more. And we would train and support them better.

Doctors, top managers and pro athletes all have access to excellent coaching, informed by solid data. They receive top-notch training and ongoing development to hone their skills.

Together, let's work to make all those elements the norm in teaching—better training, better resources, better support, and smarter accountability, tied to better information about student progress.

Part of great teaching is personalizing instruction, meeting the needs of 30 or more individual students—that's a huge, complex task.

Let's make sure teachers have access to the technological tools that can help them meet that challenge—and make sure that student data remains secure and private.

In schools, and school systems, that are serious about preparing our children for the future, mastery of learning—rather than time spent sitting in a seat for a particular class—will become the deciding factor in when the student is ready to move ahead. That means schools will need better ways to assess students' continual progress.

Parents need to know that, as well. Parents have the right to know whether their children's schools are in fact teaching them what they need to know—and they deserve better information than what comes from today's simplistic bubble tests.

Smarter assessment means providing teachers, students, and families more timely and useful information—while taking less time out of the school day. Where schools and school districts test excessively, they should cut back.

And where schools are spending too much time prepping for tests, they should cut back there as well. Great teaching, that's what leads to real learning and strong results in assessments—not time spent on test prep.

Support and evaluation for teachers should take into account student growth and gain—as one part of a mix of measures including things like observations, surveys or portfolios of student work.

When asked, parents strongly support that idea. Better information means more thoughtful, targeted, and effective support—and nobody gains when school systems treat all teachers as indistinguishable. In fact, some systems actually devalue the critically important and complex work that teachers do, every single day, on behalf of our children.

Schools ready for the future also set high expectations for learning.

Thanks in large part to efforts the PTA led, 43 states will be moving forward this fall with new, higher, better academic standards that they chose. That's a sea change in the right direction, and I thank you for your leadership.

As I travel the country, teachers constantly tell me that higher standards offer an opportunity for them to innovate and be creative—and to focus on critical thinking and problem solving, skills that our children desperately want and need.

Yet, on standards, misinformation is circulating. So let me just take one minute to go through the facts.

First, teachers and principals will always, always decide how to teach and what books to read—everything that happens in classrooms. No bureaucrat in Washington will change that. Ever.

Second, state leaders, parents, principals, policymakers, and education experts from across the country came together to develop these college- and career- ready standards.

Third, higher standards of learning give parents more information about how well their neighborhood schools are performing.

Change is always hard, and raising the bar is never easy. The transition to higher standards has been difficult in places, and communication and support for teachers have sometimes fallen short.

But it is clear to me that principals and teachers who have worked through this transition together are finding enormous rewards and better serving their students.

Let me just give you one quick example. A few months ago, I visited Orchard Gardens, a school in Boston that has made an amazing turnaround under an arts-focused turnaround effort. In just a few short years, Orchard Gardens has gone from being one of the worst schools in the city of Boston to a school today that has a waiting list, with families trying to get into that school.

I talked there with an amazing eighth-grade English teacher named Andrew Vega. Andrew said the transition to the higher standards was tough and scary at first, but it ultimately opened up huge opportunities for him and his students.

In an article he wrote, he said he is now—and I quote—"a better—and happier—teacher than I've ever been."

Of course, students will need more than just the traditional academic skills in English, math, and science. They'll need to study history, languages, and have high-quality arts instruction.

They'll need to be physically active and civically engaged. They'll need to be challenged to work hard—and as parents, we have to support that work ethic.

As parents, we know that grit, resilience, patience, and many other skills can have just as great an effect on our students' long-term prospects as their math and reading—their academic—skills.

Schools ready for the future will help them develop those skills and habits as well. And that work must begin in the early years—one more reason we must give every child in America the opportunity to attend high-quality preschool.

But it's not enough for our children to be college-ready—they also have to be able to afford to go to college. College must be in reach for every hardworking family in America.

That's why we are doing all we can to make college more affordable for every student and family.

The president and I have embarked on a comprehensive college cost agenda to ensure students are not taking on unsustainable debt, and families have the information they need, and the transparency, to make good decisions.

And to keep debt from overwhelming our young people, we are proposing to expand the Pay As You Earn plan, which caps student loan repayments at 10 percent of monthly income, to all Direct Loan borrowers.

Let me be very clear: we simply can't do this alone. This has to be about shared responsibility and mutual accountability. States must reinvest in higher education. States cut their investment. Universities jacked their tuition up. Colleges must do a better job of containing their costs and building cultures that focus not just on access—yes, access is important, but it has to be about completion and graduation at the back end.

And as we move forward, we will constantly strive to be a better partner, and to work with the recognition and the clear understanding that what matters most will never, never be ideas that come from Washington.

What actually matters most is great, exciting ideas from around the country, putting all these pieces together to build schools that are truly ready for the future.

You can see it in places like Leslie County High School in Hayden, Kentucky—a place so rural that some students travel 30 miles just to come to school. In 2010, that high school was ranked 224th out of the state's 230 high schools.

Leaders, parents, and educators joined forces with extraordinary commitment and a laser-like focus on data. Just a few short years later, today, that school—that was ranked 224th—is now ranked 16th in Kentucky, and graduates 99 percent of its students.

You can see it in Los Angeles at the Incubator School, where teachers blend online and in-person instruction and coding—which is so important for the jobs of the future—is now a core skill, taught to all 11-year-olds.

I saw it at New York's Harbor School, where students prepare for college and career simultaneously—learning subjects from marine biology to boat building.

And I saw it at El Paso, at Transmountain Early College High School. Students there, the vast majority low-income and Latino, can earn a high school diploma and an associate's degree in four years without paying a nickel of college tuition.

I visited a biology class there, where 13- and 14-year-olds, high school freshmen, are taking college-level classes for college credit.

Leadership matters. Opportunity matters. High expectations matter.

Nationally, we're seeing the impact of the hard work and commitment of teachers, families and students.

Our nation's high school graduation rate today stands at 80 percent—the highest in our country's history. I want to thank you so much for contributing to that success.

I'm pleased to report that dropout rates are down dramatically—since 2000, the dropout rate has been cut by more than half for Hispanic students, and by more than a third for African-American and low-income students.

College enrollment has hit record levels as well. Reading and math scores for fourth- and eighth-graders are at their highest level since the National Assessment of Educational Progress, the NAEP exam, began.

The improvements that we are seeing should make us all hungry to do more.

These big changes are hard. But it is an immensely important moment—not an easy one.

Teachers and principals are working to usher in the largest changes our schools have seen, literally, in decades. If it feels like things are moving fast, that feeling is right: it's because they are. If we can begin making these improvements now—we owe it to our children to do it, to not wait.

Collectively, you've already shown your commitment. You demonstrate it every single day . . . from teaching students every day to volunteering to helping with homework to reading to your children at night. You know what's at stake for them, for our communities, and for our country.

As a nation, we have so much more to do. Our nation needs your help. Our communities need your help. And our children need your help.

In conclusion, I ask you to hear my remarks as a call to action.

Like your organizational motto says, every child needs one voice.

I ask you to be a voice for higher expectations, for elevating the teaching profession. I ask you to be a voice for supporting educators as they strive to make their schools ready for the future—to transform them into the schools our students need to succeed.

I ask you to continue to work with urgency and with courage to make these important changes a reality for every single child.

I'm excited to do this work together.

Thank you so much.

Creating a Culture of E-learning Quality: The Case for Continuous Innovation

By Susan C. Aldridge

In this speech, delivered at the Distance Learning Administration Conference held on Jekyll Island, Georgia, on June 11, 2014, Dr. Susan C. Aldridge, president of Drexel University Online, speaks about the growth and future of digital learning alternatives. Aldridge begins with an anecdote demonstrating how many in America remain skeptical of the benefits and quality of online education options. Aldridge then cites statistics from several sources demonstrating that e-learning yields outcomes similar or superior to traditional classroom learning. Aldridge also cites statistics and individual stories demonstrating the benefits of integrating technology and traditional classroom education. Aldridge believes that the turn in favor of e-learning is largely due to increasing pressure on institutions to provide greater informational value to students, and argues that the global market increasingly demands "self-directed" learners with excellent digital literacy. Aldridge believes that e-learning and mixed online/classroom programs are the best means of cultivating students who are able to take an active role in facilitating their own education. Aldridge describes several innovative programs utilizing technology and digital integration to great effect. She closes by arguing that it will be necessary to create new benchmarks for evaluation and measurement to better evaluate emerging e-learning programs as they become a more critical part of global education. Susan C. Aldridge has been president of Drexel University Online since 2013. Before coming to Drexel, Aldridge was president of the University of Maryland University College.

Thank you for that very warm welcome. I am indeed honored to be here in beautiful Jekyll Island, with such distinguished and accomplished colleagues. Like pioneers in any evolving field, you continue to blaze new trails in distance education . . . which have made it possible for your institutions to transcend the boundaries of time and space with high-quality academic and professional development opportunities.

And today, there are millions of students, in many parts of the world, who are beyond grateful for your tremendous innovation and unwavering commitment. Even in the face of what has often been at best, blatant disbelief . . . and at worst, scathing criticism.

In fact, here's a true story from the annals of distance education about a talented woman named Genevra Webb-Conlee . . . who back in 1999 decided it was high time to finish the four-year degree she had started years earlier . . . but put on hold indefinitely to work full-time and raise a family.

Delivered June 11, 2014, at the Distance Learning Administration Conference, Jekyll Island, Georgia, by Susan C. Aldridge.

So she began looking for a program that would somehow fit her busy lifestyle . . . which included a significant commute, a 10-hour workday, and occasional travel as the business development manager for an aerospace company in Virginia.

After researching her options, she came up with an online degree program that seemed like a good prospect . . . but her company refused outright to pay for because it wasn't accredited. Undeterred, she started looking for one that was. Genevra's search led her to a regionally accredited public university with an academically rigorous online degree program that met her criteria.

Gearing up to sell her managers on the idea . . . she prepared an exhaustive presentation in four, two-inch binders, complete with section tabs. And armed with this information, she headed into a marathon, two-hour meeting on the merits of online learning . . . ultimately emerging with a tenuous agreement.

Still determined to prove her point, Genevra went on from there to graduate three years later with an impressive 4.0 GPA . . . subsequently earned a master's degree . . . and has since enjoyed enormous professional and personal success.

As we all can attest, traditional academics were even more resistant to e-learning than employers were back then . . . and at times, could be downright unpleasant.

Long-time faculty member and fellow distance pioneer, Scott Freehafer, ran into a real brick wall some years ago at a college where he once taught business education. After uploading major portions of his course into an online format . . . a move he saw as a real benefit for his students . . . he received a nasty rebuke from his boss about this bold initiative . . . pointing to, among other things, Scott's "obvious propensity for deviant behavior."

Needless to say, it didn't take him long to pack up his laptop and move on to a more progressive campus environment at the University of Findlay in Ohio . . . where as an associate professor, he is still teaching graduate courses online . . . and with increasingly positive results, given both his enthusiasm and his expertise.

I'm sure that for most of you, these stories are hardly surprising. But I use them to show how much progress we've made since then . . . with employers, academic leaders, and students alike rapidly coming around to the idea that online and traditional education are indeed created equal.

For example, in an often quoted survey conducted by Excelsior College and Zogby International, 83 percent of the fifteen hundred business executives polled agreed that an online degree is every bit as credible as its campus-based counterpart, when provided by an accredited institution with a reputable academic brand.

Likewise, the Sloan Consortium's 2013 Online Learning Report noted that nearly three-quarters of the academic leaders it surveyed . . . from among twenty-eight hundred colleges and universities . . . rated e-learning outcomes as the same or superior to those in the face-to-face classroom.

And let's not forget the millions of students . . . both traditional and non-traditional . . . for whom digital technology is a way of life. To be sure, most of them rely on it almost exclusively for meeting their day-to-day information, entertainment, and communication needs . . . while many also see it as an indispensable tool for learning.

After polling three thousand undergraduates from nearly twelve hundred colleges and universities, the Educause Center for Applied Research found that students frequently favor and may actually learn more in technology-enhanced courses . . . citing such academic benefits as greater engagement . . . easier access to resources . . . and higher quality work.

No doubt, this shift in attitudes across the board has led to a steady uptick in the number of public and private institutions either entering the online market or expanding their share. And even among those that aren't . . . a growing number of their faculty members are using digital technology in some form to complement the face-to-face learning experience.

But the e-learning boom is also being fueled in large part by the ever-increasing pressure on higher education to produce a measurably greater value on academic investment . . . in the face of rising student loan debt, shrinking public resources, and evolving workforce demands. Consequently, presidents, provosts, and trustees on campuses across the country are beginning to see technology as a magic bullet for reinventing their business models.

That's why in making their case, far too many of these academic leaders are fixated on institutional survival . . . rather than focused on student success . . . out of their desire to teach more students with fewer resources, while rapidly uploading courses ahead of the competition. As a result, access and affordability are still driving the change in most schools . . . when quality should be taking the wheel.

Marketing professionals have long understood the critical role that quality plays as a brand differentiator in a highly competitive market like ours. To be sure, it is the benchmark of value . . . and our single greatest asset when it comes to attracting and retaining online students . . . who are far more likely to seek out and stick with academic options that provide a quality learning experience.

And while quality means different things to different people, you know you've achieved it when your students have acquired the knowledge, skills, and credentials they need to hit the ground running in a changing world and a changing workforce.

Indeed, to find and move ahead in a job, today's graduates must be creative and critical problem-solvers . . . who are able to think on their feet and out of the box as they tackle the increasingly complex and ambiguous challenges ahead. Likewise, they must have the capacity to reach beyond their own experience and expertise . . . to connect and collaborate across disciplines and viewpoints . . . cultures and generations.

Employers are also looking for self-directed learners, who have the capacity to discover and disseminate relevant knowledge, as well as the knack for synthesizing it across multiple modalities . . . which is why digital literacy and good communication skills are a must-have in the 21st-century job market.

So as distance educators, we have a unique opportunity, as well as a real obligation to reframe the case for technology-enhanced education. Because after decades of research and practice, we have moved beyond technology's transactional value as a medium of delivery . . . to embrace its experiential value as a transformative tool for providing a quality education as defined by today's professional standards.

In fact, with the amazing array of digital technologies and techniques at our disposal . . . we have an extraordinary capacity to develop, evaluate, and refine the active, authentic, and customized learning experiences our students must have to succeed.

And given our considerable expertise, we also have both the credibility and the leverage to help our campus leaders harness these transformative tools . . . by creating a culture of quality that enables our institutions to forge new and better directions in technology-enhanced teaching and learning.

To be sure, cultural transformation of any kind requires a fundamental change in prevailing beliefs and behaviors. Or as organizational theorist Russell Ackoff once wrote . . . a different world-view rooted in a new reality.

Yet as technology-enhanced education continues making its way into the mainstream of higher learning, it is becoming the new reality on college campuses everywhere . . . as an integral part of the academic fabric. Which means that as experienced distance educators, we can play an essential role in cultivating a different world-view . . . predicated on quality.

In seeding the change, it's always good to define an effective process for innovation . . . and not the disruptive kind that continues to feed the emphasis on transactional value. I'm talking about a very different approach that is first and foremost intentional from the standpoint that it begins with the outcome in mind and works purposefully to achieve it . . . which means that it is responsive, rather than reactive.

This process is also inclusive because it engages everyone who has an investment in that outcome . . . from campus administrators and trustees . . . to faculty, staff, and students. And it's above all continuous in that innovation doesn't end with implementation only to start up again when the next big idea or challenge comes along.

Of course, egos and emotions often get in the way of real innovation . . . especially in higher ed where those egos and emotions belong to a lot of very smart people who are used to operating in certain ways. And this barrier is especially difficult to hurdle in schools where the virtual campus is distinctly separate from the physical one.

Therefore, in building support for quality innovation, we can all take a leaf from Thomas Edison's book. In describing Edison's approach, Andrew Hardagon at UC Davis wrote that the great inventor worked hard to create the future from the best pieces of the past that he could find and use . . . combining existing ideas in new ways to bridge old worlds and build new ones around the innovations that he saw as a result.

For our purposes, this composting strategy helps mobilize campus commitment and talent around merging the best of both worlds . . . online and face-to-face . . . in the service of effective teaching and learning.

Under this scenario, president, provosts, and deans assume the role of quality evangelists, who then empower their faculty, staff, and students to create a safe and open environment for mutual support and collaborative experimentation . . . rooted in the credo that all ideas are on the table and every voice will be heard.

In my experience, open and equitable dialogue . . . facilitates valuable and ongoing discovery . . . by enabling campus community members to define concerns, address impediments, and examine alternatives from within a broader context or systems perspective. So like Edison, we have the ability to see emerging patterns that lead to creative solutions.

Equally important, participatory communication such as this encourages both individual and collective ownership of the innovation process itself . . . which is essential if we ever hope to fully close the chasm between online and in-person that still exists in far too many institutions.

Composting also encourages everyone involved to think about quality improvement as a journey, rather than a destination . . . with the explicit goal of creating, capturing, and delivering progressively greater value on academic investment.

But before the journey begins, we need to develop a realistic blueprint for innovation . . . that is strategic and evidence-based . . . measurable and adaptive . . . with well-articulated goals and objectives. As such, it should reflect the values, as well as the circumstances that drive both the school's mission and its students' personal and professional needs . . . while taking into account external variables . . . such as the regulatory environment or the economic climate . . . that might have an impact on progress.

We must also have a clearly defined framework for implementing this blueprint. And given the nature of continuous quality improvement . . . design-thinking is a powerful choice . . . because it focuses everyone squarely on the student experience.

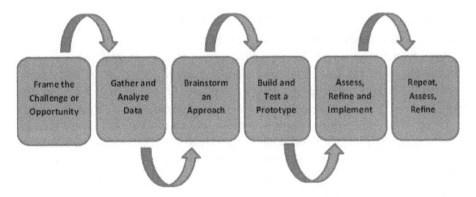

For starters, design-thinking is actually more mindset than method . . . in that it exploits the process of design to inspire fresh perspectives and novel approaches, while also paving the way for a culture of quality.

Consequently, every member of the campus community becomes a designer . . . invested in building, piloting, evaluating, and refining new and better forms of technology-enhanced teaching and learning. And by working in self-organizing teams, from within and across campus disciplines and functions, they have an even greater capacity for real innovation.

Likewise, this approach enables us to think big, start small, and scale as we go, by orchestrating short cycles of rapid iteration . . . and using continuous student feedback to add value with each successive round. So over time, campus stakeholders come to think of technology as more of an experiential tool than a transactional medium for meeting academic objectives and supporting student success.

Here's a really good example of this from within the ranks of my own university.

For years now, budding trial lawyers have had the experiential learning advantage of moot courts and mock trials for mastering litigation skills. On the other hand, their transactional counterparts have been expected to learn the art of negotiation by reading textbooks and listening to lectures.

At least until one of our law professors at Drexel . . . Karl Okamoto . . . donned his design hat and created LawMeets . . . a "moot court" experience for emerging transactional attorneys, who want to practice and perfect their deal-making skills. Although Karl originally launched his brainchild as an in-person competition, he gradually realized that it might have an even greater educational impact in the on-line environment.

So working with a team of fellow designers, he created an interactive website that law students across the country are now using to post videos of themselves counseling "clients," which are peer-reviewed through a digital voting device. Top-rated performances are then evaluated by a cadre of seasoned practicing attorneys, who furnish a demonstration video of their own, as well.

Of course, given the dearth of experiential learning opportunities in this area of legal education, Karl's colleagues in other law schools have enthusiastically incorporated these technology-enhanced exercises into their own classroom activities, with excellent results. And like any good designer, he has since added value to his original innovation . . . by developing a MOOC that combines LawMeets simulations with short vodcasts from some of the best legal minds in the country.

This open online course has received rave reviews from students, who over-whelmingly agree that the challenges are realistic, and the experience, worthwhile . . . citing the unique opportunity to connect online with recognized experts in their field. Inspired by the response, Karl is now gradually expanding his course roster.

Design thinking also encourages us to learn and adapt . . . quickly and effectively . . . which makes this framework highly compatible with our mission as educators. In fact, it can be a powerful, hands-on learning experience for students to use in developing career-relevant skills . . . as well as a great way to get them actively involved in the quality improvement process.

Several years ago, Utah State University put students in the driver's seat of innovation when it launched a student-led, expert-supported design project on its campus . . . aimed at finding fresh new approaches for supporting student success . . . from enrollment all the way through graduation.

This unique, yearlong studio course attracted 15 students of different ages, backgrounds, and disciplines . . . from international studies . . . to language pathology . . . to crop science . . . who self-organized into four teams . . . where as one student put it, they "quickly learned to play to each other's strengths and make the most of their combined abilities."

After framing the challenge, the next step was to research current practices for supporting student success . . . with the goal of identifying both how and why they were failing to hit the mark. That meant interviewing and collaborating with fellow students and prospective employers, as well as campus experts from a variety of relevant areas like academic advising, career development, and administrative services.

Using this data, they brainstormed a myriad of ideas for improving the student experience . . . which resulted in a succession of prototypes to test and refine. And with each iteration, they were able to capture, create, and deliver the unique value their campus peers were looking for.

After months of trial and error, these student designers emerged with an effective solution. A user-friendly, Web-based "one-stop shopping" service delivery portal, which is not only seamless, but can also be customized to meet each student's evolving personal, strategic, academic, and financial objectives.

And in the process, they mastered a number of critical workforce skills, including adaptive thinking and creative problem-solving . . . collaborative design and data-driven decision-making.

The university also learned its own important lesson. By empowering students to play a leading role in the quality improvement process, it could ensure an educational experience that was as meaningful for them as it was relevant to their success. What's more, by knowing what works and what doesn't from the student perspective, its leadership team was in a far better position to allocate precious institutional resources.

Of course, quality learning begins and ends with quality teaching. So in addition to student success, we should also be focused on faculty success in the technology-enhanced environment. That will mean working with our campus leaders to design, deliver, and continuously improve faculty development experiences that support quality instruction.

The University of Wisconsin-Milwaukee embraced this challenge head-on when it began making the transition to hybrid teaching and learning more than a decade ago.

The idea was to provide a multi-faceted training program that would enable faculty members to rethink and redesign their courses . . . while creating student-centered learning activities that effectively incorporated online and face-to-face components. Faculty also needed to learn effective skills for managing online interaction . . . in addition to new methods of learning assessment.

With all of these objectives in mind, the university not only researched the burgeoning literature, but also looked at similar efforts around the country. And after synthesizing all of this information, it designed, evaluated, and modified as necessary a hybrid faculty development model that could be easily deployed into a variety of academic program areas.

This model is grounded in experiential learning through hands-on assignments, group discussion, and individual reflection. Modules are taught in the hybrid format, which intersperses face-to-face workshops with online learning activities.

As a result, instructors get to experience a hybrid course from the perspective of their students . . . an important first step in quality teaching. There are also ample opportunities for emerging hybrid faculty to work with their more seasoned peers as a way to reinforce new skills and share promising practices.

Of course, you have all had a hand in realigning the attitudes and principles; norms and practices that have traditionally driven the academic enterprise. And conferences such as this one offer an extraordinary opportunity for us to build even stronger pipelines for innovation and investment . . . by disseminating groundbreaking research . . . exploring creative solutions . . . and forging robust coalitions.

So as we move into the future of higher education . . . I have no doubt that your remarkable work will set the bar for high-quality, technology-enhanced education that is as customized as it is authentic . . . engaging as it is transformative. Because when our students succeed . . . we all succeed.

Technology in Education: Privacy and Progress

By Arne Duncan

In this speech, US secretary of education Arne Duncan addresses privacy issues surrounding the use of technology in education at the Common Sense Media School Privacy Zone Summit in Washington, DC, on February 24, 2014. Common Sense Media is a San Francisco–based advocacy group that rates and reviews technological products in terms of their appropriateness for children. The organization's "School Privacy Zone" campaign is an effort to address personal security in the utilization of educational technology. Duncan discusses his personal feelings on privacy for children, as a father of a twelve- and a ten-year-old, and argues that technological advancement must not be allowed to come at the sacrifice of security and privacy. He provides examples of several school districts in which computers are being utilized to great effect within the classroom to give students personalized learning options and to provide immediate data for teachers and administrators. As only 20 percent of teachers report having access to the appropriate kind of technology, Duncan asserts that greater effort is needed to bring advanced technology into the classroom. He also argues that, while federal laws already place significant restrictions on using student data, it is necessary for educators and parents to keep a close watch over how students are using technology in schools to identify potential risks involving the volunteering of sensitive information. Duncan was appointed US secretary of education in 2009 under President Barack Obama. Before joining the cabinet, Duncan was the chief executive officer of the Chicago Public Schools system.

I want to thank Jim Steyer and Common Sense Media for bringing this event together and starting this important dialogue—and for your tireless efforts to keep the digital world that our kids inhabit safe and healthy.

America's families, including my own, owe a debt of gratitude to a lot of people here today. Anyone who has children, or works with them, knows that keeping children safe and secure is the most important thing in the world. Privacy is a part of our children's safety and security—especially in our fast-changing world.

Technology has brought the ability to do things that would've seemed like science fiction not long ago.

Our two kids get to hold conversations in full-color video with their grandparents in Australia on a quarter-inch-thick screen that they can hold in their hands—in my childhood that would've seemed like something that Q invented for James Bond.

Delivered February 24, 2014, at the Common Sense Media School Privacy Zone Summit, Washington, DC, by Arne Duncan.

But technological advances have also brought a host of new worries to parenting. My wife and I constantly feel the need to get smarter about those issues—and so many of the folks in this room are helping America's parents do just that.

I'm also glad to know you will be hearing shortly from Senator Ed Markey, whose work in this area has been so important. And I know that my partner Jim Shelton is going to have a great conversation with Commissioner Julie Brill of the FTC, who is fighting for consumer privacy.

That effort could not be more important now.

A generation ago, a phone was a thing with a wire plugged into the wall, a file went in a drawer, a tablet was something you took if you had a headache, a text was a book that students carried in heavy backpacks, and social media meant watching some TV with your friends.

The new normal embraces a stunning variety of tools and connectedness. In schools, like everywhere else, these new tools and connections have offered extraordinary learning opportunities.

Schools now have not just new ways of working, but vast amounts of new information that can empower teachers, students, and families.

But technological advances have brought with them new cautions. Online banking and email have improved our lives—but they have also given us more to defend. Our identity and privacy are treasures that we must protect in ways we wouldn't have conceived of not too long ago.

People—especially young people—are creating vastly more information than ever before—everything from pictures to news articles to restaurant recommendations and much more.

We can do our banking from a coffee shop or a ski slope! Yet we've never been more worried about inappropriate access to, or use of, our personal information.

This is something we think about a lot at home, with our 12-year old daughter and 10-year old son. Ours is not a low-tech home, although my kids, correctly, claim they have a pretty low-tech dad since they have to share my iPad, and because my wife and I limit their noneducational screen time. We've been learning to code together, though they are ahead of me.

Our kids can access their school assignments on the web, and turn them in, using document sharing. They track their own grades and progress. And we use some web-based tools to support their learning, including online video lessons and foreign language courses.

Of course, all that just scratches the surface of what's possible. We're far from the most advanced house in America.

In education, it would be easy to see the benefits, and the cautions, of this new world as a zero-sum game. I'm going to ask you not to look at it that way.

What I want to say to you today is that the benefits for students of technological advancement can't be a trade-off with the security and privacy of our children.

We must provide our schools, teachers and students cutting-edge learning tools. And we must protect our children's privacy. We can and must accomplish both goals—but we will have to get smarter to do it.

Let's start with why technology matters.

In schools, technology—when it's used wisely—can enable teachers to focus their time on the things they do best, like teaching critical thinking and helping kids who are struggling.

It can provide them up-to-the-minute information on where students are doing well and where they need more help. And it can help them reinvent the most traditional school experiences.

Take what's happening at the Brenda Scott School in Detroit. In one classroom I visited, a teacher named Kristie Ford was working directly with just a few students who immediately needed her help.

The rest were engaged in small-group projects, building 3-D models or working on laptops—a flexibility made possible by digital technology and independent learning plans.

In New York, some schools use a similar strategy to let kids work at their own pace on the material that's right for them—while teachers focus on those who are struggling. Each day, teachers receive a report on each student's progress, and recommendations for learning the next day.

At Nashville Prep, school leaders and teachers analyze data about student achievement, attendance, and discipline every week—as a team—to spot trends and sync up about each student's needs.

And in Huntsville, Alabama, teachers and school leaders can get real-time snapshots of student progress in math. That helps educators to help kids.

The direct benefits to students can be big, too. Just imagine the inspiration that two high school girls, in Kentucky and Virginia, felt when they used open government data to discover a super-fast spinning millisecond pulsar star.

Technology also can empower parents, giving them a stronger connection to what their kids are learning.

Look at Khan Academy, which lets parents look at their children's progress in the language the parent speaks—regardless of the language in which their children are working.

Look at the programs used in Newark and here in DC that generate notes for parents about their children's progress in reading or math—as well as advice about what parents can do to further their kids' learning at home each night.

Now, parents don't have to just ask "what did you do in school?" (and, if they're teenagers, have them say, "Nothing"). Now they can start a dialogue about what their kids actually were learning that day!

Here's what these examples—and thousands and thousands more like them—are starting to add up to.

It's about helping teachers work smarter, and helping students learn more quickly and stay more engaged.

It's about helping school systems support teachers more effectively, and helping families stay informed about their kids' education. And it's about parents partnering more actively with children's teachers.

All of that can be transformational. But we must increase access and take on the digital divide with a greater sense of urgency. Some of our international competitors are well ahead of us in providing broadband to their schools—an unacceptable opportunity deficit in our system that President Obama has laid out a plan to fix.

But that's just the beginning. We're behind our international competitors in so many important ways.

Technology can help us catch up—it can help us increase both equity and excellence—if everyone works together to produce solutions that serve students well.

Smart policies will support—not impede—educators who want to put technology to work for kids.

We live in a new, fast-changing time. And in fact, many teachers aren't waiting.

Every day, teachers face the challenge of making education work for each individual child in their classroom, and finding ways to tailor learning to each child's gifts, skills and needs. We need to give teachers every possible tool to help them succeed—but frankly we haven't.

According to a PBS survey, 91 percent of teachers have access to computers—but only one fifth say they have access to the right level of technology.

So no one should be surprised when hard-working, committed teachers go out on their own to find the best tools they can for their classrooms. Whether it's an online grade book, or text message homework reminders, teachers are often finding their own solutions.

Schools and districts need to develop policies that allow rapid adoption of technologies that meet privacy and security standards—and rejection of those that do not.

The practices of districts and schools are changing rapidly as well. Like many organizations, school districts are striving to get smarter about using data to drive improvement.

School systems that have been especially thoughtful in their use of data—like those in Tennessee and Washington, DC—have reaped real learning benefits for kids. And, increasingly, school systems are looking for outside, expert help in analyzing their data.

Like most other organizations these days, district and state educational systems are managing much more digital data. Partly, that's because new technologies are producing more data, and partly because traditional data like bus routes, attendance, food service and business records have moved online.

Like other organizations, school systems often opt to store those data "in the cloud"—meaning, in remote data centers.

To be clear, the motivation here is entirely positive: To find better ways to engage students, to give teachers new tools, to improve instruction, and to help strapped school systems operate more efficiently.

The consequence of all these changes, however, is an exponential growth in the variety and quantity of data. As the use of technology and the quantity of digital data have grown, so have the concerns of parents, and of advocates, like many of you here today.

The questions you are asking are vitally important: What steps are being taken to keep student data secure, and, just as important, to keep outside businesses and other organizations from making inappropriate use of those data?

No one should make the mistake of thinking that these are unreasonable or unimportant questions. In fact, failing to take privacy questions seriously means failing to understand the modern world.

Most days, you don't have to turn far past the front page of the paper to learn something new and unsettling involving personal data. Unwanted revelations can do real and lasting damage. And obviously, the stakes are that much higher when our children are involved.

So I want to be absolutely clear that school systems owe families the highest standard of security and privacy.

No one makes you sign up for Facebook, but you have to go to school. Our expectations for the protection of children must be paramount.

The truth is, in every generation—perhaps now more like every five to ten years—a new revolution in technology forces us to contend with new questions about how to keep our kids safe.

Privacy rules may well be the seatbelts of this generation. I'd like to see vigorous self-policing by the commercial players. Frankly, it's in their interest to do so—and I'm glad to see the conversation starting here.

But I'm not going to wait for industry or rely on promises. It's on all of us—government leaders, advocates, and educators—to act.

This can't be a choice between privacy and progress. It doesn't mean—it can't mean—rolling back the availability of technology.

We know that's a historical impossibility. The toothpaste isn't going back in the tube, and we shouldn't want it to: we cannot stand between teachers and the tools they need to do their jobs and reach every child where they are.

On the contrary, we need to do a far better job of getting useful technology to educators, students, and families that deepens and accelerates learning.

We cannot ask our schools to choose between privacy and progress. School systems must have the ability to use data to get their basic business done—whether that involves organizing bus routes or analyzing instructional information.

None of that conflicts with a powerful commitment to privacy.

Protecting our students' information is more than a legal requirement—it's a moral imperative. Our children's privacy is not for sale and must not be put at risk.

Personal information that students and families provide for educational purposes should be used for educational purposes only. And both school systems and technology providers should have appropriate policies for how they handle data.

Taking action on those principles involves laws and policies, but it's also a matter of priorities and clear, consistent communication.

On the legal side, as most of you here know, three keystone federal laws protect student privacy: the Family Educational Rights and Privacy Act, the Protection of Pupil Rights Amendment, and the Children's Online Privacy Protection Act.

Together, these statutes place significant limits on how student information can be used.

But these are complex issues, and the field is developing rapidly—which is why we're committed to stepping up the pace at which we provide guidance to help school systems and educators interpret the law, including examples of best practice.

Tomorrow, we will release new guidance, with more coming in the weeks ahead.

Our administration takes these issues seriously. That's why I appointed the first-ever executive-level Chief Privacy Officer in the Department of Education, Kathleen Styles, who has helped us to start offering technical assistance to states, districts and schools, around student privacy. Kathleen has been fantastic, and I thank her for her leadership. We established the Privacy Technical Assistance Center to provide that hands-on help.

But federal law provides only some of the guard rails for data and privacy practice. Much of the control over these issues lies in the policies of states and districts.

And, for the record, the Department of Education itself isn't allowed to create a national database of individual student-level information, aside from mandated purposes like college loans. We don't, we haven't, and we won't do that—period.

And nothing about the new assessments, developed by consortia of states as part of new, higher standards, changes that.

But there's a lot of hard work ahead. As an education community, we have to do a far better job of helping teachers and administrators understand technology and data issues. And we need to do a better job reaching the general public too.

Too often, the public discussion on these issues has become muddled, conflating separate issues.

For example, the mere fact that student data is stored in the cloud doesn't mean that it is used for an improper purpose, or that unauthorized parties or vendors have access to it. Data stored in the cloud can actually be more secure than data stored on a computer at a school. But too many families today have been led to believe that remote storage of student data means it's up for sale.

Put plainly, student data must be secure, and treated as precious, no matter where it's stored. It is not a commodity. In truth, while we have seen security breaches in schools—with both paper and digital records—we have seen few significant instances of systemic misuse of student data.

As you know, though, many of our school systems have work to do to bring policy into line with fast-changing technologies. This isn't a matter of bad intention; it's a matter of priorities. And for our schools, privacy needs to be a higher priority.

Schools and school systems should be asking themselves some hard questions. Here are five quick examples:

- Do you know what online services your schools and teachers are using?

- Are you offering teachers timely approval of technology they want to use?

- Do your contracts explicitly lay out the ownership and appropriately limit the use of any data collected?

- Are you transparent with parents about how your district uses data?
- Do your schools allow students to bring their own devices as tools for learning, and do your policies protect them?

Some districts and states are demonstrating real leadership and thoughtfulness in these areas, and we all can learn from them. For example, the Kansas State Department of Education has developed an innovative data quality certification program to train staff on data quality practices and techniques, including privacy and security.

And closer to home, Fairfax County tests software and applications to verify that vendor security and privacy promises are accurate.

But the responsibility here doesn't lay just with school systems. Technology providers need to shoulder their responsibility for ensuring the privacy of our students as well.

There's plenty of energy, in this room and around the country, for stronger regulation of your work. Let me say this clearly: It is in your interest to police yourselves before others do.

In part, that means being transparent—not with hundred-page user agreements spread across multiple screens, but with language that parents and educators can easily understand.

It means offering districts something better than take-it-or-leave-it "Click Wrap" agreements that allow the provider to unilaterally amend its privacy practices—without even telling the district. That doesn't build long-term confidence and trust. Please demonstrate that you know what it means to be a leader for our kids, and for us, as their parents.

While I am challenging everyone in this room, I want to make clear that we challenge ourselves, every day, at the Department to be part of the solution.

First, we enforce the statutes we administer. There are important legal safeguards against misuse and commercialization of student data, and we will enforce these safeguards.

Second, we will continue to offer guidance and technical assistance to schools and districts around student privacy—as well as guidance and technical assistance around the use of education data and technology.

As the field develops, we are working to stay current and be helpful. Where we fall short, please push us. We need your best ideas—we want to be challenged.

Let me close with the bottom line: Personal data in education should be used only for educational purposes, not to sell students snack foods or video games.

Parents and schools need clear information that enables them to make good choices. In protecting our children, we all have a role to play.

So I want to challenge advocates, tech leaders, software vendors, educators, policymakers to make protecting our students' privacy a higher priority.

I want to applaud the hard work and leadership of so many of you here to make that happen.

Together, we can and we must harness the extraordinary potential of technology to empower teachers, students and families—without faltering in our duty to protect them.

When Learning Matters: The Case for Technology-Enhanced Education

By Susan C. Aldridge

In this speech, Dr. Susan C. Aldridge, president of Drexel University Online, speaks about technology in education at the New Mexico State University Teaching Academy on March 20, 2014. Aldridge begins by refuting the commonly held belief that e-learning is inferior to face-to-face education, citing statistics from several sources indicating that e-learning can provide results that are similar or superior to those yielded by traditional classroom learning. Aldridge then discusses the recent development of massively open online courses (MOOCs), which were first offered in Canada in 2008, and allow an unlimited number of students to participate in the class online. Aldridge explains that, while MOOCs are innovative, they still operate using the traditional "drill and grill" model and, by doing so, are failing to embrace the potential of the technological digital learning environment. Referring to a variety of past analyses, Aldridge argues that the most effective learning systems are collaborative and multisensory, and that future e-learning programs could make better use of this innate learning tendency. Aldridge cites the online "moot court" LawMeets as an example of supplementing education with online options. Aldridge also mentions new programs that utilize adaptive learning strategies similar to those employed in video games to enhance participant interest and involvement. Aldridge argues that integrating technology and cyberlearning to create hybrid classrooms can help to shift the predominant education model from "teacher-directed" to "learner-centered," giving students more control over the direction of their education. Aldridge finishes by giving examples of how tools like smartphones, blogging platforms, Twitter, MediaWiki, and whiteboard applications can be used to integrate technology into current classroom models. Aldridge has been at Philadelphia's Drexel University since 2013. Prior to her position with Drexel, Aldridge was president of the University of Maryland University College from 2006 to 2012.

As experienced administrators and faculty members, you undoubtedly know that nothing sparks a heated debate in higher education quite like e-learning does, particularly among the *nonbelievers*. And there are still a good number of them, many of whom are voicing reasonable objections. Some say it's too expensive for the average institution to sustain; some contend that only the most motivated and disciplined students will actually succeed (although the same could be said for far too many traditional face-to-face classes these days); and still others see it as the domain of

Delivered March 20, 2014, at the New Mexico State University Teaching Academy, Las Cruces, New Mexico, by Susan C. Aldridge.

proprietary universities that are often accused of sacrificing the purpose of knowledge for the limited utility of profit.

There is also the all too familiar argument that e-learning of any kind is somehow inferior to the face-to-face-only variety, although the evidence we have gathered thus far seems to refute that claim when it comes to *well-designed, technology-enhanced courses*—both hybrid and online-only. It wasn't all that long ago when the resistance to technology-enhanced education was virtually insurmountable among most traditional academics and at times, could even get pretty ugly. In fact, one of the many online pioneers I have met in my travels, Scott Freehafer, told me a rather humorous story about the brick wall he ran into at a college where he once taught business education. After uploading major portions of his course into an online format, a move he saw as a real benefit for his students, Scott received a nasty rebuke from his supervisor, pointing to, among other things, his "obvious propensity for deviant behavior."

Undaunted, however, he soon packed up his laptop and moved on to the University of Findlay in Ohio, where as an associate professor, he continues to teach graduate courses online with increasingly positive results, given both his enthusiasm and his expertise. Of course, for most of us who have been blazing distance education trails for some 20 years now, Scott's story is hardly unique or surprising. But having worked hard to overcome these hurdles, we are making real progress in moving online into the mainstream of higher education and not only because of its convenience. After polling 250,000 students from 523 universities, the National Survey of Student Engagement found that those pursuing their education online reported higher levels of academic rigor than in the traditional face-to-face environment. They were also more satisfied with their educational experience overall, claiming greater academic gains in many cases. Likewise, technology-enhanced education is gaining ground among administrators and faculty.

According to the Sloan Consortium's 2013 Online Learning Report, which is based on responses from twenty-eight hundred colleges and universities, nearly three-quarters of the academic leaders polled rated e-learning outcomes as the same or superior to those in the face-to-face classroom. And even employers are coming around. In another recent report published by Excelsior College and Zogby International, 83 percent of the CEOs and small business owners surveyed said an online degree is every bit as credible as its campus-based counterpart, when provided by a reputable institution such as this one. With results like these, it's no wonder that a steadily increasing number of traditional colleges and universities, public and private, have either quietly entered or quickly expanded their share of the distance education market. In surveying more than 100 traditional colleges, the audit firm KPMG reported that the percentage of higher education leaders planning to invest additional resources in online education rose significantly in only 12 months' time, from 41 percent in 2012 to 59 percent in 2013. Still more remarkable is the startling speed with which massively open online courses, better known as MOOCs, have captured the imagination of educators around the world, even in the most elite universities.

Then in 2008, a group of Canadian online learning experts, Stephen Downes, George Siemens, and Dave Cormier, became the very first academic team to offer what Cormier called a MOOC, which was appropriately titled *Connectivism and Connective Knowledge*. It was massive in the sense that it enrolled twenty-five fee-paying students on campus, along with twenty-three hundred others who paid nothing for the privilege. It was also open from the standpoint that anyone with an email address could register. And it was entirely *online*. Yet while it was billed as a *course*, it didn't meet the traditional definition for one, in that it was far less bounded and structured. Even more important, it linked anytime anyplace learners in what its creators termed *"collective sense-making,"* by providing multiple avenues for them to interact with both the content and each other. Thus, in keeping with its name, this course was later described as a connectivist or cMOOC. Course modules were available through RSS feeds and students used an array of digital learning tools, such as blogs, Second Life, and synchronous online forums, to interact, as well as to develop web-based learning artifacts. Daily e-mails also provided links to course announcements, blog posts, and Twitter messages.

Three years later, Andrew Ng, a Stanford University computer science professor, stepped into the ring to offer his own MOOC, which was basically an online version of his oncampus Machine Learning course, attracting more than 100,000 registrants. Ng called it the achievement of his lifetime, declaring that it would have taken him 250 years to reach that many students in the face-to-face classroom, although only 13,000 actually completed his MOOC. But, convinced of its transformative potential, he joined fellow faculty member, Daphne Koller, in founding Coursera, and began enticing elite institutions like Harvard, Duke, Princeton, and MIT to jump aboard their bandwagon. Thus, the xMOOC was born, along with a vast array of MOOC providers, including such other well-known enterprises as Udacity and edX.

The truth is, massive, passive online courses with enrollments in the thousands, or even tens of thousands, are not really designed for the average, inexperienced student, who is new to the discipline of college study. According to a recent study at the University of Pennsylvania, the typical MOOC user is, in fact, a lot like all of you in this room, college-educated, intellectually curious, and genuinely interested in the topic under study. So it would seem that MOOCs do indeed serve a useful purpose as self-directed professional development, continuous learning, or even advanced study. I'm sure you've all heard about the MOOC master's degree in computer science at Georgia Tech. While program courses are free, qualified students can also earn credit for the degree, at an astonishingly low tuition price of around $7,000. Still, completion rates remain exceedingly poor overall in these supersized courses, even among educated, motivated learners. And research to date has uncovered at least two possible explanations. For starters, MOOC users are generally busy people. And while it's one thing to enjoy the occasional TED talk or YouTube podcast, it's quite another to invest the time and energy it takes to complete an eight-week course—particularly when the content is unfamiliar. Likewise, non-completers often blame their waning enthusiasm on lecture fatigue, poor course design, and the lack of meaningful faculty-to student feedback. Indeed, for the most part, xMOOCs are only barely on the cutting edge of tradition, in that they use technology to replicate the very same teacher-centric, "drill and grill" instructional methods we know are failing to engage students in the large lecture hall environment. What's more, with extremely limited or, in many cases, no opportunity for interaction with professors, content, or other students, it's a lonely learning experience within a disembodied learning environment. Put simply, these massive experiments fail to capitalize on the real power of technology as an innovative tool for supporting what we know from both years of experience and hundreds of research studies. That is, our brains are wired to learn best through repetitive and meaningful experience that is collaborative, multisensory, and authentic.

As seasoned online professors will certainly attest, truly effective technology-enhanced education is all about quality rather than scale, active learning rather than passive transfer. And when done well, it should enrich the traditional face-to-face experience, not merely replicate it. With that in mind, practiced distance educators are beginning to transform the MOOC landscape, by creating well-designed courses that are far more connectivist and experiential in their approach. By that I mean they facilitate interactive learning environments, where learners engage in authentic learning activities and co-create tangible learning artifacts. Or as cMOOC pioneer, George Siemens, once put it: courses that are far more focused on knowledge creation than they are on knowledge duplication. Let me give you an innovative example from my own university. For years now, budding trail lawyers have had the hands-on learning advantage of most courts and mock trials for mastering litigation skills. On the other hand, their transactional counterparts have been expected to learn the art of negotiation by reading textbooks and listening to lectures. At least until one of our law professors at Drexel, Karl Okamoto, created LawMeets, a "moot court" experience for emerging transactional attorneys who want to practice and perfect their deal-making skills.

Although Karl launched his brainchild as an in-person competition, he has since moved it online. And today, law students across the country use this site to post videos of themselves counseling "clients," which are peer-reviewed through a digital voting device. Top-rated performances are then evaluated by practicing attorneys, who furnish a demonstration video of their own, as well. Of course, given the dearth of experiential learning opportunities in this area of legal education, Karl's colleagues in other law schools have enthusiastically incorporated these online exercises into their own classroom activities, with excellent results. And like all good entrepreneurs, he took his concept to an even greater scale, by offering a MOOC that combines LawMeets simulations with short vodcasts from some of the best legal minds in the country. His first such course (Basics of Acquisition Agreements) met with rave reviews from students, who overwhelmingly agreed that the challenges were realistic and the experience worthwhile, citing the unique opportunity to connect online with recognized experts in their field. Inspired by the response, Karl has since added a few more options to his course roster, including a low-cost version for mid-career professionals, who are interested in earning continuing legal education credits. Like you, administrators and faculty members at other universities are having the same discussions and sharing the same concerns around what, if any, benefits MOOCs will provide for both their students and their institutions. In fact, according to a Gallup poll conducted rather quietly back in April, among nearly nine hundred college presidents, the jury is still very much out on the subject—particularly with respect to boosting student learning outcomes and reducing college tuition rates. Only 3 percent of these leaders strongly believed that MOOCs will improve student outcomes across the board. And an even smaller number, around 2 percent, were convinced that these massive courses would solve the financial challenges their institutions were facing. On the other hand, they were more likely to favor using MOOCs as a way to promote and support creative teaching approaches.

More recently, the Sloan/Babson survey published similar MOOC data collected from among the 2800 colleges and universities it polls. Only 5 percent of these institutions are offering MOOCs, although the number has doubled over last year's number. That equates to around 140 colleges and universities, most of which are large institutions with more than 15,000 students. When asked if these courses were meeting their stated objectives, nearly two-thirds of those administrators who had invested in MOOCs said it was way too early to tell. Even more telling, over half of all respondents are still undecided about MOOCs in general, while just under a third of them say they have no plans to move in that direction. And the numbers are dropping when it comes to the long term. Only 23 percent of these academic leaders believe that MOOCs are a sustainable model for delivering online courses, down from 28 percent the previous year. But interestingly enough, among those who either offered or were planning to offer MOOCs at their universities, there was general consensus that, when well designed, they can be effective tools for driving student recruitment and experimenting with effective pedagogies and innovative technologies.

Like I said earlier, experienced online educators are stepping up to design and customize MOOCs that truly harness the power of technology as an interactive platform for connecting, communicating, and collaborating. By the same token, there are plenty of administrators and faculty members exploring creative ways to deploy MOOCs in better meeting the academic and financial needs of their students and their institutions. And by doing both, we are making great headway in the distance education arena. For example, Longwood University in Virginia took a far more interactive approach to MOOC development, after teaming up with a learning platform creator Badgestack to help high school students get a head start on career success. This open access, non-credit course entitled 5 *Skills You Need to Succeed* exploited the latest gaming technology to provide hands-on exercises and continuous feedback, both of which create an engaging and effective learning experience, a big factor in the MOOC's unusually high retention rates. And although it attracted nearly 3,000 students from across the country and around the world, the largest percentage of them lived within a 200-mile radius of the university, which made the MOOC an exceptional student recruitment vehicle, as well.

Gaming technology has, in many ways, greased the wheels for *adaptive learning*, which allows us to customize the online learning environment, by spontaneously adapting content and delivery to meet the needs of individual students. Even more impressive, we now have the capacity to do it on a massive scale, which will undoubtedly enable us to produce high-quality course exemplars to use in designing far more effective MOOCs going forward. One of the earliest efforts involves a partnership between Google and CogBooks, an adaptive, web-based learning platform. Together these companies have produced a pre-college math MOOC that is massive in scale, yet personalized in its delivery. NovoEd, a MOOC provider that grew out of a Stanford University project called Venture Lab, has also made headway in breaking these massive courses into smaller groups of learners. As such, it offers a variety of open online classes in entrepreneurship and business that focus on group interaction and peer-to-peer collaboration, by creating computer-selected cohorts according to geography, ability, and type. These MOOCs also provide access to mentors and facilitate peer review.

Along the same lines, our College of Nursing and Health Professions at Drexel University is experimenting with what they call a "mini-MOOC" called *Gateway to Online Learning* as a way to stimulate enrollment in its fully online RN to BSN degree program. Given that most of their prospective students are in their 30s and 40s, relatively few of them have ever experienced an online course, much less an entire program, which makes them understandably hesitant to enroll in one. So this mini-MOOC was designed to give them a risk-free chance to test-drive the e-learning environment, while reacquainting them with such other important college-level skills as conducting research and writing scholarly papers. They would also earn three free credits toward their degree if they chose to keep moving into the tuition-paying program. What's more, the faculty wanted to make it as interactive as possible. Which meant, limiting open enrollment to dozens, rather than thousands of students, and incorporating all of the usual tools for connecting and communicating with instructors, as well as other students. And as an added bonus, they embedded a variety of effective resources, including YouTube videos; hot links to journals, library tutorials and reference; helpful hints from previous students and professors; and a popular podcast on the Fear of Writing by our Dean of Nursing, Gloria Donnelly.

All in all, this pilot was a successful one, with nearly half of all completers continuing on into the program. Even more important, we have gathered a great deal of highly useful feedback for improving upon both course design and student outcomes going forward. In yet another interesting experiment, Ithaka S&R, a nonprofit research group, teamed up with University System of Maryland to test how a variety of interactive online learning platforms might be used to improve student outcomes and reduce college cost in then of the state's public universities. And the results have been extremely promising, as a faculty member continues discovering a variety of ways to use MOOCs as an adjunct or supplement to their regular coursework. Some professors saw them as an opportunity to flip classes, using readily available online content they didn't have time to create on their own to supplement experiential projects and group discussions. One in particular decided to use a well-designed, well-received MOOC on genetics to replace textbook content in the hopes of improving student engagement. Still others saw MOOCs as a way to add expert voices-sages on the side, so to speak, to complement their own areas of expertise, thereby promoting a more interdisciplinary approach to learning. For example, one instructor is using MOOC content on macroeconomics as an added dimension in his comparative politics course.

A department chair who had, by his own admission been slow to adopt technology as a learning enhancement, came to see the light when he found that MOOC strategies such as peer review were "incredibly empowering" for his students. Consequently, he is enthusiastically reinventing his courses to incorporate these effective instructional approaches. Although we have explored a few of the more innovative ways that MOOCs can be designed and used to enhance the learning process, developing your own here at New Mexico State University may not be particularly feasible. So before you undertake such a resource intensive process, I would suggest asking yourselves a few basic questions. For starters, will they fit well with your current online learning strategy? Likewise, will your IT infrastructure support them? And specifically what do you hope to accomplish in the process: Instructional enhancement, institutional recognition, tuition reduction, recruitment tool, or something truly novel?

How important is scale, after all, and how do you define it (massive versus smaller, degree programs versus individual courses, for-credit and fee or non-credit and free)? Who will coordinate and track these courses from the institutional side, and are external partners a necessity? On the other hand, you might find it far more feasible to experiment with MOOC content that's already available out there, much in the same way the University System of Maryland schools did. Because as e-learning experts like Gardner Campbell at Virginia Tech are quick to point out, it's not the technology itself that's important, it's what we do with it to engage our students in mastering the skills they need to be successful in today's emerging innovation economy. In fact, as the "bricks versus clicks" debate rages on, it seems increasingly more logical that the solution lies somewhere in the middle. So rather than choosing one option over the other, we should be capitalizing on the best of both to create innovative and result driven hybrid models that are as empowering for our students, as they are sustainable for our institutions. Or in other words, models that add real value to academic investment by creating rich learning experiences, interactive learning environments, and vibrant learning communities. While it's tempting to view this approach as a temporal construct, a pre-prescribed division of time between campus and cyberspace, it is actually a fundamental change in the learning paradigm.

To begin with, the hybrid environment generally shifts the focus from teacher-directed to learner-centered, thereby affording students greater control over and engagement in the learning process overall. It also fosters increased interactivity across the board, student-to-student, student-to-instructor, student-to-content, and student-to-outside resource. Equally important, it enables us to integrate a variety of learning assessment mechanisms beyond the standard test and papers. But above all, the hybrid environment offers a unique and truly cost-effective opportunity to bring the digital devices and applications we use in our everyday lives into the classroom, where they can be deployed as powerful, interactive learning tools. Given the hours our students spend browsing in cyberspace, digital devices have become as fundamental to their learning process as pencil and paper once were for most of us. One recent survey revealed that the typical 18- to 34-year-old college-goer comes to campus armed with, on average, seven digital devices. The most popular of which are laptops and smartphones, followed closely by game consoles and MP3 players. On top of that, students reported spending a little more than 14 hours a day multitasking across these devices. And although much of this activity is devoted to entertainment, a considerable portion of it is spent on learning. Seventy percent of them said they used their laptops for research and coursework, and 47 percent, for taking notes in class at least some of the time. Ninety-eight percent of those who owned an e-reader occasionally downloaded textbooks, while 65 percent employed a wide variety of digital tools for creating class presentations, complete with impressive multimedia enhancement. Not surprisingly then, college campuses everywhere are struggling to get their arms around the Bring Your Own Device (BOYD) phenomenon. Can your IT department support this? While there are still plenty of administrators and faculty members who believe students should leave their personal devices at the classroom door, there is an ever-expanding circle of BYOD supporters like myself, who are convinced that it's an inevitable, if not indispensable, practice. In fact, as far as I'm concerned, students should not only be encouraged to bring their own devices, they should be required to; and not as a distraction, as in texting friends or updating social media sites, but as a gateway to technology-enhanced learning. By doing so, we are helping our students use these devices to cultivate personalized lifelong learning networks that when connected empower complex knowledge ecologies, in which innovative ideas and new information flourish and cross-pollinate.

Given the mobile devices we now have at our disposal, it's hard to imagine our lives without these gadgets. And as they become ever more compact and ubiquitous, they provide us with a unique opportunity to foster flexible and adaptive learning experiences that are active and authentic, individualized or collaborative. They can be used either in the classroom for structured learning activities or on the move for independent study that extends beyond the classroom. By the same token, they enable rich content for interaction, as in multimedia simulations and social networking sites, as well as discrete content, such as quizzes, simple games, and class announcements. Likewise, we can push content out to our students or ask them to pull it in for themselves, depending on their individual interests and needs, both in and out of class. And in the process, they will also have the option to consume it or produce it, an important factor in promoting knowledge synthesis and co-creation. Of course, digital devices of all sizes and types are virtually useless without the software applications that power them and there are literally thousands of them at our fingertips, many of which can be downloaded for free. In fact, my friend Dr. Robbie Melton at the Tennessee Board of Regents has reviewed and catalogued more than

70,000 of them, which is why she appropriately calls herself an *appologist*. Needless to say, it's difficult at best to forage through them all on your own. So I want to spend the rest of our time today talking about and playing with a few of the better ones.

Let's start with back channel media like Twitter. Not only is it free and easy to use, it has also proven especially effective for engaging students in active learning under even the most passive scenarios like large lecture halls where there are few, if any, meaningful opportunities for student participation or content clarification. But thanks to Twitter, students can work their devices to jump in quickly and quietly with mid-lecture questions and/or observations for the instructor, while maintaining a steady flow of commentary with fellow classmates, much in the same way we used to pass notes under the desk. Indeed, one of our colleagues at the University of Texas, Dallas has successfully incorporated Twitter into her history courses, using weekly hashtags to organize the comments, questions, and feedback her students tweet during class, which she projects on a giant screen at the front of the room. By the same token, this approach makes it easier for her students to reference and review important discussion points once the hour is up. Twitter is also being deployed in some academic circles as a tool for developing effective reading and writing skills, For example, a professor at Holy Cross College uses it to help his students to communicate more concisely, by having them summarize major political texts without going over the imposed 140-character limit.

Blogs are great for getting the creative, collaborative and conceptual juices flowing, and can be employed to promote active and authentic learning. Instructors sometimes develop course blogs for disseminating content and encouraging student feedback through posted comments and/or discussion questions. In addition, blogs can serve as a hub through which to coordinate essential course information, such as syllabi, learning assignments, class schedules and supplementary resource materials while facilitating group projects, as well. As group sites or individual journals, blogs are also learner-driven, enabling students to share, evaluate and reflect on course-specific information and ideas while also building their personal learning environments. Not surprisingly, this digital enhancement offers a variety of academic benefits. From the instructor's perspective, blogs provide an ongoing record of work for measuring student progress. And learners who are more or less "invisible" in the face-to-face classroom often flourish in the blogosphere, as they become increasingly more proficient communicators and collaborators both of which are essential career skills. There is a host of user-friendly blogging platforms from which to choose, many of which are not only free, but also equipped with all sorts of advanced features, including anti-spam filters, sophisticated template widgets, and search engine optimization.

Word press is still considered the granddaddy of them all for posting in class or on the go, on laptops, smartphones, and tablets, on iOS, Android, and Blackberry systems. And it's free to use for publishing and sharing content, which can also be connected to popular social networks like Facebook, Twitter, and LinkedIn. Equally impressive, it is more than just a blogging system. It's also a content management system that can be easily customized, with thousands of plug-ins, widgets, and themes. That means you can start a blog or build a full-fledged website. Wikis are also turning knowledge consumers into knowledge creators, while strengthening higher order thinking skills such as creating, analyzing, and evaluating new information. In addition to providing collaborative and asynchronous workspace for both authoring and editing, wikis are incredibly easy to use, even for digital novices, and can support any size effort from small-group class projects to worldwide mega-libraries like Wikipedia. Consequently, they are being incorporated on campuses across the country for any number of purposes from conducting mini–research projects and compiling collections of case studies and field reports. They are also being used to foster group discussion around specific concepts and create collaborative annotated bibliographies for students to summarize and critique course related readings. And there are a growing number of free, open source wiki engines to choose from, including MediaWiki (which was originally developed for Wikipedia), TikiWiki, and DokuWiki. All of which can be configured for mobile devices.

For those of you who prefer the personal touch of the face-to-face classroom, there are a variety of videoconferencing options that can be used to remotely connect students with professors, students with students, and students with outside experts over any number of devices. Simple mobile applications like Skype and FaceTime enable one-to-one connection via webcam. On the other hand, one-to-many video-conferencing systems with multipoint controllers use cloud based services (such as Blue Jeans, Zoom.us and Google+ Hangouts) to manage these linkups across multiple platforms and mobile devices. With Google+ you can also tune into live video broadcasts on a wide range of topics. Aside from the more ubiquitous applications, however, there are thousands of others to choose from that can be incorporated as additional course resources and enhancements. So I'd like you to power up your own devices so we can play with a few of them. Let's start with dictionary.com app on your device and download from there. With more than two million definitions, synonyms and antonyms, this is a fast-loading, user-friendly mobile app that will benefit students in any course. As you can see, it can be downloaded for free on any platform. There is also a voice-activated search feature, along with other bells and whistles like "Word of the Day" updates and a "Hot Word" blog. I would also like to introduce you to Babylon.com, which is all available on most systems, including Kindle and Blackberry. Go to Babylon.com and look on the mobile menu for your app. As you can see, this is an indispensable app in today's global village because it provides free mobile translation on demand from single words to full-text translation by accessing more than seventeen hundred glossaries in multiple languages. So imagine how useful it might be for your students as they study abroad, prepare foreign language presentations, or simply converse with a dorm mate from overseas.

Let's go to TED.com now and scroll down to "More Ways to Get TED" at the bottom of the home page. Now look for the app that will work with your device. Earlier, we discussed the option of using pre-recorded expert voices for supplementing in-class readings and discussions. And a heavy dose of genius from among the TED Talks archives will give both you and your students access to some of the real thought leaders of our time. Now for those iPad users, I want to share a free app called ASK# that enables you to create a mobile classroom anywhere anytime by connecting with your students' iPad devices.

Essentially, this app turns your iPad into a recordable whiteboard, enabling you to do any number of virtual activities. For example, you can teach once and record it for the class, annotate content, or host a virtual discussion forum. It also allows for peer-to-peer teaching and collaboration. So for those of you who teach hybrid courses, this is a perfect digital learning tool. Explain Everything is another easy-to-use interactive whiteboard tool that will let you annotate, animate, narrate, import, and export almost anything to and from almost anywhere, which also makes it great for creating dynamic lessons, learning activities, assessments, and tutorials.

As many of you know, well-designed virtual learning environments and activities offer risk-free, ethically sound, and cost-effective opportunities for your students to learn by doing, under real-world, real-time conditions. And there are more than an a few apps that provide high quality, media rich, and immersive simulations that can be used to master discipline-specific knowledge and skills. For instance, here's one that would definitely enrich a freshman biology lab, by providing a human vehicle for dissecting frogs. It can be downloaded for less than $5.00 on a variety of tablets and laptops. (http://frogvirtualdissection.com) Of course, in addition to planning for designing high-quality hybrid courses and content, we also need to think about how to make these digital enhancements available to our students. For years, distance educators have been wedded to the learning management system approach. These systems are not only robust and secure; they also incorporate a fairly standardized set of tools for downloading courseware; giving and grading exams; and evaluating student performance. What's more they pave the way for coordinating virtual learning activities; sharing digital files and learning objects; and furnishing online support services, including vast digital libraries. But as many benefits as they offer, learning management systems are still, for the most part, course-based and campus-owned. Likewise, they can be expensive to manage for smaller schools with fewer online offerings. Students also complain that these systems often fail to support personal learning environments because they are typically device-dependent, which makes them difficult to access from mobile phones and tablets.

With that in mind a growing number of professors are accommodating their students by providing them with online webmixes of course-specific virtual resources. And SymbalooEDU is an especially popular application. Bring up symbalooedu.com and hit "start now" on your projected screen. As you can see, there's a free version for individual student use, along with a relatively inexpensive premium account for instructors and campuses that provides additional features for creating, customizing, and managing multiple, course-specific webmixes and sharing them with an unlimited number of users. Symbaloo is also easy to organize and effortless to update. What's more, it can be accessed from any device, and allows for hosting almost any platform, from learning management systems, to social networking sites, to collaborative cloud tools. Consequently, students can add and share new resources, as needed, which makes it a wonderful tool for supporting self-directed, continuous learning.

Well, we've now come full circle from MOOCs to personal learning environments, and I want to thank you for the opportunity to be here today for what has certainly been a stimulating discussion for me, and I hope for you, as well. If we have any time left, I would be more than happy to entertain a few more questions or comments.

My sincere thanks to Dr. Sharon Lalla, New Mexico State University Teaching Academy, for the invitation to speak at NMSU.

Index

❖